"Dr. Chang has 'four unswerving ideas' which his book illustrates by reviewing the history, the philosophy, the poetry and the moral concepts of the past, which he finds living in the present. First, he asserts, 'communism' in China has not destroyed and never will destroy its ancient cultural ideals and essential humanism, but Marxism will be absorbed and modified, just as were Buddhism and other alien importations. Second, the present-day leadership represents merely a few minutes of time on the long day's clock of the nation's history, but this leadership has won mass support because it has performed necessary tasks in the restoration of unity and independence, and in rapid technical modernization. Third, world stability requires that China now be recognized as a great and responsible power in a role commensurate with her former glory, and that her sovereignty be fully respected. Finally, Sino-American mutual tolerance, if not active friendship, are indispensable for the maintenance of international peace, and not in the distant future, but immediately.

"Dr. Chang's 'new approach' to a reconciliation would require the United States to do most of the approaching, by accepting the foregoing basic ideas or assumptions. By that means, and only by that means, Dr. Chang seems to believe, could state relations be brought within the compass of rationality. *America and China* is an important book, full of valuable teaching and deeply informed by a breadth of knowledge and wisdom concerning the human condition in various cultures. If it succeeds in making Americans realize that the proper objective of their China policy is not the erasure of the present social, economic and political structure of recent Chinese progress under the Communists, but the good will of 700,000,000 neighbors, it would justify the author's most cherished hopes and the immense industry invested in this work. *America and China* should be mandatory reading for all alert citizens on both sides of the Pacific. Much of it will be as unpalatable to Chinese Communists as to some American congressmen, but none could fail to benefit from reflecting on its highly civilized—and profoundly and frankly pro-China but not pro-Marxist—point of view."

About the Author

Dr. Chang was graduated from Tsing Hua College, Peking, China, in 1918, and was awarded an A.B. by Johns Hopkins in 1919. He then went to Harvard where he received an A.M. in 1920 and a Ph.D. in 1922. His interest was English philology and comparative literature. Returning to China in 1923, Dr. Chang held a succession of academic posts as professor, department chairman, dean and vice-president in four leading Chinese universities. He was also Director and Counselor in the Chinese Foreign Office, and became Ambassador for the Republic of China in many European countries. He was Director-General of the Chinese United Nations Association. He returned to this country in 1941 and now lives here with his wife and children, who have become citizens. Dr. Chang is currently Professor of Humanities on the Teaneck, New Jersey, campus of Fairleigh Dickinson University.

AMERICA AND CHINA is a vitally important book.

It is a detailed and brilliant analysis of China's position in the world today, which offers a constructive plan for the solution of the present impasse in Chinese-American relations.

The book is not a "survey" or a history, but a startling and provocative plea for a new approach by the United States to Asia generally and China in particular.

The book explodes many cherished convictions of cold-war dogma. It has, prior to publication, already excited widespread interest.

Edgar Snow, the author of *Red Star Over China* and *The Other Side of the River,* writes of it:

"Professor Chang Hsin-hai has had an unusual career and his book is likewise unusual, if not unique. In pre-Communist China he was a patriotic nationalist and held important diplomatic posts. The revolution found him abroad, and out of sympathy with the Kuomintang government, but evidently he could not wholly reconcile himself to the new regime, either. He became, as he himself puts it, 'for all practical purposes an expatriate,' and chose to live and teach in the United States, where his children have married and made their homes.

"A scholar and writer at ease in two cultures, Dr. Chang is as familiar with the history and values of the American tradition as with those of his native China. In his book he is therefore able to present a bifocal view of problems of adjustment to revolutionary challenges emerging from Peking, which bedevil and bewilder United States strategic planners. His effort is candid and even confessional, to a degree obviously painful, at times, for the author himself. It is also likely to shock some complacent Americans in its honest and determined correction of misinformation concerning the nature of Chinese character and civilization and background facts about current controversies—our ignorance of which he sees as a basic cause of misunderstanding. His emphasis is on the long view of China and on the durable qualities of the people who live there whom we must try to comprehend not as Communists but as human beings whose genes and cultural legacy remain, and will remain, intact.

Books by Chang Hsin-hai

America and China: A New Approach to Asia
The Fabulous Concubine (a novel)
Within the Four Seas (on World Peace)
Matthew Arnold and the Humanistic View of Life
Letters of a Chinese Diplomat
Chiang Kai-shek

AMERICA
AND CHINA:
A NEW APPROACH TO ASIA

by

Chang Hsin-hai

SIMON AND SCHUSTER
NEW YORK

FIRST PRINTING

LIBRARY OF CONGRESS CATALOG CARD NUMBER: 65-24280
MANUFACTURED IN THE UNITED STATES OF AMERICA
BY VAIL-BALLOU PRESS, INC., BINGHAMTON, N. Y.
DESIGNED BY EDITH FOWLER

The author is grateful to the following for permission to reprint material
in this book:

George F. Kennan and *Foreign Affairs* for material from Mr. Kennan's
article in *Foreign Affairs,* October 1964.

Walter Lippmann for material from his article in the New York *Herald
Tribune,* May 18, 1961.

Joseph Needham for material from his January 1, 1965, letter printed
in *The New Statesman.*

The New York *Times* for material from its editorial "Asian Confrontation," June 12, 1964, © 1964 by The New York Times Company.

Harrison E. Salisbury for material from his article "China Border
Claims," the New York *Times,* September 10, 1963.

FOR REN-MAI (PAMELA), REN-DA (CHRISTOPHER),
AND REN-TAI (DAVID)

CONTENTS

PREFACE

THIS BOOK is in the nature of a confession. Like all confessions, it is not worth making unless it is sincere. My judgment of events will not satisfy all my readers, my assessment of situations may often leave much to be desired; but they are made with no preconceived notions. They do not serve any ulterior motive. All they express is the wish to see the development and consolidation of understanding between the two great nations on either side of the Pacific—without which it is futile to talk about world peace.

For all practical purposes, I have been living the life of an expatriate, with the rest of my family. I received a large part of my advanced education in this country. So did my wife. Our two children, though born in China, have reactions and responses that are typically American.

But all the same, we are Chinese. And the steady deterioration of the relations between China and the United States drove me to think hard and to find out if there is any possibility of a dissolution of a seemingly implacable hatred. What is the cause of this hatred? Need it be prolonged into the distant future, even though the two nations, so completely different in their backgrounds, are in their character and basic instincts so similar? I have, therefore, attempted in the following pages to delve into the core of the difficulties that, I like to believe, only for the moment divide these two peoples.

I am dominated by four unswerving ideas. The first is that whatever Communism has done for China and will do for her in the years immediately ahead, it cannot produce more than a mere dent on the personality and character of her people. It is only a moment in history. There is no reason to believe that it will alter the texture of the soul of a people. When Buddhism came to China in the early days of the Christian era, she had had already more than two thousand years of a fully developed culture of her own. The new religion enriched the life of the Chinese in a variety of ways, but no one can say that it brought any structural or organic change. In fact it was the Chinese character that brought profound changes in Buddhism, and it was because of this perhaps that Buddhism has been able to survive in China.

Now, two thousand years later, China is confronted with Communism, which is merely a new kind of political and social orientation. It cannot stir the Chinese soul from its depths as can a new religion. I believe therefore that it is mistaken to suppose that it can have more than a superficial impact on the Chinese character. Already the changes in the ideology have been phenomenal. When it is applied to serve an immediate end or to help solve practical problems that are of a peculiarly local nature, it is inevitable that it should be shaped and adapted to specific requirements before it can be effective. With the passing of the years these changes will be more numerous and fundamental, while all the time the Chinese personality continues to regain its equilibrium and the full measure of its identity, perhaps much the richer for having gone through a new experience. If Buddhism, which made an assault on the very foundations of the Chinese character, did not succeed in modifying it, it is unlikely that a mere economic system can go very far.

My second thought is that China may be said now to have found a way out of the prolonged national crisis which began with the Opium War in 1839 and the subsequent Treaty of Nanking of 1842. The atmosphere of surrender and capitulation has been of long duration, longer than in the history of any major nation. The dark, suffocating clouds grew thicker with the passing of every decade, resulting in repeated acts of humiliation. The weight of oppression has been too heavy. It is only now that this oppressive air is dissipating.

My third thought is that it is not only for the benefit of China, but also for the world generally, that she should regain the stature of her historic past. I have often had occasion to speak with my friends about the rise of China. I would sometimes ask why there is so much opposition toward the new regime, knowing that, in spite of its many shortcomings, it has already done so much for the common people, in contrast to the corruption and utter incompetence of the regime that it superseded. Is it really because it is Communist? Or is it because China is beginning again to be strong and a power to be reckoned with? It was amusing to watch the expressions on the faces of these friends, especially when the question took them by surprise. At first there would be a look of blankness; it would then melt into either a faint smile or a stern grimace, depending upon the closeness of our relationship. How often have I received the answer that it was indeed uncomfortable to see a strong and powerful China. Would there not be acts of reprisal against the Western nations for what they did to her in the course of more than a century?

It is on this question of vengeance that I feel it my duty to offer some explanation. I also feel that the Western peoples have an inadequate understanding of the Chinese people and their psychology in this regard. Perhaps to be vengeful would be the normal reaction of the Western peoples themselves if they were in the position of the Chinese. But the Chinese do not act in this way. This is not to say that the Chinese are morally superior. It is simply because their long experience as a nation and the pragmatic instincts they have acquired from that experience have taught them that it is more profitable in the long run to forgive and forget than to commit acts of reprisal, which in turn sow the seeds of further hostility. Again and again, the lesson was brought home to the people that it was the better part of wisdom never to pursue ancient grievances. There is always a time to heal and to cover up open wounds. In fact, the Chinese admire a man's ability to bury old feuds. It is a measure of his character and moral courage. The belly of the prime minister, so it is said, is so capacious that even a boat can sail in it.

I believe that the new China, if she is sure of herself, will tread on these ancient paths. As long as she was weak and powerless, her voice could not be heard. She was an invitation to friction and international rivalry of one kind or another. But as a fully independent and self-assured China, which she has now again become, she has a chance to implement some of her traditional ideas. When the world deals with China, I hope it will realize that it deals with a great country and a great people, that it deals with a people which has known power and its responsibilities.

My final thought is that good feeling between China and the United States is absolutely essential and indispensable. Without it there can be no peace in the world. I would urge Americans to consider if the long-range goal of Soviet foreign policy may be to prevent the coming together of these two countries. It is not impossible. The Kremlin has some meticulous planners, and this policy, if it is one, has had a remarkable degree of success from the time of the Korean War—itself the product of an overriding Soviet desire to see China converted into a Communist state, but weak and, if possible, permanently dependent upon Soviet Russia.

Since then, China and the United States have been pitted against each other. Has all this perhaps evolved according to the plans conceived and executed by the masterminds of the Kremlin? The leaders in China are probably aware of the Soviet design. But it is obvious they can neither speak out nor do anything to avert it. In America it is otherwise. The conditions of an affluent society and the good nature of its people are fertile breeding grounds for gullibility. The grievance against China has now become so emotionally massive that it seems nothing can satisfy the average American but the total collapse of the Chinese regime. The manifestation of anger on de Gaulle's recognition of Communist China is an example of this absence of emotional balance. If this is a trap into which both China and the United States have fallen, then is it not obvious that the sooner we jump out of it, the better it is for the world?

I hope these two great nations can collaborate, not in the distant future, but now.

> In matters few and many,
> Always in a hurry;
> The universe spins away,

Time presses on.
Ten thousand years—too long,
I strive only for the morn and eve.

This is part of one of Mao Tse-tung's latest poems. He is not an example of classical Chinese patience. He has always been a man in a hurry. At seventy and over he is even more in a hurry. His prestige and influence are great; if he were given a chance to help break down the thick wall of misunderstanding between China and the United States, which is now all but impenetrable, what a welcome relief it would be to a distraught world.

There is no need to add that only here in the United States can I speak out in the way that I have. I would not exchange that freedom for anything in the world. But freedom is genuine only when it rests on responsibility. What I have attempted to do, in however faltering a manner, is to dedicate myself to a fearless exploration of the legacy of a great young President, who in his Inaugural Address asked "that both sides begin anew the quest for peace." "So let us begin anew . . ." he reiterated, "let both sides explore what problems unite us, instead of belaboring those problems which divide us."

My thanks are due to the many men and women on the staff of the New York Public Library and the Dag Hammarskjöld Library of the UN for constant help in finding references. But of course to my wife always I owe more than I can ever acknowledge. However I am alone responsible for the views expressed in the book.

Mei Lodge
Great Neck, N. Y.

I THE SITUATION

WHAT IS the policy of the United States in Asia today? It is un-
clear and ineffective. There has been no New Frontier in
East Asia.

Yet there is no reason why there should not be truly a "new frontier." If it was conceived originally in terms of the extension of
American power, far beyond its natural limits, to areas where the
American will must hold undisputed sway and be obeyed, then
that frontier is bound to come into contact with serious obstacles.
But there is another sense in which a new frontier can be constructed. It need not be a frontier beyond which one will prevails
over another will. For that would mean confrontation, and confrontation brings mutual mistrust, friction, and eventually conflict.
Is it at all possible to imagine a frontier that reduces these elements of discord to their minimum, or perhaps even creates a
sense of mutual accommodation and harmony? I believe this is not
impossible. Was not the nuclear test-ban treaty meant to create a
new spirit and to make it prevail in our relations with all nations?
The treaty has been described as a "first step," which should lead
to other steps to reduce tension—not with Soviet Russia alone but
with other nations as well.

The dominant motive in American foreign policy, we have been
told, is to prevent the spread of Communism and of Chinese Communism in particular, in Asia and elsewhere. At any rate, the most
recent of the foreign aid programs is tailored with that aim in view.
The concept of containment still haunts us. Not so long ago it was
the containment of Soviet Russia. That, it seems, is now all over.
Not that Soviet Russia has been contained, but a new situation is
thought to have arisen which made containment unnecessary. Is it
then quite impossible to conceive of the rise of another situation in

19

which the containment of China becomes equally superfluous? A member of the Belgian parliament, after visiting Communist China for a month, came out with the statement that what has taken place in Russia will in time take place in China. Would it not be better for us to help create the conditions that will hasten the change? A bridge would seem to serve us better than a frontier. In fact such conditions always exist, waiting for the United States to show the initiative and make use of it. But Washington has chosen to see only what it wants to see. It has remained adamantly uncompromising.

The same Belgian gentleman was also reported to have said that many competent observers are strongly of the opinion that it would take some eighty years for China to catch up with the West. He said that he agreed with the view, except that it seemed to him to be on the optimistic side. Have not the Communist Chinese leaders themselves said on repeated occasions that it would require at least half a century for China to be an adequate industrial power? Yet we are made to labor under the deliberately cultivated fear that she is a new monster which must be leashed. That fear has been stressed again and again in all the mass media, on the public forums, and in the whispering galleries of many countries. People do not spell out the words "yellow peril" as bluntly as before. But the implications are clear. They are being made clear to members of the Caucasian race. If China becomes a strong power, so it is argued, it is not just another Russia—it will be a strong nation of people with a different pigmentation of the skin.

This explanation, it seems to me, is the key to the understanding of the present international situation. It is the key to the purpose of the nuclear test-ban treaty. The major political aim of that treaty was to make it quite impossible for China to become "a full-fledged nuclear power." Behind it is the same motivation that inspired the latest foreign aid program.

Despite her new atomic bombs, China is still virtually impotent as a nuclear power. But if Chinese nuclear power is being prevented from growing, surely the same concern should apply to France. This is where the sincerity of the nuclear test-ban treaty will be severely tested. If France continues to pollute the atmosphere without arousing the same hue and cry that followed in the wake of a Chinese explosion, then the element of race will be seen to play a part. My own conviction is that wherever we turn, the consciousness of race and the unwavering desire of the Caucasian race to dominate the rest of mankind are the biggest factors in today's international affairs to watch and curb. The Confucian concepts that "within the four seas all men are brothers" and "among men there is difference in education but not in race" have little practical value for the Caucasian peoples. Their passion for dominance over the other races will die hard. One of the major pressures on the Soviet Union from the free world has been to make the Soviet leaders realize that their people after all belong to the Caucasian race. I think all intelligent people must work to dispel this sense of racial superiority. But even highly intellectual people often fail to do so. One amusing incident is that of Dr. Arnold Toynbee, who, writing for the New York *Times* on August 7, 1960, said definitely that there was going to be no racial conflict. Then, three years later, on September 29, 1963, he was just as definite that a racial war was about to begin.

One example of racial sensitiveness was shown when, in August of 1963, the Chinese Communist leader Mao Tse-tung issued a statement on the Negro problem in the United States. In it he said, "I call upon the workers, peasants, revolutionary intellectuals, enlightened personages of *all* colors in the world—*white*, black, yellow, brown, and so forth—to unite against the racial discrimination practiced by U.S. imperialism and to support the American Negroes in their struggle against racial discrimination." Isn't the civil rights bill meant to carry out just that purpose? But the New York *Times* immediately took the statement as "the opening of a major worldwide racial campaign by Communist China." This interpretation is the very reverse of what was meant by Mr. Mao. The *Christian Science Monitor* was even more hysterical. It called the statement "a summons to colored peoples to unite in war against the white race." Also "his call for worldwide racial war reflects a degree of hate and desperation which can only be described as psychotic." The editor concluded by saying that it was a "policy of collective racial suicide." The subject is so important that I feel a full discussion is called for.*

General de Gaulle, we have been told, has declared on many occasions that he is resolved to pursue a policy of independence, especially as regards nuclear testing and atomic strength and development. He has made it clear also that he is not going to submit his country, which he will presumably lead as long as he lives, to the hegemony of the "two privileged states" of the Soviet Union and the United States, which now have a monopoly of power, for such submission would mean "turning the world over to a double hegemony" that he cannot accept.

The point I am trying to make is that the world will continue to live in a state of uneasiness and tension as long as the foreign policies of the stronger powers are based on the concept of the dominance of one race over the rest, or on the pursuit of national self-interest at the sacrifice of the interests of other nations. We should at least make an endeavor to exploit some other alternatives. There is no indication that those who have the power now are willing to do so.

Instead of that, we continue to spread the impression that China is determined to follow the path of expansion, of aggression, of military conquest, with no regard for the consequences. All of this is neither true nor just. I am reminded of one remark made by a sympathetic student of China, which deserves some study. Mr. C. P. Fitzgerald † observed: "The history of China is a record of cultural expansion, not of military conquest." I believe the observation is profoundly true, not only of any one particular period, but throughout the long history of that country. It does not mean that military power has played no part, but it does mean that the major emphasis has always been on cultural and moral persuasion.

But the picture of China now is that of a monster, of a maniac, bent on destruction. Yet the government on the Chinese mainland, though Communist, consists of practical men. They are men who

---

* See Appendix B.
† C. P. Fitzgerald: China: A Short Cultural History, p. 1.

have an intense awareness of the facts of life. They have not lost their senses and they cannot believe that war, even atomic war, is the only means to solve their problems or the problems of the world. The now famous saying, attributed to Mao Tse-tung but actually made by Tito, that even an atomic war is worth having, because then the world would be made safe for Communism, is a part of counterpropaganda, and should be taken as such.

When, as the Albanian representative to the last UN General Assembly said, China "has not a single soldier on foreign soil and not a single foreign base," and when China asks not for a partial ban on nuclear tests, but the "total, final, and complete destruction and prohibition of nuclear weapons and their testing," surely the stand taken is not for war, but for peace. The treaty, hailed by President Kennedy and by all the other responsible leaders of the world as the "first step" toward total prohibition of nuclear weapons and the achievement of general and complete disarmament, is meaningless if we stop only at the first step. Even a Chinese proverb was quoted to sustain the view that a first step must be made to cover a distance of a thousand miles. We may accuse China of being too impatient, but surely her aim is identical with that of the rest of the world. And she is impatient because it appears to her that it is going to be a long, long time, if ever, before any second step will be taken. The first step alone only insures supremacy for those countries that are already in possession of nuclear power.

As long as this is true, can we blame China for thinking, as Bertrand Russell said, that she "continues to be treated as a pariah"? "The Chinese mood," he went on to say, "will change only when Russia and the West become less hostile to China . . . The present hostility of China is an echo of the hostile noises that have come from the West. It will cease when these noises cease, but not before." * I think these words are fair and just.

People even talk about China having a "grand design" for the conquest of the world, as if it falls within the same category as Hitler's or Tojo's plans of world domination. The New York *Times*

* *Letter to the New York* Times, *August 9, 1963.*

editorial for September 14, 1963, called it "a Napoleonic phase of expansion" and suggested that "it would seem elemental prudence for all the threatened nations to get together in common self-defense"! But it is neither just nor wise to impute designs to another country where they do not exist. I hope to be able to show this sufficiently clearly in the course of these pages. When intelligent people indulge in such inaccuracies, I think their mistakes should be pointed out to them. One very good example is the article by Mr. Harrison Salisbury written for the *Times* on the same day that the editorial appeared. It was called "China's Border Claims" and was accompanied by a map purported to have been printed by Peking in 1954. The two were advanced as convincing evidence that Communist China does indeed harbor designs of expansion and conquest. It happens that the article was entirely misinformed. I was very much amused by it and had the feeling when I was reading it that I had seen the map a very long time ago. It was the same map that I used to study and pore over when I was a child, and that was nearly in the last century! So I wrote a letter to the *Times,* which they were good enough to publish. Among other things I said:

It was the time when China's fortunes were at their lowest ebb. She was almost on the point of being cut up and becoming even nonexistent. Surely she was then in no position for any expansionist policy. Yet the children were made to study these maps so that they might know what their country looked like at one period of its history. It was one means to stimulate their love of country. The same maps, we feel reasonably sure, are being studied by the people in Taiwan. It is as if Britain should publish a map of its colonial possessions in the nineteenth century for her school children. Must it mean therefore that she has decided to reconquer the colonies?

In the case of China, no Chinese now or in the past has been taught that countries like Burma or Cambodia or Malaya have been a part of China. They only had a special kind of relationship—that of bearing tribute to the then Chinese court. Or they have a large Chinese population and the influence of Chinese culture is strongly felt.

These are historical facts. But to imply, as Mr. Salisbury does, that these countries are now "China's border claims" and that they must be incorporated again into the future map of China is a gross inaccuracy.

There was no reply or comment from Mr. Salisbury. Eminent journalist as he certainly is, I take it his silence meant that he was willing to be corrected.

I have singled out this incident to show how a great many of the remarks made about China being a militant nation bent on conquest are really distortions of the truth, do injustice to that country, and willfully create wrong impressions about her.

II SOME ACCOMPLISHMENTS

A LADY FRIEND from a conservative stronghold of New England was recently thumbing through the pages of an illustrated magazine from mainland China. It was printed in German—*China im Bild* (China in Pictures)—a language she could not read. But the picture on the cover page of a working girl, with blooming, rosy cheeks and a face as round as a peach, looked enticing. Much as it was against her wishes, she quickly went through the entire issue and looked pleasantly surprised. She asked for more copies. There were altogether only three copies. By the time she came to the middle of the last copy she was anxious to make a few comments.

"I cannot believe," she said, "that in China there are such modern homes for the ordinary working people. Look at these," she continued, as she pointed to a row of clean, well-kept, though modest, homes. "Why, they are as good as any in this country."

She turned over the pages with pictures of the countryside, with ducks swimming peacefully in the pond, and the branches of the willow trees hanging over the shores of a lake covered with patches of the divine lotus. The scene was idyllic. But again the lady could not reconcile it with her image of an old, beaten up, and poverty-stricken country called China. She became irritated. Should she continue to nurse that image or should she discard it and make room in her mind for the new realities of the picture magazine?

At long last the lady just asked one question and went away. "But why was China so poor before?" Like Pontius Pilate she did not stay for an answer.

I could not have given any adequate answer to her in one hour or even in a day. For little did she realize that she had raised a difficult, even a "profound" question.

What I had meant to say to her was not just that what mainland China has accomplished within a brief span of fifteen years, against obstacles of all kinds, is nothing short of miraculous. But the story of that poverty, so widespread and so widely known that the outside world could not believe there had been anything but poverty in China, how it all came about, how it ultimately engulfed hundreds of millions of people who became so destitute and sub-human that even their own people could contemptuously spurn them, as when the son of China's revolutionary leader used to say of them, "They have nothing to lose but their miserable lives"— this story remains to be told. It is not a simple story. It is not a story of economics. It is not a story of imperialism, though that was an important contributing factor. That poverty was the result of cir-cumstances, both domestic and foreign, of which poverty was the logical conclusion.

The Chinese people are not yet free of that poverty. The stand-ard of living is still very low notwithstanding the pictures of well-being that my lady friend saw in the magazine. But there has been a profound psychological change, and that is what is so important. There is now a feeling that a long national crisis has been lifted. Where before there was unrelieved chaos and confusion, unremit-ting humiliation, and abject poverty, there is now hope, confi-dence, and faith in the future. The people are beginning to have a sense of pride in what they are able to accomplish. This is espe-cially true of the young people. Sometimes that pride seems to be excessive, and that led to restlessness and a lack of cautiousness for which the people had to pay dearly during the three years of 1959, 1960 and 1961. But just as the people in this country had the fortitude and resourcefulness to overcome the harrowing days of the Great Depression, so the Chinese people tasted the fruits of their bitterness and learned lessons from the Great Leap Forward which should be of value in the future.

It has been sometimes said that whatever the Chinese people might have gained during this period of strenuous exertion, the loss of personal freedom is something nothing can replace or compen-sate. If a people lost its freedom, it is argued, it has lost everything worth living for. This is an argument that is entirely valid, and the

Chinese are the last people on earth to wish the loss of that precious heritage. But there are differences of circumstances which we need, I think, to take into consideration. Knowing as we do the utter hopelessness in the life of the average common person in China only fifteen years ago, we must bear in mind that today his conditions have so far improved that personal freedom is not of much weight in his immediate circumstances. This does not mean that his desire for freedom has been destroyed, for I believe with President Kennedy that freedom is at the very foundation of human existence. As living conditions continue to improve, the desire to have freedom will become more insistent, and there is no way in which the government can suppress it.

But let us consider the condition as the average person sees it today. Before, he would be lucky if he had the opportunity, as thousands did in a wealthy city like Shanghai, to pick up discarded cigarette butts from the streets in exchange for a small bowl of thin rice soup. Today he can look for honest work and be paid a wage, however meager, with which he can buy food, even though strictly rationed. Before, he would be lucky if he could be hired as a coolie for a few cents a day. Today he is a proud workingman, and gets paid for every ounce of energy he puts in his work. The coolie has disappeared. When he is sick, he is sent to a hospital and receives proper medical attention, such as it is. When he marries and becomes a father, his wife and infant are taken care of in state infirmaries. When the child grows up, he receives proper education. When he becomes old and can work no more, he receives a pension. The state steps into every phase of his life to provide for him. It is true the state does not allow much room for the exercise of personal freedom. No one in an advanced industrial society such as the United States or Europe can tolerate this state interference. Even if he had no knowledge of Aristotle, he would say, quite correctly, that the state exists for the good of the individual and not the individual for the state. If the state makes no provision for whatever he wants to say or do, then, he would ask, what is the purpose of having a state or any organized society? In time the Chinese common man on the mainland will clamor for these same inherent rights, and the desire to enjoy the exercise of his rights will grow stronger. But for the moment he can only compare his lot with the miserable and inhuman conditions that prevailed only yesterday. The satisfaction of having personal freedom can wait till better days have arrived. Besides, the conception of personal freedom throughout the long history of China is entirely different from that in the West. Man has been regarded not as an absolute individual, but as a part of a social unit, with duties and responsibilities that no one can ignore.

I quite understand that this picture of the Chinese on the mainland is at variance with the views that are generally entertained. We have been reading accounts of a new China where the conditions are much worse than they were before and where the regime is at every moment on the verge of collapse. I think common sense will not allow us to believe that this can be true. However patient the common people may be in China, should there be real oppression, they will burst into open rebellion, regardless of the consequences, if oppression goes beyond a certain point. This has happened repeatedly in Chinese history. It is not for nothing that Mencius developed the theory of the right of popular and open rebellion if the ruler has forfeited what is known as the "mandate of heaven." The founder of the glorious Han Dynasty himself was a leader of the labor gang in charge of the construction of the Great Wall. In fact, practically every new dynasty in China was founded upon the widespread belief that misgovernment had become intolerable and that the "time for a change" had arrived. The government of Chiang Kai-shek, to which the United States still attaches so much importance, fell, if I may say so, for the same reason. If the present government on the mainland is no better, it will suffer the same fate. This is a kind of inexorable law that no government in Chinese history has been able to avoid. At any rate, this belief seems to receive the corroboration of Mr. Roger Hilsman, Jr., former Assistant Secretary of State for East Asian Affairs of the State Department, as late as December 13, 1963, when in his considered speech before the Commonwealth Club in San Francisco he said that there were no indications of any such collapse. "We have no reason," to quote his own words, "to believe that there is a present likelihood that the Communist regime will be overthrown."

We have also been informed that in China, the family, the main-stay of her social structure for thousands of years, has now all but disappeared. Children live away from their parents, and husbands and wives are separated at long intervals. They are brought to-gether only as the state desires. They live like robots, born into this world, as Koestler used to say "without umbilical cord." The much vaunted Confucianism, we are led to believe, is also dead and gone, Buddhism a mere façade, and all the humanistic values that took China thousands of years to cultivate and nurture have all been thrown into the gutter. The indictment of the new regime has been hard and merciless.

But it is gradually becoming clear that all these reports are false. The new regime is apparently doing everything it can to develop a sense of pride in the achievements and accomplishments of the past. From the moment that the Chinese Communists were in power, they immediately put a stop to the vandalism, the pillaging and pilfering of all the objects that would be useful in the rehabili-tation of China's historical personality, which had been going on for at least two generations since the Boxer Rebellion. If the Pe-king government had done nothing else but this, it would go down in history as having made an inestimable contribution to Chinese history.

I have myself seen and learned more of the grandeur of China's artistic creations from the museums and private collections abroad than during all the years I lived and taught and worked in China. As late as the 1930's, when I was with the Lytton Commission in Peking, at a time when I could afford to buy a few things for my-self, I saw cartloads of treasures transported to the foreign diplo-matic missions and displayed before the wondering eyes of my Western friends while I stood there completely speechless and helpless. Magnificent old silks and brocades with the most beauti-ful designs and colors, ivories and porcelains showing the most ex-quisite artistic sensibility and subtlety of the T'ang, Sung, Ming, and Ch'ing dynasties, jades of incomparable workmanship, bronzes, sculptures, paintings, even furniture—everything that ex-pressed the profound spiritual accomplishments of the Chinese people was looted and sold for export. The Chinese themselves, even if they had the means, could not acquire any of these objects. As the war with the Japanese was going on, when the last of the emperors was completely destitute, he began selling, or his eunuchs helped him to sell, the priceless Sung and Ming paintings which eventually found their way to private collectors in Europe and America. All this was part of an unspeakable tragedy which no words can fully describe.

Now this has stopped. But after over sixty years of relentless and continuous desecration it stands to reason that there is hardly anything left. All that now remains is a collection of headless torsos from the Buddhist caves of Loyang and Yunkang, too heavy to be towed away, which serve as mute reminders of a glorious past.

The destruction of the pride of race and the consequent loss of any sense of historic personality, among the Chinese generally and the official class in particular, was almost complete before the Communists took over. Is it not ironic that it should be they, the purveyors of a completely alien ideology, who began to recover that personality? It is they who realize that nationhood and a corrosive inferiority complex cannot exist side by side. What they have done since then to awaken the sense of belonging, of personal identity by the people with their rich and glorious heritage, is something quite unbelievable. If the treasures have been depleted, they put their spades to work, dug into the soil, and unearthed archeological finds. Traditional music, theater, dance, from every corner of the land, have now been developed to an amazing degree, side by side with their modern counterparts. In the field of medicine alone no one will deny that the people have established a record, on the basis of limited means and experience, of which any people can be proud. British doctors and specialists who have visited China have written articles in *Lancet* and other journals attesting to the notable results that have been achieved. And even *Time* magazine, so vigorously opposed to the mainland China on whose soil its publisher was born, sang a chorus of praise when it learned that within the space of four short hours the hand of a machine worker, completely severed above the wrist, was rejoined with the arm, and he can now not only write, but also lift a weight of over ten pounds. It was the first case of such successful surgery in medical history.

Dr. Wilder Penfield, one of Canada's leading neurologists, went to China recently where he traveled with Mrs. Penfield "at least 4,000 miles by train and car." In an interview of March 10, 1963, which was published in *Yale Reports* (a weekly published by Yale University), he made among other things the following comments:

> The development of neurology is rather remarkable . . . I made rounds (in a hospital in Peking) twice and was very much impressed by the level of work. Certainly there is no clinic in Europe which excels it, and they have already done some original work.
>
> In thirteen years they have trained 104,000 Western physicians, if you want to call them that.
>
> The college hospitals in the big cities, for example, are absolutely first-class. They are doing heart surgery with equipment for extracorporeal circulation, which they made themselves, since they were unable to get it from the United States. (I wonder how American specialists feel about such a sad situation.) In the university hospital in Shanghai I saw a large ward filled with patients who had had open heart surgery and who were being handled by a man who had never studied outside the country.

Asked about what one single impression of the Chinese people he would bring back to his own people, Dr. Penfield commented: "I think I was most impressed by the attitude of those that I met. It was a feeling of enthusiasm, exhilaration and pleasure that at last they were doing something on their own. They were working, especially the younger people, and they are working with a will . . . I would say in general that there is a feeling of excitement and enthusiasm among the people." One of the most interesting parts of the interview was Dr. Penfield's comments on the conditions of famine which were so widely reported.

> Of course, I was prepared to find evidence of malnutrition and innutrition. I have been in a famine in Calcutta and I saw the effect of deficient diet in England towards the close of the war.

I know what it looks like, and there is none of that in China. I was not in every corner of China, of course, but you can't hide these things. If you travel in public conveyances, you see the country as it is. We saw no beggars all the time we were in China, and I saw no evidence of food lack. The people are energetic as they would not be if they had not enough food, Chinese or any other nationality, and they are working with a will and with great enthusiasm.

It is not the accomplishments themselves, remarkable as they are, so much as the appearance of a new spirit and the awareness of a national purpose for which we must give credit to the Communists. There is hardly any area in the national life of the people where they have not introduced, or attempted to introduce, drastic reforms. Of course the collapse and failure of the Great Leap Forward is an example of immaturity and lack of experience in the application of economic and social ideas. It was a leap into the dark, and all China suffered from bruises and cuts which, it was even thought and hoped by many people, would prove fatal. And then adding insult to injury, Soviet Russia began, as the Chinese saying goes, pulling the faggot from underneath the caldron. Having failed to convert China into a satellite, Soviet Russia chose a moment of difficulty to recall all her technical personnel. With that, she thought, China's industrial plans, agriculture, or any other kind of modern development would have to be suspended. But it is clear that Mr. Khrushchev had neither read Chinese history nor acquired any knowledge of the Chinese character.

For today the whole nation is back on its feet. The *Herald Tribune* described it as "The Red Chinese Miracle." "Though its errors in industry were unparalleled and its failures in agriculture exceeded even those of Premier Khrushchev's Virgin Lands program, Red China's human miracle of recovery in the last two years is likely to confound the skeptics. Alone, unaided . . . by . . . Khrushchev, Red China is back in business . . . Today, once again, Red China is riding high . . ." *

A miracle it certainly is. But in the last analysis it is another

* *New York* Herald Tribune, *January 2, 1964.*

proof that spirit is stronger than matter. For the government, in those critical days of disillusionment, frustration, and disarray, never really lost faith in itself and made the people realize that salvation comes only through one's own effort. That is another way of saying that, for all their Marxism-Leninism, the Chinese Communists are still basically Confucian and even Buddhist in spirit. For did not the old Master say, "When you have committed an error, do not be afraid of correcting yourself"? Or "Rely upon yourself for rejuvenation." Or again, "Ceaselessly work to make yourself strong." Or, as Buddha said before he passed on to parinirvana, "Struggle without rest to work out your own salvation." The people on their part did not lose confidence in their leaders, for if they did, nothing perhaps could have been accomplished. Their pride of identity with the government and the awareness that the government had been working only for their welfare, performed the almost impossible task of overcoming all the difficulties. "The eyes of the people," as they say, "are dazzlingly clear"; they are fully aware of the vast differences between what they are now and what they were before the present regime was established.

Then the government was honeycombed with corruption and incompetence; *now* no single individual is rich. *Then* the wealth of the country was concentrated in the hands of the privileged few; *now* they share equally, even if they are all still poor. *Then* education was reserved for a fraction of the people; *now* everyone has the opportunity of free schooling, from the nursery and kindergarten to the university itself. *Then* there was hardly any health or sanitation to speak of; *now* everything is kept immaculately clean: cholera, typhoid and dysentery, which were endemic, are now either under control or eliminated. Even the prisons have become truly reformatories where the inmates have a chance of rehabilitation and emerge as useful citizens.*

---

* *I have no personal knowledge of these new facts of life on mainland China. For a full discussion of these and other facts* The Other Side of the River *by Edgar Snow and* China: The Country Americans Are Not Allowed to Know *by Felix Greene should be consulted. I have no reason to doubt the integrity of these able writers who visited China.*

Before it was impossible to live on one's wages, as the deprecia-
tion of the currency took place from hour to hour or even from
minute to minute. In 1948 (August 9) a lunch at the Palace Hotel
in Shanghai cost millions of Chinese dollars. Vegetable soup was
$800,000, onion soup $1,100,000, spaghetti with meat sauce was
$2,800,000, and chicken liver with mushrooms was $3,500,000!
Today the Chinese dollar on the mainland is in the neighborhood
of forty-two cents in American money, and has not fluctuated
since it was introduced.

The results of national reconstruction since the advent of the
new regime were so impressive that the former Acting President of
China, General Li Tsung-jen, had the courage and the honesty to
say that he was happy his fight against the Chinese Communists had
been a failure.* For nearly half a century, since the early days of
Communism in China, it was his duty as a soldier and government
official to help stamp out this curse of alien origin. Little did he
suspect, he admitted, that in so short a period these same Chinese
Communists could have done such wonders. General Li, who returned to Peking in mid-July 1965, after having been living in
retirement in New Jersey, is perhaps one of the most colorful and
democratic personalities in modern China. Simple, of farmer stock,
a man of absolute integrity and honesty, he made himself a model
governor of Kwangsi Province, where he was born. During the war
with Japan he became a national hero by defeating over one million
Japanese soldiers at the Battle of Taierhchwang in 1938. The
Japanese themselves admitted that General Li wrote "an immortal
page in Chinese military history." Shortly after the war ended he was
elected, against opposition from Chiang Kai-shek, by overwhelming
popular vote to the vice-presidency. When Chiang resigned in 1949
after being roundly defeated by the Communists, Li became, according to the Chinese constitution, not the acting president but the
substantive president of China, serving out the term not completed
by Chiang. Li soon after came to the United States for surgical care.
During his absence Chiang went to Taiwan, decided to take back
the presidency, and did. When Professor Edward S. Corwin of

---

* L'Europeo (*Italian weekly*), *July 14, 1963.*

Princeton, of constitutional law fame, heard this he laughed and said "This is a new one on me." And then he continued, "But then the Chinese have been the first in many things in history." When General Li returned to Peking in July, Professor C. Martin Wilbur of Columbia made the fitting remark: "He simply went home. He was an old man [aged seventy-four] who just went home. To say anything more than that would be an unworthy act."

The record of the Chinese leadership seems quite incredible. For the first time in the history of modern China, for one thing, the leaders in the government have worked in complete harmony.* In Soviet Russia there are still rivalries, struggles for personal power, purges and liquidations. But in China, where for over half a century, there was not one year in which civil war of one kind or another did not take place, there has now been peace and order from one end of the enormous country to another. Personal jealousies, selfishness, ambition, greed, avarice, the unsavory desire to amass fortunes through the abuse of political power, and most of all the willing surrender to feminine charms after all these have been satisfied and the harvest of enormous wealth is safely in the bag—all of a sudden, as if with a magic wand, these failings vanished into thin air. What has happened? Surely in a conversion as dramatic as this, some spiritual force, some power of cohesion must have developed. I believe there has. And this intangible something is what makes all the difference between the Chinese and Soviet styles of revolution. The Yenan group of elder statesmen went through identical experiences of extreme bitterness. The Long March of 6,000 miles, every inch of which along the way being as frightful as that *citta dolente* of Dante's *Inferno,* was the anvil on which all who took part surrendered themselves to be beaten and forged into that unbreakable chain which today binds the country together. When one day its authentic story is written, as it certainly will be

---

* *Assistant Secretary of State Roger Hilsman's speech at the Commonwealth Club in San Francisco on December 13, 1963, which stated the official view of the State Department on the prospects of the "second echelon of leadership" in China eventually abandoning the stand of the older Yenan group, is neither timely nor wise. It gave the impression that he was trying to break the solidarity of the leaders by promoting fissiparous tendencies. It was, to say the least, somewhat inept.*

(if it is not already done), there is no doubt in my mind that it will be considered an epic in the history of man. No other group of men anywhere, to my knowledge, has gone through such an ordeal in the teeth of such fearful persecution. When they sometimes had to swallow urine to quench their thirst, taste their own feces to assuage hunger, doze off, out of sheer fatigue, in swamps infested with malaria-carrying mosquitoes and poisonous snakes, and still had the iron will to survive and carry on their mission, then we realize what stuff these people are made of. They finally arrived in Yenan, but only a fraction of them, and there in the caves and wind-blown mud walls of the loess soil they sheltered and nurtured that indomitable spirit which ultimately made them the masters of China. Are we to believe that people with such doggedness and determination are merely interested in advancing their personal material well-being now that they are in a position to do so? And when they are called upon to shape and mold the destiny of 700 millions of their countrymen, are we to believe that they are fulfilling their mission by merely wanting to raise their standard of living? They do not say that it is unimportant to do so, but it is wholly secondary. It is a mistake to believe that the aim of Chinese Communism is to improve the living conditions of the Chinese, so that in time every family will have a radio, or TV set, and perhaps a car or two in the garage. This may be the Soviet wish. But it is definitely not what Chinese Communism wants.

One of my students, Mr. William Liebler, made a shrewd observation when he wrote, "How can the Soviet Union remain true to the social ideals of communism if she attempts only to imitate the United States in so many matters? The Chinese Communists, while they are determined to provide their people with an adequate standard of living, tend to feel that there are more important social and cultural ends to be achieved in life than mere accumulation of material goods."

One of these ends is obviously to create a society which is not only classless, but in which the exploitation of one person by another or of one group of people by another, will be made impossible. The Chinese Communists' position is based on the actual experiences which China went through. A social system in which an entire nation, dedicated to the arts of peace and culture, could be made to suffer for so long in order to satisfy the acquisitive instincts of an alien minority, it is felt, must have been intrinsically unhealthy. There is no desire on the part of the Chinese Communists to establish an affluent society in the American manner. They demand changes in human nature itself, if that is possible.

The Chinese Communist movement has more of a religious overtone than the Russian. Every individual is required to go through a process of self-analysis. It is a kind of spiritual exercise on a social scale, in which one fearlessly lays bare one's own faults and shortcomings for everyone else to see and to criticize. It is not a comfortable exercise by any means; but it has a cathartic effect, and one emerges with a feeling of humility, because the balloon has been pricked and the inflated ego becomes no more than a mere pinpoint, which it should properly be.

This discipline is in one sense analogous to what was demanded by Confucius when one of his disciples said, "I daily examine into my personal conduct on three points: first, whether in carrying out the duties entrusted to me by others I have not failed in conscientiousness; second, whether in intercourse with friends I have not failed in sincerity and trustworthiness; third, whether I have not failed to practice what I profess in my teaching." In Confucianism the emphasis is on a detached appraisal of one's conduct in the light of its moral principles: it is a strictly personal affair. In the Chinese version of communism the emphasis is on a judgment of one's conduct in the light of the approbation or disapprobation of the community: it becomes therefore largely a social matter, using the criterion of social needs as the standard of measurement and acting on the assumption that the community always has the correct sense of justice—which is, of course, open to question. But the procedure in both cases is an internal one. In the case of Confucianism, constant exercise sharpens one's conscience and increases one's moral stature. In communism, the anti-social disease of selfishness is reduced to the minimum. The energy of a person is expended not for the satisfaction of the ego, but for social advance. It is in this sense that the individual has lost his personal freedom.

The results, socially speaking, have been impressive. Trees have been planted by the hundreds of millions. Roads are even and well paved. Houses for the ordinary workmen have grown up like mushrooms. Water in many places can be drunk straight from the tap. Sanitation is so well taken care of that most of the common diseases are now under control. The list can go on indefinitely: even the fly makes a rare appearance nowadays, as there is always someone after him with a swatter.* Of course it must still be asked whether or not it was necessary to have recourse to communism in order to make these advances. But in the case of China, some form of control was perhaps essential to reawaken the people's sense of social responsibility.

Further, when we recall that these results have been achieved under the most difficult circumstances, we cannot deny that somehow, as Dr. Penfield pointed out, a new sense of purpose must be responsible for this change. With 1952 as the base of calculation, it is said that the annual rate of economic growth for 1950–57 was 8.6 per cent. It was 7.4 per cent with 1953 as the base. Even in Japan, the most rapidly developed country in Asia, the rate was only 4.6 per cent between 1898 and 1914, and 4.9 per cent between 1914 and 1936. Only in 1956–59 did it rise also to 8.6 per cent.

It is generally believed that Soviet Russia was a major factor behind this phenomenal growth in China. But, as we have said already, this is not so: it is to her interest to keep China in the permanent position of a satellite. The present rift between the two Communist powers has given us more knowledge about their relation than we had previously. If, as Premier Chou En-lai said in October 1959, "Soviet Russia has sent over 10,800 experts to the East European satellites and only 1,500 [to China] during the decade from 1949," and even those were mostly withdrawn in 1960,

---

*Among the casualties also was the harmless common sparrow. But the verdict was that it eats the grain that should go to fill the human stomach. All the village children were trained to beat their gongs, and the poor things dropped down dead, as they could not remain long in the air on their wings. But drought, locusts, and failure of the Great Leap Forward have, we have been told, brought back the sparrow to restore the balance of nature. This is another one of the lessons that the people on the mainland learn by trial and error. There are endless examples of knowledge through experience.

it should be clear that Soviet assistance was extremely restricted from the very beginning. Soviet credit available for investment in China was not more than 3 per cent of the total state investments. The fact of the matter is that China had practically no long-term credits from any country.* Without long-term credits it is obvious there can be no development of heavy industry of any scope; and without heavy industry it is difficult to see how any nation can base its policy on aggression. Doak Barnett, who is not regarded as being sympathetic toward the Chinese Communists, made some remarks that are just plain common sense. From a study of the available material he is of the opinion that, "there are many reasons to believe . . . Peking's leaders do not think primarily in terms either of Chinese historical conquest abroad or of exporting revolution by overt Chinese aggression." Elsewhere he said, "As of early autumn of 1959 there is little to indicate that the Chinese Communists have in fact decided to pursue a general policy of large-scale military aggression. The new pressures they have been exerting on China's neighbors have to date been limited pressures and apparently Peking's aims both in regard to the Sino-Indian border and Laos have also been limited." One of the best examples of the truth of this statement is what happened in November of 1962, when in just thirty-one days, much to their own surprise, the Chinese Communist forces found themselves at the southern foothills of the Himalayas, threatening the rich province of Assam. Any other army in such a position would have continued going south for a few more days, without any difficulty (Tezpur and the surrounding areas having already been evacuated), and detached Assam from the rest of India. But instead of that, the whole army was withdrawn to the original line.

---

* Doak Barnett pointed out in his Communist China and Asia, p. 231, "As China embarked on its second Five Year Plan, it appeared to be proceeding almost completely on a pay-as-you-go basis, and this may have been an important factor behind the radical changes in domestic policies 1957–58. The dramatic decisions to set up decentralized, small-scale, labor intensive industries, to mobilize labor on a mass scale for irrigation and other projects requiring little capital investment, and to regiment China's population and resources further by establishing the communes, may all be related, in some respect at least, to the fact that by 1958 Communist China has been carrying out its development programs without long-term foreign loans."

China still talks about Marxism-Leninism, but, as we have seen, the kind of dialectical materialism at the heart of Marxist teaching, that a politico-economic system should be constructed with the principal aim of bettering man's material condition, is not entirely what Chinese Communism is working for. It goes beyond that aim. According to Marx, after man has managed to proceed from a condition of necessity to a condition of affluence and abundance, the state will wither away because the need to perpetuate its dominance over the minority will have ended. But it is, I think, the wish of Chinese Communism neither to witness the disappearance of the Chinese state nor to be satisfied with merely acquiring the means of survival. As early as the seventh century B.C., fully one century before the time of Confucius, a minister of the State of Chi, named Kuan Chung, was already saying that it was all very well to provide adequate food and clothing to the people, but these were only the basis for the building of a society that should be impregnated with moral values and in which men and women would have a better chance to develop their qualities as human beings. This is what makes Chinese Communism, I believe, something different from what is aimed at in Soviet Russia: It seeks not only to raise the level of economic existence, however important that may be, but also to improve the quality of life itself. This again brings the Chinese version of communism in line with many of the reformers of the past.*

---

* The recent observation by Sir Alec Douglas-Home, half serious and half in jest, that a "fat" Communist is less dangerous than a "skinny" one, does not seem to hold true in the case of Chinese Communism. The fat Communist is defined as one who has a car, a TV set, a refrigerator, and many other material luxuries. The skinny one is supposed to have none of these. The Chinese Communist desires, I presume, to emerge from a state of being skinny, but he does not strive to be fat either. His emphasis is not entirely on material acquisitions. As Jacques Marcuse correctly pointed out in his article "It Doesn't Matter Who Succeeds Mao" (New York Times Magazine, July 11, 1965): "Chinese party members are warned that Marxism-Leninism cannot be accepted in its foreign 'standard' form, but must be rethought to fit 'the characteristics of China.'"

III THE RECORD

THE THEORY that civilization, like any living organism, grows, attains maturity, and then declines and passes away to make room for a new civilization, is a fascinating one. As yet no one has said whether it has an element of truth or is all nonsense. The Chinese, at any rate, do not think that this is the law of history. History, they believe, works in cycles. It is interesting to see how these differing attitudes have been responsible for two patterns of historical evolution represented respectively by the West and by China. The West forges ahead in violent upheavals. In the East, or in China at least, even though the change of dynasties might have been brought about by military activity, the spirit of culture itself maintained an even flow, gathering as it went along its course a rich accumulation of past experience, never wasted, which has given its life a unique flavor. In the West there is an urge to begin all over again. In China the instinct is to conserve and preserve.

Shortly after the First World War, when I was in Germany as a student, I used to go about in the company of its young people on bicycles, and I found invariably they carried in their knapsacks two books, one the two-volume work *The Decline of the West* and the other the flimsy little book by the founder of Taoism, Lao-tze. I was curious to know why it was that those two books, so different in spirit and conception, were inseparable. The reason was simple. The defeat of Germany, the Germans liked to think, was not merely an isolated fact: it was part of the process of decline which held in its grip all of Western civilization, which had reached a final stage of technological perfection, but the lack of any vital content and cohesive power was leading it to certain dissolution. The war was therefore inevitable, and after the war there would be chaos, confusion, and finally extinction. It was a sad theory. But the human soul revolts against this kind of determinism; it seeks consolation even as it feels that the inevitable stares in its face. Hence the *Tao-teh Ching,* perhaps one of the most profound and wisest books ever written, made a deep impression on the minds of even these young Germans.

How much they understood the thinking of Lao-tze is immaterial. But he fascinated them with his short, crisp, brilliant, and often witty remarks in sharp contrast to the verbosity of Oswald Spengler. The *Tao-teh Ching* has a mystical quality, it has flashes of insight or *prajna* as the Hindus call it, it is intuitive, but above all, it must have seemed to have made some sense to these young Teutons when it taught that the universe was essentially in the nature of a cycle where, as Emerson said, "every end is a beginning," and therefore contention, strife, and fighting were clearly out of place. Like the Yankee farmer who said, "Blessed be nothing. The worse things are, the better they are," the aphorisms and paradoxes of Lao-tze appeared to have fortified the sagging spirit of a lost generation. Humility, non-assertion, peace, harmony, willing submission to the forces of nature because in the end all things would evolve to where one desires them—these ideas were new to these youngsters, and for that brief moment these preachments from China provided the consolation they were looking for. But in less than ten years, these same young people had perhaps become Nazis, and were once again in the full swing of the Hegelian view of history.

I think it is fair to say that Western civilization is founded on the principle of self-assertion, of a sudden rise and fall, which is alien to the temper of the Chinese. As Professor Joseph Needham observed, "Europe, more intrinsically unstable, suffered violent changes." But both the violence and the instability, in this now terribly restricted world, can of course be a source of intense worry to others. Violence can bring to an end what, with a more effective sense of control and a more evenly distributed temper, may blossom forth into a new land of promise. The Chinese concept of the cycle has not been sufficiently analyzed, but the pattern of a gradual rise and fall has taken place by and large within a period of some eight centuries, when a cycle is completed. Be that as it may, with what is being done in China today, it has become pertinent to ask whether she is emerging from her low fortunes of the immediate past to another period of creative purposefulness comparable to any in the past? If it comes, as it may well do, I believe it should be welcomed, rather than resisted and feared, by the rest of the world. Already there is apparent a feeling of uneasiness among the Western peoples, as if a strong China will harm them. This perhaps explains more effectively than anything else why there is so much antagonism on the part of the United States toward China.

China would not be the China that we know in history, nor could she endure for so long if she frittered away her time and energy in devising ways of how to pay back what she received. Her political and moral philosophy has been based on the concept that the world is large and spacious enough, even as it is today, for everyone to live happily with everyone else. But before this thought finally takes root in the mind of the Western peoples, there will be doubt because they have not been accustomed to the habit of true neighborliness. That is why, unfortunately, for some time to come, the specter of Chinese aggression, Chinese imperialism, Chinese expansionism, Chinese invasion of her neighbors, will be placed before us. These are all terms that have long become familiar in the Western political dictionary, or in the pattern of its political behavior. Have we reason to believe that China is also following that pattern? The question will be answered when we come to discuss the Tibetan region of China, India, and Vietnam, all three of which have been taken as glaring examples of Chinese intransigence and aggressiveness.

For the moment, let us confine ourselves to what it will mean to China herself when she regains the position in the family of nations that has been denied to her for so long. We are apt to refer to China's long history as if it is something mystical, or something that other nations have not enjoyed. Doesn't Egypt have a longer history, or for that matter India? Both are good examples. In fact, in the case of Egypt, she was already mature and a full-grown civilization when China was young. That was almost what Premier Chou En-lai said in Cairo, looking at the ancient mummies during his recent visit to Egypt. But at the same time no historian will gainsay that the Egypt of today is organically and structurally not the same as the Egypt of the Pharaohs. Its continuity had been broken in a violent manner. The blood of the peasants today may to a certain extent be the same blood that flowed in the veins of the fellahins of Ramses II. But the language is no longer the same. Nor is the religion the same. The whole network of social beliefs and manners has changed. For somewhere around A.D. 640 there came to the city of Heliopolis, which was dedicated to the worship of the sun and therefore the most sacred city of all Egypt, the Islamic general Amr ibn-al-As. To him Egypt was the "color of a white pearl, then like golden amber, and then like a green emerald and a carpet of colors." He coveted the city with its "four hundred theaters, four thousand palaces with their four thousand baths and forty thousand tax-paying Jews." So he defeated the Byzantine army, and the ancient civilization of Egypt then began to disintegrate. For the Arabs built a civilization of their own, and by the sheer weight of this superstructure, everything that belonged to the Egypt of old was crushed out of existence. What was once the center of the Near Eastern world now became a mere periphery to a vast desert empire controlled from Mecca or Damascus or Baghdad.

But there was no such violent upheaval to disturb the flow of culture in the history of China even when her political fortunes might sometimes be very low.

As for India, it is again a different picture. Even if Hinduism took its rise from the Vedas and the Upanishads, trying to mold all of India according to its ideas and beliefs and thus to create a sense of unity, the divergent factors of race, language and caste, have always prevented any kind of organic unity. It was not only the Aryans who came in to desecrate the people of the Indus valley; they were followed by the Kushans, then the Pathans, then the Arabs, then the Rajputs, then the Moguls, and finally the British, each of whom in their own way imposed their rule upon the subcontinent, one on the top of the other. Neither the Egyptians nor the Indians have been as fortunate as the Chinese in preserving, nurturing, and deepening that massive homogeneity and identity

which remains their priceless possession. Its roots are planted
firmly and undisturbed in the same soil, and that is why it has a
peculiar flavor of authenticity which is unmistakably its own. That
is why, even during its days of decadence, Westerners could live in
Peking and enjoy "its fabulous ease and physical comfort," not the
kind of comfort that comes with modern plumbing, but something
more subtle and agreeable. "Peking," so says one writer, "in the
gentleness of manner of its inhabitants, in their courtesy and their
good humor, had become for those lucky enough to have found it
a sunlit haven difficult to describe, superb for the enjoyment of the
mere sweetness of existence, unlike anything they had known before . . ." *

How very true! To have known Peking is to have had an experience "difficult to describe." One can feel it soon after one is im-
mersed in its atmosphere. The usually clear bright sun shining on
the multicolored tiles of many palaces and temples, the bracing air,
the strange and unfamiliar sights, all these create a sense of exhilaration rarely known in the other cities of the world. Even the moon
and stars, as Simone de Beauvoir testified only recently,† shine
differently in Peking. "In all China," she says, "nothing can compare with the beauty of a gray *hutung* under a moon as cold as an
iceberg and stars as sharp as icicles." And then she adds, "The
voice of a vendor crying his wares reverberates between blind
walls; far off, a door-knocker bangs on a wooden door; not another sound. The acid smell of earth pervades the night. Peking is
one of those rare places in the world when certain moments are
perfect."

One would think that this is pure nostalgia, fondly written to
recall from memory delightful experiences which have long vanished. But this description is of a Peking which the French au-
thoress visited long after the Communists, who are supposed to
have swept away everything authentically Chinese, had come to
power. How often have we been told that Communism in China,
as elsewhere, is out to destroy, to strike at the roots of the ancient
traditions and to install in their place the monstrosities of a techno-

---

* *George N. Kates, in the preface to his* Chinese Household Furniture.
† *Simone de Beauvoir:* The Long March.

logical age. Obviously this is not so. In fact, the truth is the very opposite of this. The Chinese Communists have called themselves liberators. In the sphere of culture they realize that the rude and violent impact of the West on China for over a century has thrown her off balance and stayed her tide of natural development. This external influence, baneful from the very beginning because it was sordidly pecuniary, was essentially antagonistic to her entire spirit and genius and has grown deformities which have warped and twisted her soul. In the true spirit of the liberator the Chinese Communist has now lifted this influence and built a confidence of the masses in themselves which is leading them to a new era of creativeness.*

Let me mention one out of the many attempts which are being made. During a recent trip to Hong Kong my wife and I were pleasantly surprised to find various types of music which we thought had become moribund but which have actually blossomed forth with extraordinary beauty. If the purpose of music—all music—is not to shock and overpower but to create an auditory realm of sheer delight, then there is a good deal in the music of the Chinese mainland which satisfies the requirement. Also some of the moving pictures based on historical themes are examples of technical perfection, comparable to any elsewhere. The music, the dance, the acting, and the development of the incidents, without the coarseness and vulgarity of much of this kind of entertainment, have shown, as in other things, that this vaunted Western superiority which has been mercilessly inflicted on the world for over a

---

* As long as over half a century ago one observant critic made this perceptive remark: "The external influence brought to bear upon her [China] has been one essentially antagonistic to her whole spirit and genius, and has served to make development of a kind which was natural to her and which was something wholly unlike and far more subtle than the progress of modern Europe, an impossibility." Hugh Clifford in "The East and the West" in The Monthly Review, April 1903, p. 133. Mr. Clifford continued: "The aggressive spirit of Europe and the spirit which, coming into rude contact with that of the East, threw the latter violently back upon itself, stayed the tide of its natural development, compelling retrogression." I may add that holding out pecuniary gains without understanding any higher values in life eventually produced a type of person in China that was no longer Chinese and certainly not Western.

century, is no longer what it was taken to be. I am not as yet discussing the world of moral and spiritual values. Even in the world of matter, the world of science and technology, in which the West has been decidedly superior, it is wise, I think, to remember the words of Dr. H. A. L. Fisher, who in his *History of Europe* said:

> This astounding supremacy in the field of scientific discovery has not always existed and may not always continue. Judged by the length of years during which human life has existed on this planet, the intellectual ascendancy [in science] of the white European race is a very recent phenomenon. Europe has not always been the tutor nor Asia a pupil. There was a time when these relations were reversed.

This was true, for instance, during the period of the Crusades and a large part of the Middle Ages, when the intellectual life among the Arabs was more vigorous and advanced than among the Christian nations. This Arab vitality and the Arab critical attitude that gradually superseded the authoritarian spirit of the Church were in fact a contributing factor to the development of the spirit of inquiry that brought on the Renaissance and the subsequent triumph of science. Scientific accomplishment is an acquisition that can be mine today, yours tomorrow. It may be of European origin, but it cannot permanently remain a European or American possession. Its attributes have universal validity, and to that extent they belong to all mankind if mankind decides to appropriate them for its use.* This distinction was discussed in the early days when the

---

* *That the Chinese through the ages made great contributions to scientific and technological advance, including silk, printing, porcelain, gunpowder, etc., all of which immeasurably increased human welfare, is a historical fact that should be widely known. Professor Joseph Needham's massive volumes,* Science and Civilization in China, *of which four out of a projected ten have been published, should be a permanent possession of every educated person's library so that he may regard the scientific capacity of the different peoples in proper relation to one another. Professor Needham also contributed a long chapter on the development of science in China in a recent book,* The Legacy of China (Clarendon Press), *in which he quoted some remarks from the* Novum Organum *of Francis Bacon that are of the utmost significance. "It is well to observe," said Bacon, "the force and virtue and consequences of discoveries. These are to be seen nowhere more conspicuously than in*

Jesuits brought science into China in the seventeenth century. They insisted on calling it "Western," with the intention obviously of increasing the prestige of the religion that they wanted to propagate, and which, of course, they wanted to show was as much "Western" as science. But the clear-sighted emperor Kang-hsi, who had come on the throne in 1660, would have none of this and insisted on using the word "new" and not "Western." The emperor won, not because he was emperor, but because he was right. However, the Jesuits made the best use of the argument and affirmed that if science, which was of European origin, had universal value and was therefore superior, then all other human activity that was European in origin must likewise be universal and superior.*

---

those three which were unknown to the ancients, and of which the origin, though recent, is obscure and inglorious [sic]; namely, printing, gunpowder, and the magnet. For these three have changed the whole face and state of things throughout the world, the first in literature, the second in warfare, the third in navigation; whence have followed innumerable changes, in so much that no empire, no sect, no star, seems to have exerted greater power and influence in human affairs than these mechanical discoveries." Those three inventions, which revolutionized European society more than any other invention, and whose origins no one, not even Bacon himself, knew, we now know to have come out of China. In other words, the Chinese capacity for science need never have been questioned. It was its incompatibility with the cosmological views of the Chinese that prevented it from developing; but from now on, under the compulsion of a previously nonexistent set of circumstances, the development of science in China will acquire a new momentum.

* Mr. John Foster Dulles, for all his stubborn pursuit of a firm and inflexible foreign policy, had some interesting thoughts in other areas. In his report to the nation given on March 24, 1956, he had this to say: "We need to remember that although we have developed more rapidly than Asians in some directions, notably in industrialization, they have preceded us in finding many of the ways to make life richer. Their culture and art long antedate our own, and in many respects have not yet been equaled by our own. . . . They have an exceptional love and appreciation of beauty.

"They possess in full measure those human qualities which all admire—devotion to family and to country, courage and willingness to sacrifice. They possess unusual qualities of patience, reflection, and repose. Therefore, let us not forget that while we have material and technical things to give, they also have things to give. And if we are wise enough to perceive and to take what Asia has to offer, the balance struck between us will not be one-sided by any true measure of values.

"The great richness of our universe is due above all to its diversity. We may take honorable pride in our own distinctive accomplishments. But we

This curious and fallacious logic has wrought havoc for three centuries. Roman law, because it is European, must be superior to any other legal system in the world, Westerners argue. That, of course, cannot be true. A study of Chinese legal concepts in antiquity will convince anyone that many of them are of value in our modern world. Western philosophical thought, it is also argued, is superior. That, of course, is not true.

Now, for the first time in a century, the inferiority complex that grew from the impact of the West has been dissipated. I think this is all to the good, not only for the Chinese, but for the world. The masses of the people are beginning to feel that they have enough resources, both of a material and a spiritual nature, to sustain and direct them. That does not mean that the growing strength will in time be employed to subdue the will of others.

Some will say that this is simply not true, that the facts of international life are pointing in the other direction. Since the advent of the Communist regime and the Korean War, it will be said, China has deliberately launched a policy of expansion, of aggression, of territorial aggrandizement, of invasion into neighboring states, until she has become the exponent of a new imperialism and colonialism, even as these are on their way out in other parts of the world.

I hope to make it abundantly clear that this is emotionally inpired and is being turned out from mass media to stimulate antagonism and animosity. It has neither reason nor sense. Take the Korean War as an example. Is there not a UN resolution condemning aggressive action by China? With due respect to that world organization and believing, as we all do, that it is the only effective organ for the maintenance of world peace today, I think we would be naïve indeed if we did not recognize that it can be maneuvered, like all international organizations, into adopting resolutions that do not necessarily represent ultimate wisdom. Is it not possible that the Korean resolution was one of such cases? After all, the United Nations consists now, as it consisted then, of a large number of independent sovereign national entities, each of which is out to promote its own interests, even as it tries to promote the interests of peace.

---

should equally be aware that the accomplishments of others are a proper subject for their pride and our appreciation."

The Palmerstonian concept of permanent national self-interest dies hard, as we all know.

Let us review briefly the history and factual background of the war itself. When it erupted on June 25, 1950, the Chinese Communist government had been in existence for barely eight months. Are we to believe that such a government, which was hardly on its feet, was foolhardy enough to run headlong against world opinion by precipitating a major war? The Communist leaders then are the same leaders today, and time has shown them to be a cautious group of people, with a firm grasp of realities. Consider also the condition of the army of the new government in 1950. In spite of its numbers, it was regarded, certainly by the outside world, as a rabble, having just gone through a long period of conflict with the Japanese and a still longer period of exhausting civil war with the forces of Chiang Kai-shek. It was ill-fed, ill-clothed, ill-equipped, and ill-trained. Surely such an army was in no position to fight with the world's most powerful armies. The most logical thing for a government under such circumstances to do, if it wished to win the support of its people, would be to disband its soldiers now that it was in the saddle, to send them back to the farms, and to have them do something constructive. That was precisely what the new government planned to do some two months before the crisis exploded.

The story of this episode has not been told. From reliable sources it is now learned that Mao Tse-tung did indeed consider the demobilization of the army. When the Korean crisis broke, he called a conference of leaders representing every shade of opinion. Two members, one of whom was the redoubtable professor of economics of Peking National University, Dr. Ma Yin-chu, were against going into the war and reminded Mao of his desire to disband the soldiers. The decision to go into the war was however, in spite of Ma's opposition, passed, but Dr. Ma did not return home. Mrs. Ma grew anxious and asked a friend to find out what had happened. Evening came, and there was still no sign of Dr. Ma. Mrs. Ma's fears grew and she asked the friend to contact Premier Chou En-lai. She then received the news that her husband was being "persuaded" to see why China had to go into the war and that he would return home the next morning—which he did. What happened was that Stalin, acting upon Acheson's remark that Korea was not within the U.S. defense perimeter, urged North Korea to take immediate action. If the war broke out and met unexpected resistance, Stalin would ask Communist China to come to the assistance of North Korea, promising logistical support. What Stalin principally wanted was to involve China in a major international crisis and to compel her to rely completely on Russia. The meaning of the Soviet move was not lost to the new leaders in Peking, but at that time there was no way in which China could ignore the wishes of Soviet Russia. She had to mobilize, and the soldiers who were sent into Korea were drawn from some of the distant parts of the country. Previously there had been no concentration of Chinese forces on the Korean border.

Chinese Communist soldiers were not sent into Korea till November, four months after the forces under the UN command were on Korean soil. Are we therefore to believe that they had been planning aggressive designs on Korea all along? Would it rather be more accurate to say that, seeing that Allied soldiers under the command of General MacArthur were crossing the Yalu River, and fearing that they might continue into China's territory to topple the newly formed government, the Chinese Communists became convinced they must enter the war. The General never denied that such was indeed his intention. He even threatened to use atomic power to obtain his end. As late as two years ago, during his visit to the Philippines, he frankly and honestly stated this position of his in public. He had the courage to say so, and the world admired him for it. But if such were his intentions, would we be wrong to say that the Chinese Communists fought out of desperation only in defense of their country? In what then does Chinese aggression in Korea lie?

There is still another historical fact which must be considered. Knowing that it was hopeless to fight against a formidable international army, the Chinese Communists attempted at all costs to avoid a confrontation, though not to the extent of completely sacrificing their national honor. They made it explicitly clear, through Indian intermediaries, that they would intervene if Allied troops crossed the 38th parallel. If they had to fight, they would. On this point, let me say that there is in America a complete lack of understanding of the Chinese character. Such ignorance could not have existed had there been some knowledge of Chinese history. A weak, backward country, which the Western world had learned to trample upon with no remorse for over a century, is not the kind of country whose opinion is automatically respected. Yet there is a fiber among the peasants and the common people which can become as tough as steel when the propitious moment arrives. It was already apparent during the war with Japan. The Roman soldier, so we have been told by the archeologists, had a Stoic sense of duty. The Chinese soldier, if the occasion called for it, willingly sacrificed his life, as the discoveries in the lonely ramparts along the 1,500-mile Great Wall, often separated by enormous distances in the sandy wastes, amply testify. History is full of such examples. While the Roman soldier is known and respected in the West, there is no comparable knowledge of the Chinese soldier. Each belonged to an empire that was harassed by nomads. But, while the Roman empire eventually succumbed, China survives to this day. The Chinese soldier has not been a weak character.

Behind all this there is yet another consideration that we should bear in mind. Is it not possible that the Sino-Soviet split of which we now talk so easily began in the Korean War? When Soviet planning is so meticulously thought out, why was Mr. Malik absent on that fateful Sunday of June 25, 1950, when the Security Council convened to consider the crisis? How could the Soviet Union be so negligent as to miss the deliberations that led to the resolutions of June 25 and 27? * From that moment on, the United Nations

---

* The United States in World Affairs *for 1950, published by the Council on Foreign Relations, has this to say: "Why the Kremlin allowed the Korean aggression to occur in the midst of its own boycott at Lake Success is one of the intriguing mysteries in the history of the Politburo's operations. It is an incontestable fact that the prompt and effective response of the Security Council was made possible only by the absence of Mr. Malik from the council table. Had a Soviet representative gone to Lake Success on June 25 and June 27, it was inconceivable that he would have refrained from vetoing the historic resolutions adopted on those two afternoons. Failure to sabotage the Council's efforts seemed, at the least, like a major tactical*

became an active part of the Korean War. Confrontation with China became unavoidable. The conclusion was thus inevitable that the Soviet Union was playing the game so that Communist China would be branded an aggressor nation. That was what happened. Also, she succeeded in embittering the relations between China and the United States.

But why would Soviet Russia want to do such a thing? For the simple reason that Russia under Stalin welcomed a Communist China only so long as China remained a satellite. But China showed no such inclination. The only alternative then was to create a set of circumstances that would compel China to become a satellite, whether she liked it or not. After all, Stalin had previously bargained with Chiang Kai-shek at Mao Tse-tung's expense. Mao, in Stalin's view, was not strong enough to carry through— and yet Mao succeeded in completing his revolution, by means of methods that were entirely his own and not those of Stalin. Mao obtained the support of the peasants, rather than that of the urban population. For a variety of other reasons Stalin came to the conclusion that Mao was a danger—to be carefully watched but not trusted. So the uneasy relations continued. After the war Stalin dismantled and took away some two billion dollars' worth of industrial equipment left behind by the Japanese in the northeastern provinces. He also coveted the rich provinces contiguous to Siberia, parts of which were themselves snatched from China during an earlier period (Treaties of 1858 and 1860). As if that was not enough to embarrass the new government, Stalin promoted a dissident movement by exploiting the personal ambitions of Kao Kang and making him lord and master of that huge area. Kao even had his own currency; and a separate political entity, like Manchukuo in the days of the Japanese, was already in the making. Kao was captured before he could do much damage, and Peking put him away.

error on the part of the Soviet Union" (p. 217–218). The resolution of June 27 asks the Security Council to call on UN members to "furnish such assistance to the Republic of Korea as may be necessary to repel the armed attack and to restore international peace and security in that area" (p. 470). This was the beginning that led to the condemnation of China as the aggressor nation.

What I wish to stress by reviewing some of these past episodes, is how one-sidedly we regard important events. Words are often used with utter disregard of their consequences. The word "aggression" has been used against China. It has now become a permanent label, and even honest people merely parrot the word without wondering if it is fair or just. As Senator Wayne Morse said on the Senate floor on March 4, 1964: "One would have thought that there no longer remains a square foot of the earth's sea or land surface outside of the Communist bloc that has not been designated as 'vital to the security of the United States' and been subjected to an American military presence of some kind." If the U.S. did this, it was right and proper. But if Communist China moved her soldiers into Korea at a time when her very survival as a nation depended on that act, it was aggression. Aggression against whom? China fought for self-defense against tremendous odds, four months after the UN troops landed on Korean soil, and after having warned the world that the invading troops must not cross the 38th parallel. If such a nation could be branded as an aggressor then there must be a mistake somewhere. I think one of the immediate tasks before the UN is to review and, if possible, to reassess the events of that war. I also think that in any dispassionate study of the Korean incident, one cannot help reaching the conclusion that, for the United States, it was the wrong war at a wrong time, for a wrong purpose, and with the wrong country. We can understand the reason why America wanted to prevent China from becoming Communist, but must that have been done through recourse to military measures? The fighting brought some 157,000 casualties to the United States. It intensified frustration and bitterness in the American mind; it made any cool and rational approach to subsequent events virtually impossible; it needlessly exacerbated Chinese-American relations. On the Chinese side it created the image of the United States as an implacable enemy. That in turn led to the present tension in every corner of the world. The only country that seems to have profited by the Korean War is Soviet Russia. However we look at the picture, Russia was and remains America's major source of antagonism. All the protestations of friendship and willingness to coexist with the United States notwith-

standing (calculated, as we may well surmise, to make Chinese-
American reconciliation impossible), it is difficult to see how that
friendship can come about when she remains the center of Communist ideology, with an ally only ninety miles from Florida. Has
the United States ever had so serious and so near a threat to its
security in its entire history? And yet the United States has chosen
China, some 8,000 miles away, as its enemy.

If, for the sake of argument, the Korean War is not an example
of Chinese aggression, then what about Tibet? What about India?
And what about Southeast Asia? Are not these glaring examples of
Chinese aggression? These are all issues that need to be gone into
in some detail, especially when the flood of information to support
this thesis has been so persistently and effectively marshaled that
there seems to be no doubt at all in the minds of intelligent people.

In the case of Tibet, it has been in contact with the rest of China
from very early days. With the Chinese court from the time of the
T'ang Dynasty (618–906) it came into closer relations. That was
when the "wanderings of the peoples" were taking place in the
early Middle Ages in Europe. Since then it has remained a part of
China. The relations were sometimes very close, at other times not
so close, depending on the circumstances and the strength of the
Chinese court. The Chinese never went in for political or territorial
annexation, which is a common feature in the Western world. If
their area grew, it was because of cultural and racial assimilation,
at best a long and arduous process, with political ties always remaining loose and tenuous. But no one raised any question about
its being a part of the Chinese empire. It has been more so than,
say, Brittany is a part of France, or Cornwall and Devonshire a
part of Britain, or Sicily a part of Italy.

In the nineteenth century, however, rapid changes took place.
That was when Chinese weakness became so evident and Western
imperialism was virtually in complete control of the entire world.
China herself, let alone Tibet, was on the point of being dismembered. There was nothing to prevent Tibet from going through a
harrowing period of exploitation from the north as well as from
the south. Russia's expansion, according to Nansen, had been at

the rate of fifty-five square miles a day for four hundred years! When asked whether there was any Russian boundary in Asia, the answer was that Russia knew no such boundary. So Russia came marching southward (and eastward also) appropriating enormous tracts of land, at the expense of China, without even having to ask for it. Most of this land has now become part of the Soviet Union, as, for instance, the Maritime Province with the port of Vladivostok and parts of Central Asia.* Russia also laid her hands on parts of China's Sinkiang. But when she came farther south, Britain made it unmistakably clear that she would not countenance any threat to India. Under Lord Curzon, Britain began sending young empire-builders like Francis Younghusband to see what they could do to make the British flag respected in the strategic areas in Tibet. Whether by so doing they were trespassing upon China was a purely academic question. If there should be any feeble voice of opposition from China, the British government could always say, as it did on many occasions, that it recognized China to have "suzerainty" over Tibet, or that Tibet remained a part of China's territorial entity. These admissions of historical realities made no difference to the fact that Tibet was virtually controlled by Britain. But all the time, in spite of her impotence, China refused to give any legal sanction to these British acts of aggression.†

---

* One huge area from the mouth of the Amur River to the west and then to the north of that river was ceded to Russia in 1858. Another huge slice to the east of that river, stretching from its mouth to present day Vladivostok, was ceded two years later.

† That Tibet has always been an integral part of China, as Alaska now is of the United States, is an international fact which no one has contested. The British recognized this as long ago as 1792. When, in 1904, as a result of Russian pressure, they sent a military expedition to Lhasa, the U.S. Ambassador in London, Joseph H. Choate, was instructed to remind the British Foreign Secretary that Great Britain had on three occasions recognized China's sovereignty over Tibet and "assumed" that they still regarded Tibet as being a "part of the Chinese dominions"! Finding it difficult, if not impossible, to establish "independence" for China's Tibet Region, the "friends of Tibet" have tried other means, which unfortunately have proved to be equally unconvincing and ineffective. "Are not the people in Tibet of a different race from the Chinese?" they ask. The answer is that the average Chinese one meets belongs to the Han race. The Tibetan belongs to a different branch of the Mongolian race, but he is just as Chinese as the fifty other minorities which together form the Chinese nation. That is practically

That was the situation in Tibet down to the early days of the First World War when preoccupation nearer home compelled Britain to bring matters to a period of suspended animation. That was also the time of the Simla Conference, which gave birth to the so-called McMahon Line.

With the advent of Indian independence in 1947 came the best opportunity for the adjustment of all these accumulated wrongs and British encroachments. For nearly two centuries India was a British colony; she was now the mistress of her own destiny. India could have then approached China, especially in view of the truly unparalleled example of the two peoples having for two thousand years conducted their relationship on a purely spiritual and cultural basis, and asked that such relations be restored and placed on a modern footing. That would have been a glorious page in the history of international relations. It would not only have reaffirmed Chinese-Indian friendship: it could have demonstrated to a profit-ridden and exploitation-minded world that it was still possible to conduct relations between nations and peoples on a plane of cultural understanding and mutual assistance, much as self-respecting individuals do. India, in other words, could have conveyed the thought to China that they were both now free from the pressure of the intruder, heavier in her case than in China's. Now that Great

---

how all nations are formed. "Well then," a further question is raised, "does not the Tibetan speak a different language or believe in a different religion?" The Tibetan believes in a form of what is called Tantric Buddhism, but then Buddhism spreads in different forms and sects over a very large part of Asia. As regards language, there are two in Belgium, three in Switzerland, and over a dozen or fifteen in India, and still they are nations. The truth is there is a considerable amount of local autonomy which the Tibetans enjoy in China as much as do the other racial minorities or as the French Canadians do in Canada. My information is that not only is this autonomy not suppressed, but it is carefully fostered and promoted to provide that diversity of culture which is expressed at least once a year in the massive displays at Peking on October 1. At any rate, if the argument is sustained that a nation must consist of one homogeneous race of people speaking the same language, then I am afraid the world will disintegrate into thousands of nations no one of which perhaps will be any larger than the principality of Monaco! Perhaps the world will be happier for this. Who knows? I think this effort of trying to cut Tibet loose from China is a case of lost labor or misplaced energy.

Britain was gone, India could have made a meaningful gesture, and informed China that the clarification of their respective frontiers should lead to the establishment of neighborly relations. For a time that neighborliness prevailed. But India noticed that the northern neighbor was having trouble of one sort or another of her own. She had no time to take care of her living room, let alone the porch. It was at this point that India wavered, surrendered to temptation, and, as I think, acted unwisely. Should she take advantage of the chaotic situation in China and follow the example of the British and re-occupy the porch where not so long ago the owner had little or no control? Or should she be true and loyal to her own better instincts born of a rich heritage and strenuously resist the temptation?

That was the critical moment. The tremendous spiritual reserve of India, accumulated through the ages, carried her through 1954, when she signed a treaty with mainland China fully acknowledging that Tibet was an integral part of China, that in fact it was only the Tibet *region* rather than Tibet to help dissipate any misunderstanding as to its being a separate entity. So far so good. President (then Professor) Sarvepalli Radhakrishnan could still say, as he did, that "all roads in Asia lead to India," meaning that it was from India that the peoples in Asia derive their spiritual sustenance. It was not true, though no one wanted to deflate the Indian balloon. But this is not the point: India has been always fond of immersing herself in the mirage of being the guardian of spiritual values. But such a guardian, in order to be worthy of the name, must have one indispensable qualification. He must have the character, the inner strength, to resist temptation, or, as the *Dhammapada* says, to subdue and conquer self. "Self is the lord of self," says that incomparable Theravada sutra, "who else could be the lord? With self well subdued, a man finds a lord such as few can find." In another part, the *Dhammapada* says that the man who conquers his self is a greater man than he who has conquered the world.

India was clearly on the horns of a dilemma in the mid-1950's. To yield to temptation or to resist it? She looked around wondering what she should do. Mainland China was Communist. She had gone through the harrowing experiences of the Korean War. She had been branded as an aggressor by the United Nations. World opinion was against her. She had many grave problems to solve and had obviously no time to look into the porch that is the Tibet region. A combination of fortuitous circumstances was acting against her but in favor of India. She acted. She decided not to follow the advice of the *Dhammapada* or of the noble tenets of Hinduism, but to follow another of her own teachers. That teacher was Chanakya Kautilya, who was adviser to Chandragupta before the time of Asoka and who in his *Arthasastra* went even further than Machiavelli in the pursuit of Realpolitik.* That proved to be a fatal decision. There were of course other reasons. But in that decision is to be found the key to the understanding of the border incident between India and China and of the sad situation in which India now finds herself.

India, I am afraid, has no one to blame but herself for the difficulties in which she is now floundering. Even though, with due apologies to Dr. Radhakrishnan, not all roads in Asia lead to India, still the long array of her great spiritual leaders, and the magnificence and profundity of much of her thinking stretching all the way from the Upanishads through the six systems and the Bhagavad-Gita, with all the Shankaracharyas and Ramanujas and the modern Ramakrishnas and Vivekanandas, have given India a respected and exalted position among the speculative peoples of the world. If only she acted in the spirit of her great leaders! But she has chosen to tread on the mundane and what has proved to be the ruinous path of the greed and covetousness of common mortality, with the result that she is now surrounded by neighbors,

---

* *Mr. U. N. Ghoshal, who has made a special study of Kautilya, says in his article in the* Encyclopedia of the Social Sciences, *"Expediency forms the keynote of Kautilya's rules concerning foreign relations . . . In sacrificing morality and religion to the interests of the state, Kautilya, who has been called the Indian Machiavelli, followed the example of earlier authors. He advocated the free resort to assassination for the suppression of ill-disposed and wicked subjects . . . Kautilya's influence upon later Hindu political theory was far-reaching. He founded a tradition of statecraft which became a synonym for unscrupulous cunning and which, although condemned by some, was adopted by many later thinkers." I think it is useful to bear these remarks in mind in any appraisal of contemporary Indian political behavior.*

none of whom has a good word to say about her. Pakistan, Ceylon,
Nepal, Sikkim, Bhutan, Afghanistan—all these neighbors at best
do not speak out and at worst, as in the case of Pakistan, bear a
deep grievance against her. One would think that mainland China,
having gone Communist and being "aggressive," should carry the
burden of ill-feeling on her shoulders. But it is unfortunately "spiritual" India which is having the worst of it. She wants to follow in
the footsteps of the former British raj and to dominate her neighbors. But this is renunciation of her ancient glorious heritage.
India's troubles will doggedly pursue her till she learns the lesson
of sweet reasonableness. Already there is clamor for a Himalaya
conference to iron out the differences which can be solved only
in the spirit of give and take, but Indian philosophy, alas, has
not taught the Indians to develop a sense of measure or proportion.
Everything about her can be described by the word "overwhelming."
She is overwhelming in her climate; overwhelming in the diversity
of her races and languages, which stubbornly refuse to be merged
and harmonized under the unifying influence of Hinduism; overwhelming in the multiplicity of her castes—three thousand of them
—which keep Indian society stratified to a degree not found in
any other society in the world; overwhelming in the luxuriance of
her vegetation which, as in the case of the banyan tree, Milton
observed:

> *Spread her arms,*
> *Branching so long and long, that in the ground*
> *The bended twigs take root, and daughters grow*
> *About the mother tree, a pillared shade,*
> *High over-arched, with echoing walks between;*

overwhelming in the immensity of her imagination;* overwhelming in the enormous rotundities of her woman's breast (in Indian

---

* No race, in its concept of time, has gone to the extent of imagining a
woman with the most delicate of fabrics, touching and thus wearing away
the hardest rock in the form of a ten-mile cube. Each touch makes some
impression on the rock, and with the trillions upon trillions of successive

sculpture) which is said to have the capacity to feed a thousand infants all at the same time; * and overwhelming in the abundant fantastic forms and shapes in her art which made Macaulay, in his speech in the House of Commons in 1843, decry that all Indian art is "hideous, grotesque and ignoble." There is in Indian art a strange combination of voluptuousness and exalted spirituality. The only exception is the chaste simplicity and beauty of the Taj Mahal, but that is Islamic and not Hindu. No art is so full of vitality, so reckless in its abandon, so profuse, so exuberant, and shows such an absence of discipline. The Madura temple alone, it is said, is ornamented with 33 million carvings. And as for the temple at Khajuraho, with its amazing display of unadulterated eroticism, all conceived within the framework of religious propriety, there is not a spot in the world that can show anything com-

---

touches the whole cube is worn away to nothingness. There you have a unit of time with which to measure periods as the Indian sages conceive them!

* The story was told by Fa Hsien (fourth or fifth century) in his Travels *about a king on the Upper Ganges whose concubine had been delivered of an unformed fetus. The queen in her jealousy said, "Your delivery is a bad omen," and accordingly enclosed it in a wooden box and threw it into the Ganges. Down stream another king, having his daily stroll, took the box from the water, opened it, and found one thousand small boys, well-formed and good-looking. He brought them up as his own sons. When they were grown up, they became brave and strong so that when they went to war, the enemies were compelled to submit. Then they attacked the country of the king who was their real father. The king became sad, and the concubine asked him why. He replied, "The king down the river has a thousand sons, brave and strong beyond compare, and they wish to come and attack my country; and that is why I am sad." The concubine replied, "Do not grieve, but put up a lofty platform on the eastern wall of the city, and when the enemy comes, place me on it. I shall be able to keep them off." The king did so. When the enemy came, the concubine called out to them, "You are my sons: why do you rebel against me?" "Who are you that say you are our mother?" And she answered, "If you do not believe me, all look up and open your mouths." She then pressed her two breasts as large as melons, and each breast gave forth five hundred jets of milk which fell into the mouths of her thousand sons who thus knew that she was indeed their mother and at once laid down their arms. The two father kings attained the rank of saints, and the pagoda in their honor is still existing. Afterwards when the world-honored one became a Buddha, he said to his disciples, "This is the place where before my time weapons were laid down." See Herbert A. Giles:* Travels of Fa Hsien. *This is the most effective way of transforming swords into plowshares on record!*

parable. The concept of simplicity or of restraint is utterly alien to the Hindu soul.

India lives apart. It is a world in itself. Her excessiveness and extremes leave the stranger in complete wonder and amazement. And it is this which makes her so profoundly different from her neighbor to the north, though both belong to the same East. For in China, as Goethe found out long ago in his conversations with Eckermann, the predominant note is not one of overluxuriance, but of moderation. "It is this strict moderation in all things," said the sage of Weimar, "which has preserved the Chinese Empire for thousands of years." There is nothing in China which seeks to overpower or overwhelm: everything is under severe restraint and discipline. The principal thing one learns from childhood is to learn when to stop. That is taught in Confucianism as much as in Lao-tze. As the Great Learning said: "It is only when one learns where and when to stop that one gains equilibrium. With equilibrium comes repose. With repose comes serenity of purpose. With serenity one can reflect and deliberate. With deliberation one attains the goal of what one aims to accomplish." Nowhere do we see so clear an application of this idea of moral discipline as in the withdrawal of the Chinese troops in November of 1962 after they had reached the southern foothills of the Himalayas. It was not a pure military victory they desired: it was the attainment of the conditions with which to convince the leaders of India that they wanted nothing but peace and the negotiations which lead to peace.

Of all the religions and philosophies in India, only Buddhism has taught the "middle way." But then Buddhism, remarkable as it is as a religion and as a *Lebensanschauung,* died in the land of its birth after a relatively brief period of a thousand years, absorbed by the same ocean of Hinduism from which it took its rise, to flourish, to prosper, and to blossom forth among the peoples to the east. It came to be transformed into something purer and, I may even say, nobler as it went farther east into China and Japan, elevating and spiritualizing the lives of the masses of their people. Why was this so? The Indian mind excels in having flashes of insight, in intuition, in *jnana* in the perception of the infinite, but it seems to be incompatible with the development of what Dante calls in the *Convivio* a philosophy that is "a loving use of wisdom" (*uno amoroso uso di sapienza*), of the kind of wisdom that we need so desperately in the ordering of our contemporary world.

IV THE UNITED STATES AND CHINA: 1

THE SAD RELATIONSHIP between the United States and China will go down in history as an unusual and, to many, a wholly unexpected development. That does not mean that it cannot be understood, though the understanding will scarcely lead to any improvement of that relationship in the foreseeable future. For that, some basic adjustment, not of immediate practical interests, but of points of view, especially on the part of the United States, will be necessary. For the issues involved are those of the classical conflicts which determine the rise and fall of civilizations, and the conflict between China and the United States, which is now only in its early stages, is likely to be long, bitter, and devastating.

The West has dominated the world since the beginning of the sixteenth century largely through the deft use of the weapons of destruction. Only once was this domination successfully challenged. That was done by Japan, and it came quite late. Her defeat of Russia in the war on the plains of northeastern China over half a century ago, because of the important implications not found in other wars, so deeply stirred the Western world that ever since it has become obsessed by what might happen to it in the future. For two generations Japan continued to expand and to symbolize a threat, so the Western world conceived, which must eventually be removed. That was not difficult to accomplish. For the Western world knew, what Japan herself perhaps did not know, that so long as the contest for supremacy was based on technological efficiency and ability, the West had advantages over her which in the long run must triumph. And triumph it did. If Japan had understood that she was involved in a war of civilizations in which the use of force was only one of many factors for success, the situation might have been somewhat different. If Japan had realized that, for all her great virtues and attributes, her civilization is after all of a derivative nature and that her ultimate strength must depend on continuing to draw upon the resources, of continental origin, that have made her what she is, the results would not have been so disastrous. Japan should not have so cruelly antagonized the Chinese people by resorting to brutal acts of domination, and blindly imitating the methods of the West. It is true her strength would not then have risen in so spectacular a manner. It would have been slower, but it would have been built on more solid foundations and therefore more long-lasting and enduring.

The Japanese war has now become a closed issue. Little did the West think that it should be followed, so soon, by what it feels to be a much more ominous threat. The threat is not of a military nature, but much more subtle and indefinable, and therefore more difficult to tackle. The awakening of the dragon is perhaps the most disturbing single event for Western man in the twentieth century. It dozed for a full century, because, as Nikos Kazantzakis observed, "the laws of nature require that even dragons have to rest sometime." Now it is awake, but the Western man remains utterly unconvinced that it is harmless, and that when it begins to stir it does not have evil designs. He cannot believe that a dragon can be benevolent, as it is believed to be in Chinese mythology.

Throughout her long history China could have conquered, annexed, and even annihilated her neighbors, if she had wanted to. Even as late as the fifteenth century, before the Portuguese opened a new chapter in the history of what has been aptly called the Vasco da Gama period in the relations between the East and the West, Chinese naval expeditions reached as far west as the Persian Gulf and the east coast of Africa. Their curiosity satisfied, they simply went home. Nothing happened. There was no subjugation of conquered peoples, no exploitation, no appropriation of land and resources which were not Chinese. There was no colonialism, which could very well have begun seventy-five years before the Portuguese started it. As Mencius said long ago, it was not a case of being "unable to do it, but of not wanting to do it." And this was because the whole of China's social and political philosophy was founded on the concept that it was "the duty of the more fortunate peoples to help raise other nations which have become extinguished and to allow those which have become discontinued to prolong their life." It was a philosophy of genuine coexistence and mutual assistance.

It is impossible for Western peoples to see how a nation that has acquired strength and power can do anything else but convert them into an effective weapon for aggrandizement. It is therefore extremely difficult to establish any rapport between China and the West without, in the first place, understanding the differences of approach in political action. All that the West can see is that an awakened China is a menacing China. Napoleon gave the warning in the early days of the nineteenth century. Since then the coordinated effort of the Western nations, for fully one hundred and fifty years, has been to keep the dragon asleep for as long a period as possible. Nor would they feel sorry if it should not awaken at all.

There are two considerations which, it seems to me, a government must attend to as soon as it is strong enough. One is the determination of its physical boundaries, and the second is to have a sense of security in areas beyond these boundaries so that they are not a source of any immediate or potential danger. These are perfectly legitimate wishes. It is to these basic and rudimentary tasks that the Chinese government addressed itself from 1949, and at once it met with vigorous opposition.

The fact that it is a Communist government undertaking these tasks is beside the point. The whole array of epithets and abusive words that are hurled at China today would, I feel sure, be used against her with equal vehemence if she had the most liberal and democratic government in the world. For to be able to undertake these tasks is an indication of the strength of the regime and of its self-assurance, and these are not attributes usually associated with China by the Western world in modern times. The image of a China strong enough to assert her will is, from the Western point of view, upsetting and may even portend more unpleasant developments in the future. The logical thing is to destroy that image in its initial stages. Hence the difficulties that Communist China is meeting at every turn, even though she may be cautious in her foreign policy and do nothing to be provocative.

The best examples of the difficulties arising from China's effort to determine her territorial limits are Taiwan and Tibet. Taiwan has become a special issue worthy of a special discussion. Tibet also is a complicated issue because India has become involved, giving rise to open warfare. But a few more words at this point are not out of place.

The immediate reaction of the Communist government in China, soon after it came into power, was that Tibet has been one of those outlying areas over which for centuries the Chinese government has exercised but limited effective control. The decision was then made that from now on it was to become as vital a part of China as any other part. But from weakness of the previous governments as well as from neglect, which had invited foreign encroachments in the nineteenth century, it realized that it had to contend with certain existing obstacles. However, the work of integration had to proceed regardless of what these obstacles might be. The first of its duties was to demarcate the boundaries. To leave them ill-defined and uncertain as in centuries past would be only to invite confusion and even disaster. But to have a clear-cut boundary in place of a borderland, which it actually was, also involves another country with which the boundary must be drawn. India was cooperative in the sense that in 1954 she went to the extent of signing a treaty with China confirming that Tibet is a part of China. There was no need of such confirmation, but it was helpful in overcoming the impression, deliberately and consistently fostered in the nineteenth century by Britain and Russia, that Tibet was a separate political unit, even though nothing in international law could substantiate such a status. India's agreement to use the term "Tibet region of China" rather than "Tibet" was appreciated. But in the practical implementation of the treaty the Chinese government soon found that India was not prepared to yield the privileges to which she thought she was entitled by virtue of what the British had acquired earlier. These came to her, India contended, as part of the legacy from the British when she regained her independence. This legacy, she argued, included some areas on the long boundary between the two countries, and on those she stood firm. China obviously could not agree to the Indian position, for the simple reason that those concessions, which had no legal sanction in any case, were made under *force majeure*. The McMahon Line was one such arrangement. The disagreement remained, and the Chinese government thought that the only possible way to remove it was by way of a conference, where both sides would present their arguments, and perhaps arrive at a solution in a spirit of compromise. The record shows that at no time did China give up hope for negotiation and peaceful settlement. Fighting broke out in late October of 1962 only when Mr. Nehru threatened to throw out every Chinese from what he considered to be Indian territory.

That the Chinese government is only interested in delimiting the boundaries and in nothing else, is amply borne out by a series of successful and conciliatory negotiations with Nepal, Sikkim, Bhutan, Burma, and now with Pakistan.

The boundary question with India in the Tibet area has for all practical purposes been solved—as of this moment. There will be no further fighting unless India takes the initiative, and India herself will not take the step unless external forces over which she has no control compel her to do so. In the meantime, conditions within Tibet itself, according to a New York *Times* dispatch of July 19, 1964, have become quite normal. Resistance, such as it was, has been overcome even in the Chamdo area in southeast Tibet. Rapid growth in agriculture, including wheat, beans, and barley, is reported. New methods of tilling the soil have been introduced. Education is becoming more widespread, hospitals are being set up, superstitions are being swept away, many forms of cruelty, including the chopping off of hands for stealing, have been suppressed. All in all, the lot of the people of Tibet seems to have been much improved. But whatever may have been done to improve their conditions, the world outside will continue to hear with horror about the unforgivable "invasion" by China and the "suppression of religious freedom" of the people of Tibet.

This border question is an interesting example of propaganda. By dint of repetition, even intelligent people are being made to ac-

AMERICA AND CHINA

cept, without the slightest hesitation, crude misinformation as something of a gospel truth. The message is that China is drunk with power, scheming to claim back all the territory that she has lost, at one time or another, "within the last two thousand years," according to a television discussion by "experts" only recently.* All the participants, in varying degrees, believed that China is out to seize all the territory stretching from Burma to Vietnam, and, in the north, Korea and certain areas of Siberia and central Asia. How the Chinese propose to conquer this enormous area, with a primitive industry barely sufficient to maintain a decent standard of living, in the face of worldwide opposition, is a question that is seldom asked and never answered. The attitude is entirely one of hysteria. If the approach of supposedly well-informed people is so irrational, what can we expect from the general public?

Among the border areas that China is alleged to be now claiming there is one that has been repeatedly overlooked, for which I now gladly supply the information. In the first century of the Christian era General Pan Ch'ao, brother of the distinguished historian Pan Ku and of the equally distinguished lady historian Pan Chao, extended the Han empire to as far as the east coast of the Caspian Sea, so that to this day there is a legend that one of the early rulers of Armenia (west side of the Caspian) was a Chinese! If Communist China is as covetous of land as she is painted to be, it is not likely that she would forget the luscious and fertile plains to the east of the Caspian Sea.

It is truly astonishing how, in performing its first duty as a responsible government, the new regime in China should have stirred up so much organized propaganda against it. Aggression, invasion, military control, new imperialism, conquest of India—words such as these have been and are still being used indiscriminately to create the image of a China that is a menace to its neighbors and to the world.

Even as the fighting with India had broken out, Mr. Chou En-lai still urged that negotiations should be continued and said that he was

---

* June 7, 1964, on Channel 5, discussion between Hanson Baldwin, Marguerite Higgins, one former U.S. Ambassador to Thailand, a professor from the East Asia Institute of Columbia University, etc.

willing to proceed to New Delhi forthwith. As to whether India or China started the unfortunate war there is hardly any room for doubt. General Maxwell Taylor, of all people, came out with a frank statement in a closed session of Congress on April 18, 1963, according to an International News dispatch, that he was of the belief that it was India who started the hostilities. Earlier, on February 14, when he was asked by the House Appropriations Committee whether he thought that it was India who was responsible for the war, General Taylor unequivocably said yes. He testified that it started when Indian troops advanced into the contested areas and began occupying them.*

In addition to the demarcation of boundary, the next question that any responsible government must face is that of national security. If the United States does not feel secure when territory some eight to ten thousand miles away is not in entirely friendly hands, surely there is hardly any reason to begrudge the People's Government of China a sense of security on its very borders. If the United States gets deeply involved in men and material in Southeast Asia, that is deemed essential for its national security. If Communist China so much as sends any supplies over her border into North Vietnam, it is downright aggression, for which the punishment may even take the form of nuclear bombs. The United States has of course the capacity to do it, but this would be neither fair nor just, and without fairness and justice, as Mencius pointed out long ago, there could be no conquest of men's hearts. There could be no peace.

The clear demarcation of the Chinese boundary and national security have thus been the two primary preoccupations of the Chi-

* In General Taylor's own words, the Indians "were edging forward in the disputed area." Also "the area [NEFA] was so rugged that there had been no accurate mapping or boundary marking." Brigadier General Linscott Hall of the Defense Intelligence Agency, who accompanied Maxwell Taylor at the hearing, said, "One thing, I think, is very important to point out—that the Chinese Nationalists, when they were in control of China, did not recognize this line [McMahon Line] either. So it is not a question of the fact that it is a Chinese Communist line vis-à-vis an Indian line. It is an Indian line that has never been recognized by either the Chinese Communists or the Nationalists."

nese People's Government as they would be of any Chinese government, including the Chiang Kai-shek government, if it became sure of its mandate and authority. We can go even further and say that this is perhaps the first duty of any government in the world, once it is installed and sure of its power, for is there any country which cannot define precisely what its territorial limits are? No government can function properly without that knowledge. In the case of China, her boundaries have been tampered with for the last hundred and fifty years. In their readjustment there is bound to be a certain amount of disagreement. The whole of China's foreign policy is basically quite simple. She is trying to set her own house in order; she has no desire to spread communism to other parts of the world. But by repeated harassment and unrelieved antagonism we have succeeded in changing the character of her policy and driving her to desperate measures.

As late as April 20, 1964, President Johnson, in a speech on nuclear control in New York said, "As for China itself, so long as the Communist Chinese pursue aggression, so long as the Communist Chinese preach violence, there can be and will be no easing of relationships . . . It is not we who must re-examine our view of China, it is the Chinese Communists who must re-examine their view of the world." Mr. Johnson went on to say, "Nor can anyone doubt our unalterable commitment to the defense and the liberty of free China. Meanwhile we will say to our historic friends—the talented and courageous Chinese people on the mainland that just as we are opposed—just as we opposed aggression against them, we must oppose aggression by their rulers and for the same reasons."

These remarks by the President are, I think, the most clear-cut and unequivocal definition of American policy toward China. They are firm—but they are frankly one-sided. America has the power and the weapons to carry out her intentions. On the other hand, the People's Government of China feels that she is entirely the aggrieved party, that she has been thwarted at every turn by America's superior military power. Communist China claims that the present situation could not have existed were it not for American intransigence and her desire to keep China weak and divided so that, as in the early days, she will be at America's mercy. There is where matters stand today. Between the two points of view is a yawning gulf. Are the two countries destined to remain apart for an indefinite period? At this point it is necessary to go back a little to their early relationship, to have a good look at China herself, and then to see what the future is likely to be.

There is, before we go into that study, one saving quality in President Johnson's remarks. He referred to "our historic friends —the talented and courageous Chinese people on the mainland." In other words, the Chinese people are distinguished from their government, and it is perhaps the hope of President Johnson and of the American government generally that one day the Chinese people may act as a bridge over what now seems to be an all but impassable gulf. But that would be possible only when the people begin to repudiate their government. The belief is perhaps quite widely spread that the Chinese people are chafing under the tyranny of their government and that, as soon as a set of favorable circumstances arise, they will overthrow that government. This myth continues to be spread by the agents of propaganda from Taiwan, for understandable reasons. Mr. Roger Hilsman, in his now famous address before the Commonwealth Club at San Francisco, was under the same illusion, though in a slightly different form. He spoke of the lower echelons in the Peking government who, in another ten or fifteen years, will assume positions of importance, and may then, Mr. Hilsman thinks, repudiate the policies of the present leaders.

As long as the United States does not either overtly or covertly extend any assistance to the propagation of this assumed disaffection, or shape its policy accordingly, I think there is no harm in entertaining such views. But from all reports, the discontent—if there is any—both on the part of the people and of the comparatively junior officials of the Peking government, is not important enough to worry Peking. The New York *Times*, like all widely read publications in the country, does not refrain from saying a few unpleasant things about Communist China when there is an opportunity, and yet on this matter of disaffection on mainland China, it made this very significant concession in an article in its

issue of May 8, 1964. "Western observers," the correspondent
said, "also concede that if a free general election were possible the
Communist regime would be returned by a great majority, though
perhaps not with anything like the degree of unanimity party workers suggest."

A simple statement like that reveals a lot. The people on the
Chinese mainland are still poor and will be for a very long time to
come. But this does not mean that they are unhappy or discon-
tented with their government. They have now not only a sense of
security and purposefulness, which they did not have before and
which quite fully compensates for the lack of personal freedom to
which we here legitimately attach so much importance, but their
conditions of living have also so far improved that a return to the
earlier despicable Kuomintang days is unthinkable. The three years
of drought and famine between 1959 and 1961 would have meant,
under the Kuomintang, unspeakable horror, with millions of corpses
over the land. This time, there was of course deprivation, but there
was no famine in the usual sense of the word. Now after three years
of great difficulty, food is once more plentiful. The same article in the
New York *Times* said, "The people look healthy enough and there
is nothing in their appearance to suggest malnutrition, much less
starvation. Many wear clothes that are plentifully patched, but
they are scrupulously clean and tidy. The people are cheerful and
smile readily." In fact the impression one gets is that the people
are attached to the government on the mainland to a degree unknown at least within living memory. "Shanghai, the country's
largest city," the article continues, "has 28 colleges, 800 middle
schools and 5,000 primary schools with a total of 2,400,000 students . . . there were only 23,000 students in the city before the
revolution." In other spheres of public welfare the improvement
likewise has been phenomenal.

"The people are cheerful and smile readily." In that one sen-
tence, I believe, we have the key to the understanding of the Chinese nature and a measure of success of the present government.
Cheerfulness, readiness to smile, and, we may add, laughter,
gaiety, and a bubbling sense of humor—all these come direct from
the heart and are spontaneous. Of all human expressions of the

human soul they are the least susceptible of contrivance and arti-
ficiality. We have long heard about repression on the Chinese
mainland, the lack of freedom, unquestioning obedience to the
wishes of the government. All this may be true, but if the people
are still cheerful and can smile readily, there is a saving quality
that Americans, of all people, should be able to appreciate, since it
is the same quality that makes the American people what they are—
large, open, frank, and perennially hearty. With all the differences
in tradition and cultural background, no two peoples are more alike
than the Chinese and Americans. It is as if they are born in two
widely separate areas of the earth, to complement one another. And
yet they are today the bitterest of enemies. Is there no way in which
this bitterness can be overcome and transformed? I believe there *is*
a way, if only men on both sides are willing to lift their minds from
the limitations of immediate interests and look into the future with
sympathy and understanding. The American people do indeed have
a manifest destiny. That destiny is to realize to the fullest extent possible the spirit so eloquently expressed by the founders of the republic in the early days of their revolution. The Chinese also are now
going through *their* revolution, following the concept enunciated as
far back as twenty-five centuries ago that when a government has
forfeited the "mandate of heaven" so that it became no longer acceptable to the people, then the people have the divine right to
overthrow that government and institute a new one more in accordance with their wishes.

The purpose of the American Revolution, if I understand it
correctly, was to establish, on the new soil of the Western Hemisphere, an orderly society in which justice and equality might prevail, and then through that society to spread the social gospel
ultimately to the distant corners of the world, so that people everywhere might live in peace and friendly relations with one another.
The American Revolution embodies an ecumenical significance
that we must not lose sight of. This, more than any other time, is a
period of revolutions and violent upheavals. With hardly any exception, the peoples of the world would gladly cherish the image of
an America from which they could derive inspiration, of an America that could place her strength and resources at their dis-

posal for the attainment of liberty and independence throughout
the world. There is no doubt in my mind that people everywhere,
Communists and non-Communists alike, still have respect for
Americans as the representatives of a democratic and equitable society. But there are moments when that image becomes tarnished
by the obstinate pursuit of a policy that sees scarcely anything beyond America's immediate national interests. For we are today obsessed with Communism to an extent that, I believe, is out of
all proportion to its real strength. For I am in complete agreement
with President Kennedy when he said that the desire for freedom is
an integral part of life itself. It cannot be suppressed indefinitely.
This is why, in a sense, the free world has no reason to be afraid of
Communism, for the innate and natural urge for freedom is always
there to work on its side. Regimentation in any form must in the
end defeat its own purposes, and very often the best way to soften
it is not to apply pressure, but simply to leave it alone and allow it
to take its natural course. This is true of Soviet Russia, where the
voice of the people is receiving increasingly more attention from
the government, and it is even more true of Eastern Europe.
"Heaven sees what the people see, heaven hears what the people
hear." "When you stop the mouths of the people, it is just like
damming the flow of a river: it is a dangerous practice, because the
water will burst out in some other direction. The wise controller of
the river deepens its bed and facilitates its flow. The wise ruler of
men encourages them to speak up freely." "The people constitute
the most important part of a state, the next is the granary, and the
least important is the emperor." These remarks, made in many
cases before the time of Confucius and under a quasi-monarchical
and later a monarchical form of government for four thousand years,
show that the Chinese people loved their freedom very dearly; they
show also that their form of monarchy was not the embodiment of
the concept of the divine right of kings, so familiar in the history of
Europe, but of the divine right of the people to rebel if the monarch
or ruler failed to promote their welfare. It can always be argued that
the present government on the Chinese mainland is not following the
ancient precepts; but it is quite aware of the danger it runs into if it
does not fulfill the wishes of the people. One of the favorite remarks

of Chairman Mao Tse-tung is that a government is like a fish, and the people are like the water in which the fish swims. Just as the fish cannot live without water, so no government can function without the support of the people.

I am of the persuasion that the present uneasy international relation between China and the Western world is the result of a faulty reading of her history and psychology. The West, for much too long a period for its own good, has taken for granted that the rest of the world must think and act on *its* terms, for whatever the West believes in must be the ultimate truth to be complied with. This is hardly the way in which individuals behave in civilized society, and this is not the way in which nations should behave in a civilized and orderly world. It is a pity that at the time when the Chinese Communists were succeeding to establish their authority over the country, the West did not seize the opportunity of showing even a small amount of practical sympathy. If they did, I am positive that the present difficult problems could not have arisen. As it was, the West immediately followed a pattern which it developed out of earlier experiences. It did everything to create obstacles and hindrances. No fair-minded person can deny that the previous government had truthfully forfeited the "mandate of Heaven," the right to rule. If it was on the verge of falling, the logical thing to do would be to allow it to fall in the natural course of events. But instead the West took a frankly partial stand, prevented it from falling, and has ever since supported it with military help and financial resources.

The West, from the Taiping Rebellion (1850–1866) on, has developed the habit always of backing the regime that was in power in China no matter how decadent it was. It was a highly successful policy because in that way it was able to enlarge and consolidate Western interests and privileges, which were extorted from an unwilling China. Also, it kept China weak by making its government dependent on foreign power, which it was in no position to renounce. The Chinese were therefore quite helpless in trying to establish a self-respecting and independent government, because that would have involved at least some infringement of the enormous Western privileges and concessions. Sun Yat-sen thought and believed that he was

strong enough to become an exception, but it did not take him long
to find out that those obstacles were truly immovable, and that was
the reason why he had to turn to Soviet Russia for assistance.

It would be obviously too much for the West to change its methods when the Chinese Communists began to spread from north
China to central China and then finally to south China. If only it
had the ability to see a little more deeply under the surface or to
realize that this time things might turn out differently! General
George Marshall could perhaps have done something of importance in the last years of the 1940's and thereby even changed the
course of history. He was the type of American whom all sections
of the Chinese learned to respect and admire. He had integrity,
honesty, a sense of fair play, and what the ancient Romans called
pietas and *gravitas*. He produced the impression of being a man of
deep sincerity and noble ideals, of being a man who could be
trusted.* These are all great attributes in dealing with the Chinese.
There is not one corner of human relationship that they have not
explored in their long history. They understand and appreciate a
man of high qualities. George Marshall was such a man. But his
own people could not appreciate him: he was repudiated, even
branded a Communist.

Albert Camus was right when he said that out of revolution comes
awareness. Awareness of what? Awareness of one's strength as well
as one's weakness, awareness of one's limitations as well as the
length to which one can go. The revolution of 1911 that began with
the overthrow of a two-thousand-year-old monarchy could not have
been otherwise than a profound and stirring event. And yet when it
came, it did not make more than a ripple. It was so deceptive, and
that was why foreign observers and many of the Chinese them-

---

* *Mr. Dean Acheson's portraiture of General Marshall is much along the
same lines. In an article for* The Reporter *for November 26, 1959, Mr. Acheson said, "The moment General Marshall entered a room, everyone in it
felt his presence. It was a striking and communicated force. His figure conveyed intensity, which his voice, low, staccato, and incisive, reinforced. It
compelled respect. It spread a sense of authority and of calm. There was no
glamour about him and nothing of the martinet. Yet to all of us he was
always 'General Marshall.' The title fitted him as though he had been bap-
tized with it."*

selves seemed to be so little concerned with what went on. The first phase passed, only to be followed by a second phase of confusion and chaos known as the period of the warlords. The Chiang Kai-shek phase proved to be only a third phase: it was still an inter-regnum. Then came the real crisis, and a new cycle was born. It was as if the vital forces of heaven, earth, and man moved into the identical orbit and conspired to create that propitious moment that is destined to herald a new dawn and start another of those histori-cal periods for the fulfillment of Chinese culture and civilization. The Chinese are notoriously addicted to the belief, born out of ex-perience, no doubt, that the life of a people consists of recurrent cycles, as the seasons follow one another in the life of nature, and that human events assume their importance according to the posi-tion they occupy in these cycles in the same way that lives of plants and animals are determined by the succession of the months. I think there is an awareness on the part of the leaders of the revolution now going on in China that the historical forces have converged at last to give birth to that moment that comes only at long intervals to the life of a people. In the long history of China there are not many such moments. The Han Dynasty was such a moment. So was the T'ang Dynasty. Those were moments of expansion. But in order to be significant, a moment need not be marked by physical expansion. It can be marked also by consolida-tion and concentration leading to the finest expressions of the human soul. The Sung Dynasty was in fact under the impact of foreign invaders; it nevertheless reached a level of cultural and artistic refinement and sensibility rarely equaled in the history of the world. Buddhism, which was then the only influence from the outside to contribute to the enrichment of Chinese life, had lost all the flavor of its alien provenance and had so completely synthe-sized with China's own systems of thinking that together they created a sense of harmony that was exquisitely and nobly ex-pressed by the great masters of Sung art.* The culture of the Ming Dynasty was perhaps in a minor key: it did not reach the grandeur

* M. René Grousset, speaking of "that Paradisical period of the Sung," says, "It is difficult to think of anything more satisfying to the eye than the monochromes of this period, which depended entirely on shape and color

of the Sung period, though I do not think it is of less moment on
that account.

---

*for their ineffable beauty." Also, "Sung pottery is the most beautiful and
perfect of all time." Chinese Art and Culture (passim).
But more important still are the observations of Mr. Laurence Binyon,
whose soul vibrated so sensitively to every expression of beauty and grandeur
by the masters of Sung painting. Here are some random remarks culled
from his Painting in the Far East: "It [the Sung period 960–1280] is the
atmosphere of an age of civilized grace, of leisured thought, of refined culture." The figures of the women have a suavity and graciousness about
them, "a smiling tenderness that yet is serious; what Dante may have meant,
addressing Virgil, O anima cortese; a kind of courtesy of the soul." Mr. Binyon then raised the question, following Matthew Arnold's example, as to
"What, in effect, do we imply by the word modern?" And he answered,
"We mean, I think, by a modern age, an age in which the interest of the
race has passed beyond dependence on the struggle for existence; in which
the mind is free, has found a clue to life, and can disinterestedly review and
estimate the forces operating outside itself; in which the state of society has
emerged from a state of warfare, such as the wearing of weapons implies,
to a state of civility and amenity. The age of Sung has this modern character,
if we are to judge it by the art it has left" (p. 134). "The great landscape
rolls had the nearest counterpart in music, in the sonatas of Beethoven" (p.
152). "Loftiness and simplicity, a deep feeling for solitary places, give their
character to the art of these masters . . . Austere at times, with a sense
of desolation in bare peak and blasted pine, yet often bathed in the mood of
serene and silent joy, the joy of the mountain-dweller gazing out on vast
spaces of moon-flooded night, their art is never trivial, never pretty" (p.
153). And now this final passage: "It was in China, in the Sung age, that
this attitude of mind [sense of harmony with nature] found mature expression. There is no longer any element of dread or discomfort in the Sung
artists' and poets' feeling for wild nature, storms and rain and snow; nothing
of the horror of mountains which survived till nearly a century ago in civilized Europeans. The life of nature and of all non-human beings is regarded
in itself; its character contemplated and its beauty cherished for its own sake,
not for its use and service in the life of man. There is no infusion of human
sentiment into the pictures of birds and beasts, of the tiger roaring in the
solitudes, of the hawk and eagle on the rocky crag; rarely is there any touch
of the sportsman's interest which has inspired most European pictures of this
kind. If an artist painted a bird with such emotions as were Shelley's when he
wrote his 'Skylark,' we should have something comparable to the Sung
painting, though different. These men painted birds and flowers as they were
in nature, with no explicit symbolism, with nothing factitious added, and yet
the inspiring thought, the sensitive feeling, that was in their minds as they
worked has wrought its effect and still finds a response in the minds of those
who understand. 'To see the world in a grain of sand / And a heaven in a
wild flower.' The words of our own Blake crystallize more aptly than any*

There is, in all of these moments, one common feature which I think deserves our attention, and that is, these moments were without exception created by the Chinese only when they were completely masters of themselves and when they were living under a set of circumstances which were conducive to the full and unhampered expression of their personality. There is still another characteristic that should be noted. When the Chinese were in complete control of their destiny, even though the Han and T'ang Dynasties are considered as being expansive, there was no effort at all to employ military force for the conquest of neighboring peoples or to incorporate their territory within the Chinese domain against their wishes. That is why all this talk of the new China being expansionist, aggressive, or imperialist strikes a false note to the ear of anyone who has even a limited knowledge of Chinese history. What was there in those "expansionist" days of Han and T'ang to prevent the Chinese from annexing not only neighboring peoples, but even distant peoples if they wanted to do so? There was no power in the world then to stop them.

What then did the Chinese do? They said to their neighbors— albeit from a somewhat elevated position, I am willing to admit— that they should become friendly to one another and exchange gifts as a token of this friendly relation. These then were what came to be known as "tributary" states; but we are quite mistaken if we think that these gifts formed a kind of one-way traffic. Burma, for instance, sent gifts to the Chinese court, but the Chinese court sent gifts to Burma in return. Throughout, there was an expression of reciprocity and mutual respect. It was in essence a viable form of coexistence. I think it was an admirable system of conducting international relations. That is why it takes understanding and perceptiveness for a man like Professor C. P. Fitzgerald to say, as he did in his excellent book on China, that the history of China "is a record of cultural expansion and not of military conquest." *

---

language of mine what was at the heart of the poet-painters of Sung" (p. 160).

   * "The history of China is a history of a nation which is continually absorbing other races from without, and impressing on them the character of

Of how many other nations in history can we say the same? The French, with a longer and more mature cultural background than other Europeans, have a better understanding of the Chinese people. There is no ground for suspecting that they are out to "sabotage" American policy. I think they are genuinely trying to point out that there is a better and more effective way to solve many of our present difficulties than the tough, inflexible policy of the American government. The interview that Under Secretary of State George W. Ball had with General de Gaulle on June 5, 1964, is one of those revealing records which has not been adequately studied and analyzed. According to the New York *Times*, the two leaders agreed on what to do with Southeast Asia, but disagreed on how to do it. "The underlying cause of the difference between the two governments," said the *Times*, "is that the United States believes the Chinese Communist regime is in an expansionist period . . . The French, on the other hand, believe Peking is in a period of consolidation." I am positive that the French approach is much more rational and in keeping with the facts of the situation. M. Edgar Faure, who made the first contacts with Communist China before the French recognition, was also believed to have said once, "I maintain that the present Chinese government is a government which needs peace. The Chinese are entirely occupied with the interior problems which they certainly regard with humility. When people tell you, 'We'll catch up with the U.S.A. in ten years,' it's a bad sign. But today in Peking, they tell you they hope to reach the level of British agriculture in twenty-five years, of light industry in fifty, while for heavy industry it will take a good eighty years. When people have such a state of mind at home, they cannot afford to be aggressive abroad."

I think this statement by M. Faure represents a type of thinking that should commend itself to all intelligent and rationally minded people. If, as I believe, there is no record in China of the kind of expansionism and aggressiveness that have marked the course of

---

its own civilization. China has expanded by absorbing her invaders rather than by going out to conquer: her Great Wall was built for no other purpose than to keep the barbarians out; to territorial aggrandizement, as such, she has been indifferent." Laurence Binyon: Painting in the Far East, *p. 94.*

Western history, why should we presume that China is now going to forsake her historical behavior and follow the bad example of the West? Is it absurd to at least give the Chinese the benefit of the doubt, and say that in Southeast Asia, as in other parts of their long border, through which foreign invasions have often taken place, they are simply trying to create a sense of national security. If Premier Chou En-lai offered to sign a non-aggression pact to include those areas, is the idea so fantastic that it must be rejected before the words were out of his mouth? I think it is nonsense to say that the Chinese are out to convert them into Communist satellite states so that they may send their surplus population there, and seize the food they so desperately need.* The bogey of population explosion has been overworked. If we only give the matter a little thought, we shall find out soon enough that it does not stand any analysis. There are no indications that any spilling of people is being contemplated or planned. If the Chinese leaders entertain any such idea, then they must clearly be out of their minds, for they would be sowing seeds for their own destruction. Is it not true that Southeast Asia, for instance, is already congested with its own people? As regards food, must it not be reserved for the people of these lands in the first place?

The difficulty is that few people are willing to exert the effort of thinking, let alone of "thinking the unthinkable." There are a few independent-minded leaders, including a small minority of senators, who have the courage of their convictions and sometimes speak out. If they had their way, or if a man like General George C. Marshall, fifteen years ago, could have done in China what he did in Europe, the present situation could not have arisen.

First, knowing that it had been fruitless to be pitted against the Russian revolution and that after sixteen years America still had to come to terms with the Soviet government, and knowing further that the revolution in China was no less violent, that in fact it was one of those historic "moments" which nothing could prevent from happening, Marshall might have moved for immediate recognition of

---

* During the Chinese-Indonesian crisis only a few years back, large numbers of Chinese residents, many of long standing, were welcomed back to China when it was known they were not wanted in Indonesia.

the Chinese Communist government, especially since he was personally aware of the worthlessness of the Chiang Kai-shek regime. Second, the American government could have proposed to the United Nations that the Communist government in China, now that it had become a reality and fact of life, should become the new representative of China, as one of the five principal powers of that organization. She would only have been doing what Britain did. Third, the American government could have approached the Chinese Communist government and admitted that Taiwan was an integral part of the Chinese territorial domain, in accordance with the letter and spirit of the Cairo Declaration, as well as of the Potsdam Declaration, which followed later. Fourth, having gone so far, the American government could have even offered to help the modernization of China by means of long-term credits and technological advice.

These proposals might seem amazing. But is it not possible that they might have represented true statesmanship? The Chinese Communist leaders would have suspected a kind of Trojan horse. But in the end we would have won their confidence. There would have been no Korean War. There would be no Taiwan problem. It could have been settled as China's internal or domestic problem, as it has always been. And the more than five billion dollars that have been invested in Taiwan since 1949 would have been a handsome investment in all of China, yielding substantial dividends from a thankful people. It is needless for me to reiterate that of all the peoples in the world the Chinese have perhaps the most profound sense of gratitude for anything they receive with no ulterior motive, but out of a sincere heart. For 2,500 years they have been taught to cultivate filial piety as the first of the moral virtues, and filial piety is simply another form of gratitude shown to those who have given, out of a loving heart, with a spirit of self-sacrifice and devotion. So also in international relations, the Chinese do not forget an act of genuine kindness. But conversely, they also do not forget an unfriendly expression or an act of animosity or an act of premeditated malice. Then they are in a fighting mood. Once they are in that mood, they do not give up till the bitter end. This is a Chinese racial characteristic which it is sometimes convenient to remember and to bear in mind in dealing with them. They are not afraid of force in any shape or form so long as they feel they are in the right.

If some or all of those propositions that I have thus far described were considered or adopted at the time when the Chinese Communist government needed them most, both to stabilize its regime and to show to its people that it was functioning in a friendly atmosphere, I am willing to wager that the world situation today, fifteen years later, would be entirely different, and better. In fact the situation would be propitious enough for a complete Sino-American understanding, in which China would be prepared to dilute its Marxist pretensions in order to accommodate American sensibilities. The astute schemers of the Kremlin need not be clairvoyant, but they saw clearly the inherent dangers to them should there be such a rapprochement. In other words, the rift between China and Soviet Russia, now entirely in the open, had its beginnings long ago. For Russia was surprised, as everyone else was, that the Chinese revolution could be so sweepingly successful, but the surprise in her case was compounded with fear and uneasiness. There is a story told that shortly after the Communist conquest of the Chinese mainland, Stalin sent out a questionnaire in which a number of high-ranking but imprisoned officials, both civil and military, were asked to express frankly their views of the impact that this conquest would have on Soviet Russia. Almost without exception they painted a gloomy picture for Soviet Russia. It so happened that among those prisoners was a German medical doctor. On representations from Dr. Konrad Adenauer this doctor was subsequently released and lived to write this story.

Whether the story is apocryphal or not, the Russian fear that the chances of China being a satellite would thereby be drastically reduced is quite understandable; and it was out of this fear, probably more than out of anything else, that the thought was generated in Soviet Russia for the United States to take on the task of reducing the proportions of China so that the continued animosity between the two countries might make China increasingly dependent on Russia. So long as the United States did not show any spirit of accommodation toward Communist China, Russia was sure of some success. It was out of that atmosphere that the Korean War came. Subsequent developments seem to have confirmed the accuracy of the Soviet analysis. The Korean War brought in its wake a complete reversal of American policy toward Taiwan and severed any relationship between China and the United States. All that remains is a thin silken thread in Warsaw, which has managed to string together over two hundred meetings, like so many little beads. This is where matters stand at present. How long do we have to wait before they grow any better?

China feels that she is being balked at every turn by what she considers to be American intransigence and America's firm resolve to create serious obstacles for her all along the way. The hope of accomplishing anything through conciliation having disappeared, the Chinese leaders must find other avenues of expression. All that is happening around the world—in Southeast Asia, in Latin America, and in Africa—is very largely the result of the vital energy of a burgeoning China being repressed and trying to seek new outlets elsewhere. With all the difficulties, which China believes that the United States continues to create for her, it is still clearly her hope that they will be solved through peaceful negotiation. For in the flimsy and fragile relation maintained by the two countries at Warsaw, the new Chinese ambassador, in the first meeting with his counterpart on July 29, 1964, said that his government "has consistently stood for peaceful settlement of disputes between China and the United States by peaceful means." And he added, "I will make efforts to this end." * We have reason not to doubt the sincerity of these words.

---

* *New York* Times, *July 30, 1964.*

V THE UNITED STATES AND CHINA: 2

W HETHER OR NOT one admits that Soviet policy in the last fifteen years was aimed at bringing China and the United States
into open conflict with each other, the fact remains that there is
now implacable animosity between them.

Thinking people see a clear danger in this animosity, and the
New York *Times* has written words of warning that are both wise
and timely. In its editorial of June 12, 1964, which is worth quoting
at some length, under the title "Asian Confrontation," the paper
said:

> Two United States planes have been shot down in Laos and
> now American armed fighter plane escorts are shooting back. The
> situation is deteriorating in Vietnam as well as in Laos and, by
> reflexion, in Cambodia, Thailand and all of Southeast Asia . . .
> The power factor . . . that really counts is the confrontation
> between the United States and Communist China. They are still
> at some distance from each other, but the gap is closing. When
> Under Secretary Ball and President de Gaulle conferred the other
> day, they agreed that Southeast Asia should be denied to the
> Communists, but they disagreed on how this goal was to be
> achieved.
> General de Gaulle insists with reason that no settlement of
> the Indochina conflict is possible without the concurrence of the
> Communist Chinese. This is the dominating factor. China is
> there; the United States is 10,000 miles away. Chinese power
> radiates over the whole of Asia from India to Korea.
> The nub of the question is the American belief that a with-
> drawal of our military support would leave a vacuum which the
> Red Chinese would inevitably fill . . . The de Gaulle argument
> is that China has enough problems with Russia in the north, India
> in the west and the United States in the east, not to mention a

strained economy, to be willing to leave Southeast Asia more or less alone—on the condition that China felt there was no longer any reason to fear a threat from the United States in that area.

There is no ideal solution; but it has seemed to this newspaper that the most practicable one is, in the broadest possible terms, a guaranteed neutralization of all states that formerly made up Indochina. What this means is that the interested powers—including particularly the United States, the Soviet Union and Communist China—would mutually and gradually withdraw militarily from that area and would at the same time guarantee the independence of the respective states, possibly with a UN presence to enforce it.

Obviously such a solution is risky and might not work out in practice, but the risks will be great no matter what is done, and will be still greater if the outcome is left to the hazards of military escalation.

The entire problem deserves exploration in another conference of the fourteen nations, Communist China included, that have been concerned with Southeast Asia since the Geneva Conference of 1962. The decisive confrontation of the United States and Red China should be over a negotiating table, not with arms. In the long run, this will only be possible when Communist China is a member of the United Nations and when Washington can speak to Peking in the normal course of diplomatic exchanges between two nations that recognize each other.

I think, in all fairness, this is about the most rational, the most reasonable approach to the whole question of Chinese-American relations. It was written without bias, without emotion; it is cool and dispassionate; and it maintains throughout those ideas which, if put into practice, can re-establish United States and Chinese friendship on a firm and durable basis.

All these objectives in time will come to pass; the international situation demands them. But in the meantime, people still talk of war. The dangers of open conflict cannot be entirely eliminated.

America has massive superiority of fighting power, and China is completely at her mercy. If armed conflict takes place, China will be completely ruined. The mistakes that America thinks she committed in the Korean War will not be repeated. The destruction of China will be ruthless and thoroughgoing.

But what good can this do the United States? What will the world think of her? And what will the United States herself become with such a record of mass murder, death, and merciless annihilation, in the years to come?

The world will come to the conclusion that this then is a clear case of a strong nation abusing its power and determined to destroy a noble and ancient civilization for the simple reason that it is beginning, once again, to pull itself together, with the potential of challenging America's supremacy. The rise, phoenix-like, of China is indeed a great drama of the mid-twentieth century as the rise of America herself was a great drama of the nineteenth century. What kind of an image will America produce on the future generations of mankind when they are told, as they certainly will be, that America cannot stand the competition of another great nation and destroyed it when it had the capability?

I believe the world is beginning to feel, if it does not feel already, that all this talk of the hatred of Communism in China is largely a pretense and a façade. It has now become no longer accurate to talk about any conflict between two well-defined groups, "the free world" and "the Communist bloc." The Communist monolith has been split. Soviet Russia has been trying very hard to edge her way into the good graces of the West by isolating China, which is presumed to be her major partner. There are also signs that the Eastern European nations are following a more independent course. Rumania is an example, and, given time, the other satellites will follow. In other words, all indications seem to point to the development of national interests, which in the last analysis weigh more heavily than ideological beliefs. In the case of China it isn't her Communism that is so annoying, for there too it will change, if it has not changed much already, as the fact that she is growing strong, that the Chinese are a different race* and of a

---

* On this subject of racial implications in the destructive use of atomic power, the usually forthright and fearless Secretary General of the United Nations, U Thant, has made some pertinent remarks. Speaking at Ottawa on May

different color, and that a strong China is unwelcome to the Western world. The United States cannot coexist with such a country, and therefore China must be destroyed. *Delenda est Carthago.* That was the conviction of ancient Rome, and this would seem to be the conviction of modern America. But China is not Carthage. Even in the case of Carthage, while she was completely ruined by 146 B.C., never to rise again, Rome soon followed suit, also never to rise again. For Rome, in thus destroying Carthage, sowed the seeds of her own destruction. The law of nemesis, in the life of nations as of individuals, is hard and inexorable. It took a few centuries for the law to find fulfillment in Rome, but it worked all the same, silently and implacably. The man that lives by the sword, it is said, dies by the sword. China too will be destoyed if America decides to let loose the arsenal of her lethal weapons. Will the law in this case fail to operate? The destruction will bring home a lesson to all those other nations, which will survive, that might, not right and justice, rules over the world. Are we so sure that what is

_____

26, 1964, with reference to the then Senator Goldwater's suggestion made on May 24 to use nuclear power to defoliate parts of North Vietnam, he said anyone who proposed to use atomic weapons for destructive purposes "is in my view out of his mind." He then gave four reasons why he thought no such desperate attempt should ever be made by any power. The last of these, he said, was "very important." "There is, if I may say so," he continued, "a racial factor in such a projected operation. In 1945, when atomic bombs were dropped over Hiroshima and Nagasaki in Japan, there was a widespread feeling in many parts of Asia that these deadly atomic bombs were dropped upon Japanese cities because the Japanese were non-whites; and it was also argued at that time that atomic bombs would never have been dropped over cities in Nazi Germany." (And Nazi Germany, as much as Japan, was then at war with the United States.) This is, I think, a fair statement, for racial or color consciousness, as a concept, was after all created, then intensified, and finally woven into the political life of the world entirely by the West. When it begins to boomerang, as it must, the West turns around to say that it is the non-whites who are responsible for the racial policy, as, for instance, when Communist China establishes friendly relations with the peoples in Africa and tries to exploit the race issue to dominate over the West. It will be difficult to lend credence to such a view when the West, for over four hundred years, itself created the issue and has in a manner so successfully used it as a weapon to dominate over the rest of the world. Throughout the long history of China there has been no instance of any racial or color consciousness, not at least to the extent of influencing national policy. The whole subject is so important that it is discussed in another part of the book (See Appendix B).

being contemplated for China will not be done to America at some future moment, if not by China, then by some other power that will have the same capability? Force has never solved any question permanently, for it always leads to retribution.

These are lugubrious thoughts and would be entirely unnecessary were it not for the fact that people are not lacking in high and responsible positions who, as Vice President—then Senator— Humphrey said in effect, constantly grope with their nervous fingers for the button that releases the ultimate weapon.

But even though China may be destroyed by America's nuclear weapons, she will survive. Not only that, she will survive longer than America can hope to survive should she follow the example of Rome, and persist in her policy of armed might and nuclear power as the means of settling international disputes. General Mac- Arthur's views on a cobalt belt in Korea * and Senator Gold-

---

*There is no reason to believe that the interview given by General Mac- Arthur to Jim Lucas in 1954, but published after his death, is not authentic. According to Mr. Lucas, the general "proposed to sow a five-mile-wide belt of radioactive cobalt . . . along the Yalu, thus permanently sealing Korea off from China." The Joint Chiefs of Staff, according to Mr. Drew Pearson in his "Merry-Go-Round" published in the New York Post on April 30, 1964, "seriously considered" the plan, but rejected it for reasons which we should know. These were given by Mr. Pearson as: First, the United States didn't have enough cobalt to create a radioactive belt all the way across Korea. Second, there was no practical way to spread the deadly cobalt. There were not enough planes to spray the cobalt by air, and it would have taken months to spread it by trucks. Third, no matter how the cobalt dust was sown, it would have been almost sure suicide for those who handled it. Fourth, radioactive cobalt doesn't kill immediately, but sometimes takes weeks. The Chinese rulers who showed no concern for the lives of their own men in Korea could have marched their armies across the cobalt field and driven for a quick victory before the slow death took effect. Fifth, at even less sacrifice of men, the Chinese could have dug or washed safe paths across the cobalt. Finally, the Chinese could have flown their men over the cobalt belt and parachuted them into Korea. These are the reasons, added Mr. Pearson, why MacArthur's great master plan was turned down. This is as good an example as any of the now famous dictum that "Extremism in the defense of liberty is no vice." One's immediate reaction is to cry out with Madame Roland: "O Liberty! Liberty! how many crimes are committed in thy name!" There was not one fraction of a thought among these reasons, if they are accurately reported, that the plan was inhuman, that it was immoral, and that it came from a Christian country which has been in the habit of sending missionaries to convert the "heathens" in Asia! What has man-

water's suggestion of defoliation in Vietnam through atomic power
are more widely shared by other people than we are willing to admit. China will survive because, if past history is any lesson to us,
the fact that she has been able to do so through five thousand years
of continuous history is an indication that she has built within her
system an indefinable quality which, in spite of innumerable vicis-
situdes and difficulties, is able to resist ultimate destruction. There
is no secret for national survival. But we know with certainty that
no nation survives by mere accident. There are always forces of
one kind or another which labor to put an end to that survival; and
if it lives on, it means that it has been able to develop some unusual vitality. Where are the other empires—ancient Persia, the
empire of Alexander, imperial Rome, the empire of Genghis Khan,
Assyria, Babylonia and Egypt? They have come but they are gone.
China is the only exception. For China knows that military power
alone is not enough to guarantee her survival.

If China has been able to survive longer than any other civilization, while maintaining continuously and without intermission her
historical and cultural identity, there is more than a military reason. This is why I feel certain that, whatever may happen to her
now, that identity will project itself into the future. There are
reasons why I believe so, but I shall mention only a few.

First, there is that deep sense of unity in China which has produced a massive solidity. Other nations, with the possible exception of France, have created that unity through political means. In
the case of China, it is entirely a cultural unity or a unity of consciousness, because every element in her civilization, from its early
formative period and well into its period of maturity, grew from
her own roots and from her own soil without benefit of any alien
contribution. That is one of the reasons why it has such a durable
and long-lasting quality. It developed a character of its own from
neolithic times, as we see it clearly in the Yangshao and Lung-
shan pottery. Then came the bronze age and the invention of
writing which further enhanced its uniqueness. For nearly thirty

---

*kind come to, that we do not even blink at the very idea of killing fellow
human beings by the hundreds of thousands or even millions! The plan was
not put into practice simply because it was not expedient!*

centuries that civilization went on growing until its unity acquired an institutionalized form barely two centuries before the Christian era. Shortly after the Han Dynasty this political unity came to be established on the basis of a Confucian orthodoxy or bureaucracy through which Confucian thought, itself the direct lineal descendant of an earlier world view, succeeded in permeating both the spiritual and temporal life of the people. That is why the unity so created became solid and impressive.

The late Professor R. H. Tawney, who was in China in 1930 on an educational mission for the League of Nations, made some remarks that are well worth remembering. As a distinguished economic historian, he could be relied upon to make some profound observations on the social scene in Europe as well as in China. In an article published in the *Manchester Guardian* in March 1931, he raised the question, "What is it that makes for the unity of China?" And he answered that it was not geography, nor political institutions, nor economic conditions, nor religion, but something that was deeper than any of those or all of them combined. "Every fact that a stranger learns," he continued, "tells him that there is not one China, but many. Every day that he passes there, he knows more certainly that China is one . . . In no country, not even France, is the impression of a nation, not merely as a political unit or territorial arrangement, but as a human being, so profound and insistent. The personality of the people surrounds the visitor like a tide; while he is peering at one point he is outflanked at another. His reason is still doubting whether China exists as a single organism, and lo! his soul has become half Chinese." Professor Tawney ended by saying, "Her [China's] unity, like that of Europe in the Middle Ages, was during the greater part of her history the unity of a civilization, not of a political system."

Europe then could have likewise maintained or developed the unity of Christendom if the spirit of the Middle Ages remained. But it was not to be. The fissiparous nature of its thinking split Europe wide apart. While in China it was entirely meaningless to consider temporal powers as being divorced from spiritual powers, in Europe that became the major issue. Even before the Middle Ages came to an end, men like Thomas Aquinas, Dante, Duns

Scotus, William of Ockham, had begun to consider them as two disparate entities. By the time of Machiavelli (1469–1527) the Pope could no longer claim supremacy or control over secular affairs; his influence was confined exclusively within ecclesiastical limits. In the political world there was nothing to hold in check the tendencies toward separate nationalities and monarchies, and in Italy alone the numerous feudal principalities and free cities emerged as five distinct units—the Republic of Florence, the Duchy of Milan, the Republic of Venice, the Kingdom of Naples, and the territory of the Roman Church—each claiming a sovereignty of its own. That was natural, as it was perhaps natural in China during the Period of the Warring States, but instead of a Machiavelli to confirm and justify the separate existences of these states, the weight of the Confucian ideas held them together and made them responsible to a moral order, so that the Machiavellian doctrine "that any means, however lawless or unscrupulous, may be justifiably employed by a ruler in order to establish and maintain a strong central government" had no chance to develop. That is why China remained a unity to the present day while Europe became cut up into national units pursuing their different national interests.* As long as the West is founded on the concept of an amoral or non-moral state, a peaceful world, in my view, is almost an impossibility. That is why the present confrontation of China and the West is not merely a confrontation of nations: it is a confrontation of two widely different points of view of what a world order should be.

Western imperialism, which reached a high-water mark in the nineteenth century, was a logical outcome of European history, for imperialism means the pursuit of national interests at the expense of others, without reference to moral considerations. And when China began to suffer from the exploitation during the early days of that century, the West claimed that she was no more than a geographical name, that, divided and chaotic, her different parts could never come together to form a national unit. Only the West, which had always been centripetal, so the argument ran, could help unify

---

* *The subject was discussed in my book* Within the Four Seas, *passim.*

China—and that, of course, provided the excuse for the further domination over her. The argument might be true of India. But it certainly could not have been true of China. In language alone how widely apart are those two peoples. If one applies the linguistic map of China where there is only one written language and where millions upon millions of people also speak the identical language—with, of course, local differences, which in many cases are never so wide as to prevent mutual understanding—upon any part of the world of comparable size, no such area can be found, with the exception of the United States. But then in this case it is America that is the aberration. It is an artificial creation, with peoples transposed from Europe made to learn the same language.

I feel that this impressive unity in China, which is the result of thousands of years of the development and evolution of a unique civilization owing no debt to any other civilization,* is something that nothing, not even the atomic bomb, can destroy. It cannot be destroyed because it is in essence a spiritual quality, and to say that it can be destroyed through some physical means would be tantamount to saying that matter can in fact triumph over spirit. This is a proposition which no religion or philosophy, either in the East or in the West, is prepared to acknowledge.

Closely related to the first reason is my second reason for believing that Chinese civilization will long survive after other civilizations, many more spectacular and dramatic, have come and gone. Chinese civilization is not only founded upon, but is the actual embodiment of a set of moral values to a degree which is not thought possible by other civilizations. That does not mean of course that the Chinese, as individuals, are morally superior to the

---

* Mr. Alan Watts in his Way of Zen said, "Confucianism is one of the most workable patterns of social convention that the world has known. Coupled with the 'let well enough' attitude of Taoism, it nurtured a mellow and rather easy-going type of mentality which, when it absorbed Buddhism, did much to make it more practical. That is to say, it made Buddhism a possible way of life for human beings, for people with families, with everyday work to do, and with normal instincts and passions" (p. 40). In other words, Buddhism came into Chinese life with an established civilization of already more than two thousand years only after it had been drastically overhauled. It had to become Chinese before it could find a place in the Chinese scheme of things.

individuals in Western society. But I think it is still true to say that China's political and social organization has been impregnated with a spirit which has provided a vitality, a stamina, and a sense of direction not found in other societies. The best example is the latter part of the last century. The fortunes of the country were then at the lowest ebb. It was surrounded and humiliated, yet, characteristically, the Chinese leaders never thought that the Chinese view of life or the Chinese approach in the conduct of life should be given up: they were willing to adopt the technique of producing wealth and power only on condition that it be modified to suit the Chinese environment. Out of that came the famous phrase *chung-hsueh wei ti, hsi-hsueh wei yung,* meaning that they should take the old learning for substance and the new Western learning for function. In the realm of political action it was thought that a government should still be one of virtue, with the addition of a certain amount of government by law, as if law itself was not sufficiently a moral concept.* The important thing was to

---

The concept of being law-abiding as a part of civilized life is now taken for granted, but I am not so sure if this Western concept of statutory law, for that is what it amounts to, cannot be overdone; and the multiplicity of legal enactments tends to reduce to a minimum the relationship between law and the moral idea of which it is presumed to be an expression. The Western concept seems now to be more closely related to the concept of original sin or to a lack of faith in human nature, without some external compulsion, in its ability to develop a condition in which law as such could be dispensed with. In ancient Greece, clearly exemplified in Sophocles' Antigone, there was still talk of the conflict of legal enactment and the unwritten laws of heaven, but the subsequent development of law, especially under Roman auspices, took progressively less cognizance of the need of human laws to be the embodiment of the divine law. In this connection the traditional Chinese conception of law, which is in consonance with the Greek idea, has still, I believe, quite an important part to play in the modern world. Confucius was supposed to have said that in hearing litigations he was no different from other justices. "If there should be any differences," he continued, "it would be found in my effort in creating conditions under which litigations would not be started or needed." This attitude toward law seems to have been borne out by an incident concerning Tse Chan who was the prime minister of the State of Cheng before the time of Confucius. It was said that the people in that state had metal caldrons on which were inscribed the laws relating to the punishment of crimes. An official Shu Hsiang then wrote to the prime minister and made the following complaint: "Formerly, Sir, I took you as my model. Now I can no longer do so. The

cultivate *wang tao,* "the kingly way," or rule by virtue and benevolence. One comparatively recent scholar put the whole idea in the following words:

> If we wish to receive the benefit of Western methods, we must first acquire a knowledge of Confucius, Mencius, Cheng Tsu and Chu Hsi [of neo-Confucianism] and keep it as the foundation to make people thoroughly familiar with filial piety, brotherly love, loyalty, sincerity, a sense of propriety, righteousness, integrity, a sense of shame, a sense of obligation, the teachings of the sages, and moral courage, in order to understand and demonstrate the foundation, before we can learn the foreign spoken and written languages for some practical use.

This view was not confined to those who kept themselves at home, but was expounded even by those who had traveled in foreign parts. In a book called *Observations on Western Countries,* another recent scholar Yang Tse-chih made some prescient remarks that make interesting reading even today:

> As to human affairs [the writer said], China emphasizes human relationships and honors benevolence and righteousness. In the West, on the contrary, a son does not take care of his father [is not this only too true?], a minister cheats his emperor, a wife is more honored than a husband; thus the bond of the three relationships is broken. Because the proper relationship between husband

---

ancient kings, who weighed matters very carefully before establishing ordinances, did not write down their system of punishments, fearing to awaken a litigious spirit among the people. Since, however, all crimes cannot be prevented, they set up the barrier of righteousness, bound the people by administrative ordinances, treated them according to just usage, guarded them with good faith, and surrounded them with benevolence. But when the people know that there are laws regulating punishments, they have no respectful fear of authority. A litigious spirit awakes, invoking the letter of the law, and trusting that evil actions will not fall under its provisions. Government then becomes impossible. Sir, I have heard it said that a state has most laws when it is about to perish." This is an idealistic approach to law which is perhaps hardly practicable under the complex conditions of our modern society, but I think it contains a warning that can still be of value to us in the twentieth century, when the legal network has become so overwhelmingly complicated.

and wife is not cultivated, the marriage ceremony means hardly anything. As soon as a girl is twenty years old, she is permitted to find a husband whom she chooses, and there are those who make many selections or trials before they make a match. They do not consider sexual relations preceding marriage as a shame [the Kinsey report and others more than confirm this]. Beautiful young girls seek males everywhere; even the silver-haired and the widows can invite male companions for intimate relations as they like. The customs are bad to such a degree!

The Chinese have always considered society as being the individual writ large, so that the moral values that are considered essential for the life of the individual are equally essential and important for the life of society. In the West, the Aristotelian and Platonic concepts of the "philosopher-king" existed, but were never put into practice, owing to the rapid disintegration of the Athenian city-state after the Peloponnesian War. The Chinese had more than two thousand years in which the Confucian and pre-Confucian concepts were tried, and experimented upon, by a system of civil service examinations through which the most accomplished scholars were allowed to be the rulers of men. This was perhaps the most marvelous political system conceived by the mind of men, and the empire constructed upon it was strictly a scholastic empire in which war, following the teachings of all of the Chinese thinkers, held no honorable place. It is therefore impossible to find China, in any of her historic periods, having recourse to war as an instrument of national policy. That does not mean that there have been no wars within China's own boundaries. There are grasping and ambitious men in all societies and at all times. But to resort to war for the conquest of foreign lands and to subjugate their peoples and exploit them for one's own benefit is a totally different matter. The Western nations have consistently done that, and their history, especially in the last four hundred years, has been a record of such conquests. No one can say that China has followed their examples. When people say that China today is warlike, aggressive, and militant, anyone who knows China's history and her view of life must doubt it. And yet this is the theme that is being persistently and remorselessly dinned into our ears. It could only happen if China should turn away from her heritage: but there is no indication that such is the case. China does admire the West—its technology, its scientific development, and all the accomplishments that are the results of this development. But she is not forsaking her heritage. If anything, she has been doing everything to preserve, to refine, and to amplify that heritage to an extent unknown before. She is convinced that what has come to her from her past is intrinsically good and beautiful, and has an important part to play in the world of the future; that it can contribute immensely to the building of a peaceful world; and that it is only through a deep love of this heritage that the millions of her people can renew their faith in themselves.

Foreign travelers who have visited the Chinese mainland can testify that the new China conforms to the ancient image of that country—a hard-working people, genial and friendly. Travelers report that soldiers are not visible. Mr. Felix Greene joined the celebrations on October 1 and saw no display of tanks or jets, no proud boast of military power, but instead millions of toy balloons, floats of pretty girls, dancing by all the national minorities, surrounded by an atmosphere of fun, frolic, and gaiety. M. Edgar Faure took pains to explain: "The Chinese have always proclaimed their adherence to the rule of peaceful coexistence in the relations between countries with different social systems." Dr. Tuzo Wilson, a Canadian and President of the Geophysical Congress, saw one part of China (around Lanchow in Kansu) covered with scientific laboratories and experimental stations, where previously there were only vast stretches of sand dunes.

The list is long of people from foreign parts who are anxious to have the world share their knowledge of the new China, of all the massive work that is being carried out. It is all the work of peace. No one, so far as I know, has testified to the building of war machinery intended to be used for aggression or invasion. It is a pity that these facts about life in China are not known to the American public. I am convinced that if they were known, the American people would say to themselves that the Chinese, so hard-working and industrious, are people just like themselves, who know no greater satisfaction than the creation of a viable and solvent society. The American and Chinese people have much in common, not least the belief that nothing is impossible. Camus was right when he said that with rebellion came awareness—awareness of the enormous potentialities for good once the inertia and apathy are lifted, awareness of the possibility of galvanizing an ancient society into a modern and vital environment. Is this something to be feared? Or is this something to be encouraged, admired, and rejoiced over? Unfortunately there are people who *are* afraid of what is going on in China, and that is why they are against her.

Chinese civilization is based not on military strength, but on moral law: this is the simple reason for its durability. It was Lao-tze who said, "The best soldiers are not warlike; the best fighters do not lose their temper. The greatest conquerors are those who overcome their enemies without strife. The great directors of men are those who yield place to others. This is called the virtue of not striking, the capacity of directing mankind: this is being the equal of Heaven." These remarks are not merely paradoxes, but contain truths that are born out of long experience and a profound knowledge of the human heart. These are not truths, I am afraid, that can be found in any Western philosophy, nor are they generally believed. Marcus Aurelius was the nearest person to a philosopher-ruler in ancient Rome, but as he wrote down his immortal thoughts, while looking across the Danube and fighting the Teutonic tribes, there was no intimation that he appreciated the "virtue of not striking." For the Western world believes that force must be and can only be met by an opposing and superior force.

The concept of ahimsa in Hinduism is the counterpart of Lao-tze's philosophy, and the success of the Gandhian movement is sufficient proof that there is something positive in what is generally regarded as a negative approach to political action. The history of what Professor C. P. Fitzgerald described as the "cultural expansion" of China was one along similar lines. It was a form of moral or cultural osmosis. The Chinese nation, from the beginning of its history, was surrounded by "barbarians." Military means sometimes had to be resorted to, but if its survival depended entirely on an opposing superior force, the chances are that it would have perished long ago. The principal thing was to develop those specifically human qualities in a man so that his approach would be regarded by those with whom he came into contact as that of a true friend and not of an enemy. Since we are all human, barbarians and civilized alike, a human approach to life's problems, made in the spirit of the utmost sincerity, can seldom fail.

And this leads me to a consideration of the concept of the ideal man, of the gentleman or *chün-tse,* which was developed far beyond any comparable set of values in Western thought.* The concept of *arete* in Homer, as exemplified in the conduct of Achilles when Priam came to ask for the return of Hector's body, was a sound beginning, but it led to no change in man's behavior. The Aristotelian concept of the magnanimous man to whom Spenser gave poetic expression in his *Faerie Queene* was an ideal never followed. The Renaissance concept of *l'uomo universale* laid too much emphasis on intellectual qualities, even though we may admire them in a Pico della Mirandola or a Leonardo da Vinci. Baldassare Castiglione's *Il libro del cortegiano,* which had a tremendous vogue in England for centuries, succeeded only in giving us a Polonius or a Lord Chesterfield. Perhaps only the French, as in other areas of moral and cultural values in the Western world, managed to evolve the idea of the *honnête homme,* but it is no equivalent of the Confucian concept of *chün-tse,* which became the embodiment of all the human and moral virtues. The *chün-tse* is not only a man of good manners, self-negating, self-forgetting, considerate of the feeling of others, and of unwavering courtesy, but he is also a man of loving kindness, humane, of unquestioned honesty, of profound sympathy and humility, of simplicity of heart, devoid of egotism, free from vulgarity, and broadly tolerant. He is, above all, a man of the utmost sincerity, so that he goes, as Confucius said, into the midst of "barbarians," armed with these spiritual "weapons," but has nothing to be afraid of. He was not unmindful of his own interests, but he was prepared to place the

---

* *Mr. Harold Nicolson, in his otherwise excellent book* The Good Behaviour, *which is a comparative study of the concept of the ideal man in different cultural areas, both East and West, unfortunately had no knowledge of Chinese culture and made a travesty of the Confucian* chün-tse, *as if he were no more than a mere robot going through the motions of observing ceremonies and rituals, and nothing else.*

interests of other people ahead of his own, or at least on a level with his own. The Western world does not and will not believe that this can be true in the relations between human beings. It would be presumptuous to claim that this ideal was realized at all times. But it hangs like a curtain in the background of the Chinese drama, and the record of Chinese history is full of examples to show that it worked. This is what one may call conquest by not conquering. It is not for nothing that China has come to be known as the home of the humanistic ideal.

The case of Vietnam gives us the best opportunity to experiment with a new policy. If some effort were made in that direction, I feel confident that there would be no problem in South Vietnam. No problem in Asia can be satisfactorily solved without the participation of China. The Anglo-Saxon world, however, finds it difficult to reconcile itself to this truth. It has long been in the habit of believing that what *it* thinks must be right, regardless of what others may feel.* In Vietnam and Southeast Asia, even though the United States is a hemisphere away, no one is supposed to have the right to oppose any measures that the United States may have decided upon. America claims the right to feel insecure, as she does, about Cuba. But China has no corresponding right to guard her borders, even if Southeast Asia is full of military "advisers" and active combatants, now numbering over 140,000. The rest of the logic is simple. America is the most powerful country in the world. She has the largest collection of the effective weapons. North Vietnam has already fallen to the Communists. The rest of Southeast Asia may fall, as North Vietnam has fallen. Since America is against the extension of Communism anywhere, whether it be one mile or ten thousand miles distant from her frontiers, she must there-

---

* This is part of "a double standard of morality" which Professor Henry Steele Commager feels is at the base of "much of our current foreign policy" ("A Historian Looks at Our Political Morality" in the Saturday Review, July 10, 1965). And he gave seven solid examples which are unanswerable. One of these is: "It is a matter for rejoicing that we have the nuclear bomb, but when China detonated her first bomb our President told us that 'this is a dark day in history.'" In other words, what America does is right, but the same thing done by another country is wrong!

fore crush it, either by aiding local governments or by fighting for them. Whether these governments are those the people want is beside the point. What former Congressman Walter Judd used to say about China is a classic example of this unique type of thinking. Whether the government there, he said, was democratic or not was none of America's business. All she wanted was a government in China whose leaders remained friendly to the United States and were willing to do what America wanted them to do.* This was how the Chiang Kai-sheks, Syngman Rhees, Bao Dais and Ngo Dinh Diems came into power and helped to make Communism popular. If they were proved to be ineffective, others were chosen to take their place. As they say in China: "You change the juice, but not the medicinal herbs that produce the juice." In the meantime, thousands upon thousands of Vietnamese have been killed; millions have been mutilated or rendered homeless, having been herded into virtual concentration camps, which are euphemistically called "strategic hamlets"; the entire country is reduced to utmost poverty; and no one has known one day of peace in these years of war and devastation—all in the name of freedom. The American boys themselves, who help in the fighting, also become demoralized, as, for instance, in the case of one pilot reported in *Newsweek* magazine †️ who goes out with his superior weapons, like the man who goes to his office with his briefcase, for the day's routine work of killing

---

* *The exact wording of Dr. Judd's astounding speech before the Executives' Club at Chicago on February 2, 1951 (reprinted in* Vital Speeches, March 1, 1951), *is as follows: "It was not necessary that they should have a good government in China. That was desirable, but wholly secondary. It did not necessarily need to be a democratic government, an honest government, or an efficient government. The key thing was that the manpower and the resources and the bases of China be under Chinese friendly to the United States, and not under the control of potential enemies of the United States." Dr. Judd was a Christian missionary in China and a medical doctor! If one extends this view of China to the rest of the world, we can see why Communism has grown so rapidly since the end of the Second World War. It has been helped by a series of governments that are sponsored and financed by the United States, whose interests they serve; and by serving the United States they serve themselves and oppress the people of whom they eventually make themselves the enemies. Is it any wonder that they rise to overthrow their governments and go over to the Communists? Mao Tse-tung used to say that Chiang Kai-shek was his best friend.*

† *June 8, 1964.*

and mutilating the Vietcongs if he could find them or just the plain natives who might after all be Vietcongs in disguise, and returns with immense satisfaction to his base to find his shoes polished, his laundry done, his dinner cooked, ready for an evening of dancing and entertainment, and perhaps a night of love. With the dawn of another day he goes out to repeat the "mission," "swooping down like a hawk on unsuspecting prey," and with his machine gun he systematically cuts the guerrillas "to pieces as they ran across open ground in search of cover." All this reminds one of young Mussolini when he felt such exhilaration in seeing his bombs bursting out like flowers and killing the innocent people on the plains of Ethiopia. War, let us remember with Lao-tze, is an instrument of evil: it has a demoralizing effect.

What has the world come to when civilized people can grow so callous, so indifferent to the suffering and misery of other people —especially when these people belong to a different race and color? What have the people of Vietnam done to deserve all the cruelty that is being inflicted on them? Napalm bombs with liquid fire know no difference between men and women, old and young, Vietcong soldier or simple peasant.

I believe there is an alternative to all this bloodshed and cruelty. It is to be found in the practical application of the words of President Johnson shortly after he went into the White House. On more than one occasion he made a plea for reason, for a rational approach to the conduct of international affairs. He showed his aversion to political extremism in his first speech to the Congress on November 27, 1964, when he said, "Let us put an end to the teaching and the preaching of hate and evil and violence. Let us turn away from the fanatics of the far left and the far right, from the apostles of bitterness and bigotry, from those defiant of law and those who pour venom into our national bloodstream." He made virtually the same plea in his address before the United Nations on December 18. "I know," he said then, "that vast problems remain: conflicts between great powers, conflicts between small neighbors, disagreements over disarmament, persistence of ancient wrongs in the area of human rights, residual problems of colonialism and all the rest." But President Johnson was not afraid of these problems. For he continued: "Men and nations, working apart, created these problems. And men and nations, *working together* [my italics] must solve them." These sentiments are an echo of what President Kennedy had said before him. "We need," Mr. Kennedy had said, in what has now become a famous line, "a better weapon than the hydrogen bomb . . . this weapon is peaceful co-operation." But have we really made any adequate attempt to "work together," or to promote "peaceful co-operation" with the de facto, the actually operating government of China since it came into existence on the mainland? *

The most eloquent words were those spoken by President Johnson during Easter Week of 1964. He then urged again "reasoned agreement" rather than "rash retaliation," for "general war is impossible . . . without risking the end of civilization." He said that he wanted to be a President who can make it possible for every boy in this land to grow to manhood loving his country— loving his country, instead of dying for it." And then he continued by saying that the only sensible approach to the solution of international problems was that of patient negotiation. For "we, the most powerful nation in the world, can afford to be patient . . . Power brings obligation and the people of this country and the world expect more from their leaders than just a show of brute force." So let us all be patient. These statements are from the lips of a great man of peace. How could he have made them if he did not mean that they be put into actual practice?

Friendly relations between China and America are not beyond our reach. For one thing, there is a reservoir of good feelings between the two peoples through the decades, even though the his-

---

* *The present recourse to retaliation and the massive bombing of North Vietnam, begun in the early days of February, 1965, which includes the use of non-lethal gas, many say, is a repudiation of President Johnson's early remarks. They believe he has even gone beyond what Mr. Goldwater said he would do if he was elected President of the United States. As one writer to the New York* Times *complained, it was only yesterday when the Americans were only "advisers," today they are active combatants in Vietnam. America seeks no wider war, and yet bombing is being carried into the heart of North Vietnam. Today it is "non-lethal" gas, in addition to "lazy dogs" and napalm liquid fire, what tomorrow is going to bring is anybody's guess.*

tory of their relations is far from perfect. For another, the national characteristics of the two peoples have much in common, with due allowances for their vast cultural differences. Above all, the two peoples have a firm grasp of realities and a rational attitude toward things and events.

If America had sincerely said to the Chinese government that, in the interest of peace and for the welfare of the people, she was prepared to seek a *modus vivendi,* I feel there would have been a hearty response from mainland China and a solution to the problems. The United States could have said, "You cannot expect us to like your Communism. We are implacably against it. You have become a Communist country: that is your own doing. But we shall resolutely see to it that Vietnam and Southeast Asia shall remain free from Communism. That is why we are there to help those governments. But you feel insecure because we are there, though there is no reason for that fear. However, you are entitled to the sense of security that all nations desire. Your boundary is contiguous for long stretches with the boundary of that area, while we are far away. But in order to provide you with that sense of security, we on our part must be certain that you will not extend your Communism southward. We must have a guarantee before we are willing to consider withdrawing from that area. If that sounds reasonable to you and if you agree, then we shall ask other nations to join us so that, if and when you contravene either the letter or spirit of our agreement, and if there is incontestable proof that, in spite of our agreement, you still try to invade, infiltrate, or conquer Southeast Asia, then we shall not hesitate to use all the military power we have at our disposal against you."

If such a position had been taken by the United States, I am sure it would have been accepted by China. China wants security and America wants Southeast Asia to be free from Communism. America should give China the benefit of the doubt, and should receive, in exchange, an assurance and a solemn commitment that Southeast Asia will remain free. Such a proposition might well be agreeable to China; it is not very different from the idea of a non-aggression pact which Mr. Chou En-lai suggested on more than one occasion. America, however, insists on believing that it is not security that China desires, but the conquest of all Southeast Asia to solve her problems of surplus population and food shortage. This is of course a completely erroneous reading of Chinese motives as well as of Chinese history. There is nothing to substantiate such a view. China has enough troubles with Russia in the north, with India in the west, and the United States in the east, to welcome further troubles from the south.

This matter of population explosion has often been mentioned, but I do not see how any intelligent person can ever give it a thought. The latest comment on China's alleged quest for space and food in Southeast Asia was made by Marshal Chen Yi in his interview on July 24, 1964, at Shanghai with Dr. Hugo Portisch of *Der Kurier* of Vienna, which was reproduced in the New York *Times* on August 7. I quote these words not because they come from a Communist source, but simply because they make sense. "There are two things to be said," began the Marshal. "China has sufficient space. We could easily feed an additional 200 million people or more in this gigantic country [China is larger than the United States]. And even if some day we should have reached the 800 million or a billion mark, the country would still be big enough for them. We have rich material resources, and we have gigantic quantities of land which can be cultivated. Take the northwest of China. There is, for one, the province of Sinkiang. Only 6 million people live there, but Sinkiang could easily provide space and food for 50 million people. There are many such areas in China. Hence we are not compelled to reach beyond our borders." And then on the subject of birth control, the Marshal said that China had sent specialists to Japan, Sweden, England, and India, and "we are now carrying out birth control on a large scale. But interestingly enough nothing of this is being reported in the world." Quite soberly he concluded, "I do not believe that there will be any more rapid increase in the Chinese population in the future." And then raising the question as to what the Chinese want in Southeast Asia and India, the Marshal answered, "Only more people, jungles, swamps, mosquitoes and snakes—all things which we Chi-

nese cannot stand. What would China want to go there for?" *
I have brought in this subject of Vietnam as an illustration of
how moral values instead of expediency can be usefully applied in
the solution of international problems. Without them I think a just
and peaceful world order is like a will-o'-the-wisp that will always
be elusive and unrealizable. The Chinese, as a race, are, I believe,
most amenable to reason. One cannot deny that this interview, attributed to Marshal Chen Yi, so free from bellicosity, is the very
embodiment of reason. Whenever there is any difference of opinion, the immediate reaction of all classes in China—the common
people no less than the educated—is "let's talk reason" (*chiang
li*). The teahouses of old, spreading from one end of the country to
the other, used to serve as a kind of people's courthouse as well as
gossip forums, as in the case of the coffeehouses in the West.
There was no need to refer to any legal compendium; those assembled in the teahouse would instinctively know what was right and
what wrong. That was your public opinion, and the two contending
parties would have no alternative but to abide by the judgment of
the public. This way of settling little differences of life which flesh
is always heir to is still being practiced, in a modified form, on the
Chinese mainland. As Confucius said, what the leaders want is to
create a set of conditions in society where litigations, even of the
teahouse type, will be obsolete.

Here I wish to cite two examples of this point of view in contemporary China. One is the case of a black market profiteer who
was selling some article of food, during the famine of 1960, at
double the normal price. The local authorities discovered it and,
instead of having the man imprisoned or shot—as we would expect
any Communist government to do—they simply took out what
they had in their reserve and quietly sold it at the usual price without so much as disturbing the profiteer. The result was that he
could no longer find buyers. The authorities triumphed without
legal penalties. It was a moral triumph, because they knew that the
man would probably refrain from any further anti-social action.
Why punish him? Is it not better that he punish himself?

---

* *This sentiment was already expressed by Ssu-ma Kuang (1019–1086) in
his great history completed in 1084.*

The second case is that of a law professor of Tokyo University, Yozo Watanabe, who was on a visit to mainland China. On his return to Japan he wrote an article for the magazine *The World* in its April 1964 issue. He said he was interested in investigating legal conditions in China and visited the courts there as well as the prisons and law schools. On arrival at Peking he asked to be taken to witness some legal proceedings and was told by the Chinese authorities that they would be glad to arrange such visits. He was surprised when he was warned that cases were very few and that they were not sure there would be any for him to attend during his period of stay in the capital. They promised, however, to arrange something for him at Shanghai in case he failed to see any at Peking. For a city of many millions of inhabitants this came to him as a surprise indeed. Before he left, there was actually no criminal case, but there was one civil case which he attended. It was a divorce case which arose out of disagreement on how to bring up the children. The three judges were all women, with the recorder a man. The case was dismissed with compromise outside of the court. The next thing the professor requested was to see the prisons. One large prison had a capacity for three thousand prisoners. There were 1,700 prisoners at the time of his visit of whom 40 per cent were special agents for Chiang Kai-shek, the remaining 60 per cent being criminals of various types. Professor Watanabe drew the following conclusion: "China has such a huge population, and yet, as compared with Japan, the number of criminal cases is exceedingly small. I said to the staff member of the prison who accompanied me that in Japan cases of murder are brought in every day. He was much surprised when he heard that, for he told me that the majority of the criminal cases in China involve counter-revolutionary activities, while the rest include theft or burglary or corruption or accidents in traffic. As regards murder, I wouldn't say that it does not exist, but cases are exceedingly limited."

This account seems to be borne out by a number of foreign visitors from the West who sometimes complain that they could not lose anything. Socks with holes in them and torn shirts which were left in the hotels to be thrown away, would be returned to them when they stopped in the next city. That was honesty with a vengeance. That was morality in an aggressive form. Mainland China can in fact be aggressive, but it is what may be termed internal aggression as against external aggression with which she is being charged.

This is why it is again a misreading of Chinese history or of the Chinese nature to feel, as many do, that just because the new government is founded on Marxist principles, it has placed a moratorium on the moral life, which has made China what she has been through the ages. The very instincts of the new leaders must tell them that if they do so, they do it only at grave risk to themselves. Marxism in China serves a particular purpose at a particular moment in China's history. There are, as I see it, two such purposes. One is, through Marxism they seek to regain a respectable position for China in the family of nations through the revival of personal integrity and pride in the heritage of the past. We may describe this as one form of nationalism or patriotism. The second purpose is to create and establish a clean and incorruptible government. The initial steps taken for the attainment of these ends have been drastic, but after all it is a revolution that China is going through, and to have a revolution on one's hands is not like going to a banquet, as Mao Tse-tung used to say.

Persuasion is a slow process. It is not drastic, but it is radically more effective. It is based on the belief that every individual has contributions of one sort or another to make to the total social welfare, and the more he is convinced of the error of his ways, the greater are these contributions. One formula has been widely applied in this work of persuasion. It is expressed in four Chinese characters *tse wuo chien tao,* that is, submitting oneself to self-examination. A person is asked to go through a psychological process of dissecting his own psyche, to look at it in as detached a manner as possible, to appraise it objectively, to admit to himself which parts are selfish and which are useful for social well-being, and then to piece the psyche together with the selfish parts suppressed or eliminated.* Another method that is being widely practiced is the total elimination of class consciousness. Though China

---

* This is commonly known as brain-washing.

has never known caste, class consciousness has of course existed. That I think is unavoidable in all societies. Now with the practice of *hsia fang,* a bureaucrat or an intellectual is periodically made to do the work of the farmer, or a common laborer, so that his pride as a "superior" species is completely eradicated, and his sympathy for the common people enhanced.

One remark may sound rather far-fetched, but by putting together the somewhat meager reports that have come out of Communist China, one gathers the impression that the new leaders are trying to build a society aptly described by Lao-tze as one in which a person can sleep through the night with doors wide open; or by Confucius, who dreamed of a society in which everyone respects elderly people as if they were one's own father and mother, and loves children as if they were one's own sons and daughters. The ideal of Confucius was not that of a Christian saint, for sainthood is attainable only by a very limited number of people, but of a sage; and sagehood is a condition, Confucius continued to remind us, within the reach of everyone. One of the poems by Chairman Mao Tse-tung has these two lines:

Spring breezes and thousands upon thousands of willow sprigs,
Within the realm six hundred millions are all Yao and Shun.

Mao's aspiration to rule the country after the manner of these legendary emperors, who were paragons of virtue and sagacity, is unmistakable. It is significant that though Confucius is considered by mainland China as the product of a feudal age, his basic ideals of human behavior have not been repudiated, and no unkind words have been said about him. Also all previous dynasties, no matter what their beliefs were, sooner or later turned to Confucius as a necessary teacher for the development of orderly society. All this merely goes to show that what is happening in China today is in lineal succession to what has happened in previous centuries. There is no hiatus between the two. Dr. Wing-tsit Chan of Dartmouth College in his *Source Book in Chinese Philosophy* has, I think, given a good explanation of this continuity.

"Mao Tse-tung," says Professor Chan, "has not claimed to be a philosopher, and he has not been labeled as such. But his ideas have determined the directions in which philosophy has been developing in New China since its establishment in 1949. Of his many works, two are of extreme importance in this connection, namely, *On Practice* (1937) and *On New Democracy* (1940) . . . The thesis of *On Practice,* which is the most philosophical of Mao's works, is simple and definite . . . 'To discover truth through practice, and through practice to verify and develop truth. To start from perceptual knowledge and actively develop it into rational knowledge, and then starting from rational knowledge, actively direct revolutionary practice so as to remold the subjective and objective world. Practice, knowledge; more practice, more knowledge; the cyclical repetition of this pattern to infinity, and with each cycle, the elevation of practice and knowledge to a higher level. Such is the whole of the dialectical materialist theory of knowledge, and such is the dialectical materialist theory of the unity of knowing and doing.' "

In Professor Chan's words, "The fact that Mao concluded his essays with the theory of the unity of knowledge and action is most interesting, for it is one of the most prominent [and I may add perennial] theories in the history of Chinese philosophy" (p. 773). It is the central theme of all philosophical thinking from Confucius to Wang Yang-ming (1472–1529) and later. Knowledge, it is held, is not a matter of epistemology: it is not complete, is in fact useless if it is not implemented by action, which is the embodiment of that knowledge.

One of the principal and typical remarks by Confucius, which is illustrative of the interrelationship and the harmonious blending of thought and action, is to be found in the *Great Learning*. It is a remark that has made China what she is and which, in effect, makes China different from the Western world:

> The illustrious ancients [said Confucius] when they wished to make clear and to propagate the highest virtues in the world, put their states in proper order. Before putting their states in proper order, they regulated their families. Before regulating their families, they cultivated their own selves. Before cultivating their own selves, they tried to be sincere in their thoughts. Before trying to be sincere in their thoughts, they extended to the utmost their

knowledge. Such investigation of knowledge lay in the investigation of things, and in seeing them as they really were. When things were thus investigated, knowledge became complete. When knowledge was complete, their thoughts were sincere. When their thoughts were sincere, their souls became perfect. When their souls were perfect, their own selves became cultivated. When their selves were cultivated, their families became regulated. When their families were regulated, then states came to be put into proper order. When their states were in proper order, then the whole world became peaceful and happy.*

I think what makes this observation so impressive is that from a single individual to the entire universe, the identical principle is at work in the guidance of one's conduct and behavior. It is quite alien to Chinese thought that man and nature, for instance, are opposed to each other, or man and society are two disparate entities unrelated to each other, pursuing different teleologies. The universe is one complete unity of massive proportions. I believe this kind of thinking is rarely, if ever, found in the Western world. The difference between Confucius and Machiavelli is the difference between the East and the West. In Confucius you have the feeling of integration, of harmony between the individual and society of which he forms only a part; while with Machiavelli there developed a dichotomy of the individual following one set of values as against society, which is conducted on a different and often antagonistic set of values. Thus it was that Professor Reinhold Niebuhr could speak of moral man and immoral society, a concept that sounds completely blasphemous to a Chinese. In the Confucian scheme of things this division has no place; for it is inconceivable to have a moral man without having a moral society, and conversely it is equally impossible to have an immoral society without having an immoral man.

It is not for me to be critical of Western society, but a correct attitude as to the proper relationship between man and society is a matter of supreme importance. I have been here in the United States long enough to love and admire the great qualities in its

* *Translation by Will Durant in his* Adventures in Genius, *pp. 6–7.*

leaders of men and in its institutions. In a few more years my contact with this wonderful country will reach a half-century mark. But I shall not be honest with myself if I do not also believe that there is room for considerable improvement—we all need it—in just this area of an adequate integration between man and society. The individual has been brought too much under the strain of a social impact, which in the last analysis is not guided by the moral imperative, and he ultimately begins to suffer. At this point it is best that I allow a keen observer of the American scene, himself an American, to speak out.

In a letter to Mr. Adlai Stevenson, Mr. John Steinbeck complained of "A creeping, all-pervading, nerve-gas of immorality which [he thinks] starts in the nursery and does not stop before it reaches the highest offices, both corporate and governmental. If I wanted to destroy a nation, I would give it too much. I am troubled by the cynical immorality of my country. I do not think it can survive on this basis, and unless some kind of catastrophe strikes us, we are lost. By our attitudes we are drawing catastrophe to ourselves. What we have beaten in nature, we cannot conquer in ourselves." These are strong and stinging words. I hope that Mr. Steinbeck is one-sided and all wrong, but it is a situation that is well worth looking into. For the New York *Times,* in its issue of June 19, 1964, published some statistics on the crime wave for the first quarter of the year which, to say the least, should give food for thought and the most serious reflection.

New York City [the report said] had an increase of 15 per cent in seven major crimes: murder, forcible rape, robbery, aggravated assault, burglary, grand larceny and auto theft.

In its breakdown of crimes in this city the F.B.I. said there were 139 murders in the first three months of 1964, compared with 117 last year; 258 forcible rapes, compared with 225 last year; 2,226 robberies, compared with 1,596 last year; 3,402 aggravated assaults, compared with 2,752 last year; 12,735 burglaries, compared with 10,685 last year; 16,718 grand larcenies, compared with 15,609 last year; and 7,501 auto thefts, compared with 6,225 last year. . . .

More than 85 per cent of all the cities in the country with populations over 25,000 reported crime increases. In all, 521,303 serious crimes in the above categories were committed in the nation in the first three months of this year, in comparison with 436,577 in 1963's first quarter, an increase of 84,726 crimes.

If these figures are regarded only as an inevitable part of a growing society, like the growing pains of an adolescent young man, and need therefore give us no concern, then there is not much we can say. But few people will believe that this is not a matter of the utmost gravity. These figures are indications of a profound malady, and what is more, it threatens to spread, if it has not already spread, with alarming rapidity.

I am persuaded that the moral life of a nation is the single factor that determines whether that nation is going to endure. For all its glamour, there was something hollow in the character of the ancient Roman. Aeneas struggled to found a new race because the rise of Rome meant for him "a new hope for the human race, a hope for peace, of order, of civilization." But this new hope was born of pride, arrogance, and the lack of consideration for others. He had nothing but contempt for the plea by Dido to work in collaboration with Carthage. The ancient virtues of *pietas* and *gravitas* were impressive at their best, but they did not have sufficient moral conviction and strength to give them vitality. The ancient Roman had no sense of humility. That was why the Christian religion, which came afterward, had to emphasize "meekness" and "humility" over and over again. The motivating spirit in the Roman was essentially aggressive. He was egocentric; had a profound sense of "mission," though no one knew who it was that gave him that mission; thrived on conquest and exploitation and depended almost exclusively on his military might for the realization of his desires, because, as Will Durant said, "he could only rule the world." When Emperor Vespasian was breathing his last, he was still saying, "Alas, I think I am becoming a god." No wonder that as early as Polybius men were already beginning to complain of corruption in the lives of individuals as well as in society. That corruption continued to increase in volume and provided the central theme for the homilies of the Christian fathers later on. An empire that was founded on such ingredients could not long last. There was no cohesion to bring them together. And when corruption began to sap its vitality, as in the nature of things it must in the course of time, and when the barbarians began to be troublesome, the ramparts just fell apart and could offer no resistance.*

The lesson of two mighty empires, existing contemporaneously, in two different parts of the world, the one succumbing to the onslaughts of the barbarians never to rise again, while the other, Han China, likewise succumbed to the same barbarians, but was able to rally its forces, even if it took three or four centuries, to emerge with renewed vitality in the T'ang empire—this lesson has never been lost to the historians. But the reasons for their differing fortunes have never been adequately explained. Professor Teggart † has made a scholarly study of the period from 58 B.C. to A.D. 107, when, he said, "every barbarian uprising in Europe followed the outbreak of war either on the eastern frontiers of the Roman empire or the western regions of the Chinese. . . . It has now been shown," he concluded, "that the occurrences in Europe were closely related, in a majority of instances (twenty-seven out of forty) to wars in Sinkiang, the extensive western province of China, and thus an enquiry into the disturbances on the frontiers of the Roman empire has had the unexpected outcome of demonstrating the highly important place of China as a factor in the history of the remote West."

I need not say that history indeed repeats itself, but the fact that Rome disintegrated and then disappeared, while China in the Han Dynasty (221 B.C.–A.D. 220) survived and still survives down to

---

* For all the "glories" of the Pax Romana, I think the consensus of opinion is that "the history of Rome is the history of Mediterranean banditry for a thousand years . . . They [the Romans] were in the habit [and the habit persisted for many hundreds of years] of collecting hundreds of captives, criminals, and minor offenders against official regulations, and, on certain festival occasions, making them suffer capital punishment at the hands of man and wild beast alike. These circuses were not put on merely for the pleasure of the masses, but were also conceived as a penal deterrent for the benefit of all citizens and slaves alike who lived in the grace of Pax Romana." Letters to My Teacher by Dagobert D. Runes.

† Rome and China: A Study of Correlations in Historical Events by Frederick J. Teggart, 1939.

the present day, is a mystery that has not been properly accounted for. There have been at least three or four dozen explanations of the fall of Rome. Some attributed it to economic causes, others political, and still others social, all of which are plausible; but they were merely manifestations of a basic cause, which remains elusive. It becomes clear, I believe, only when we understand the nature of the difference between the two forms of society. While the impact or challenge was identical, the responses owing to the differences of social behavior were decidedly not the same. Through the centuries there had been built into the social and political fabric of Chinese society a moral reserve fund that the Chinese could copiously draw upon for replenishment in time of difficulty. That reserve was used in two different directions. One was that, since the desire for conquest and exploitation of the kind that was so typical of the Roman empire was practically nonexistent, there was no bitterness of a "confrontation." Like the Romans, the Chinese had built a higher civilization, but it was not used as a weapon to overcome or subdue their neighbors, but to be shared and enjoyed by them equally with the Chinese themselves. There were thus large numbers of aliens who willingly and on their own accord became assimilated and identified with the Chinese so that they were ready to defend Chinese civilization as if it had been their own from the beginning. One of the most eloquent examples is that of Ye-lu Chu-tsai of Khitan origin, for whom there is, I believe, no counterpart in Roman history. He acquired all the characteristics of a Chinese scholar and gentleman. His calligraphy to this day is a visible testimonial to the degree of his absorption in Chinese culture. He not only thoroughly merged with the society in which he lived, but helped even to save the country from the ravages of Kublai Khan. To quote Professor C. P. Fitzgerald again: "No territory once fully subjected to this [Chinese] civilization has ever been wholly lost, and no territory permanently incorporated in the Chinese area has withstood the penetration of Chinese culture." This is something that political or military force alone cannot accomplish. That, in essence, is the difference between Rome and China. The second use of the moral reserve is that, when the Chinese were crushed by barbarians, they did not feel as if the world had collapsed. They went through a period of self-examination, then re-emerged all the stronger.

The dissolution of the Han empire drove the people to their inner resources. That was when Buddhism made great inroads into their souls, but they embraced the new religion only after they had reshaped and remolded it until it served their own specific purposes in agreement with their own nature and requirements. That was why Zen had no equivalent in India, the home of Buddhism. The same kind of transformation, I believe, is going on with communism today. Already it is vastly different from the Marxist version even though it still bears its name, and different from what is being practiced in Soviet Russia. In China it is working for the transformation of the whole person, and its reconstitution has to proceed from the recovery of the moral content of his traditional beliefs. There is no denial of the importance of raising the standard of living for the people and the need for technical development. But that is not the whole answer. Man, as man, depends for his happiness on the fulfillment of those specifically human qualities that have been the concern of China's traditional thinkers. The ancient humanistic tradition under Communist rule is not moribund but very much alive. If the reports of unbiased observers are to be believed, there is an attempt on a majestic scale to create a society in which the people can genuinely love and respect one another and be considerate of one another's feelings and welfare. Rightly or wrongly, they regard the cult of self as being at the center of our modern malady, and all our evils have arisen largely from the desire to pursue selfish interest, economic or otherwise, at the expense of others. That applies to the individual as well as to the entire international order. It is the root of colonialism and imperialism. Communist China does not have any self-appointed "mission," but she does believe that by going through a profound spiritual revolution of her own, the example may very well have an impact on the rest of the world. When, as we have been told, not only soldiers but even policemen are not seen on the streets of mainland China today (girls in uniform direct the traffic), when people actually sleep without locking their doors at night, when

THE UNITED STATES AND CHINA: 2

personal possessions cannot even be lost, when black market profiteers are given the opportunity to feel their own sense of shame for doing something they should not do, when law courts for long stretches of time have no criminal cases to handle in cities with millions of inhabitants, that is hardly carrying out a Marxist program as we ordinarily understand the word Marxism: that is an attempt to put into practice what the Chinese thinkers taught over two thousand years ago. There are four characters in China that, I understand, form a kind of slogan wherever people congregate for work. They are *pee, hsueh, kan,* and *pang,* which mean "compare" (that is, compare your work with that of others to see where you fall short), "learn," "follow up quickly" (that is, make good one's shortcomings as quickly as possible), and "help" (that is, help those who struggle to raise their level of work).

Sometimes people are inclined to feel that the Chinese Communists are impractical dreamers trying to establish a utopia. However, they clearly do not feel that human evils, in so far as they are expressions of human weakness, can really be suppressed or removed. But they can be controlled through moral discipline, which again is in line with the Confucian thought that man by nature is basically good, a concept that played no important part in Western thinking until the time of Rousseau. One has the impression that the Chinese Communists, without expressly saying so, are trying to put into practice some of the basic ideas of China's classical thinkers. These ideas have at times been eclipsed, but even during the worst of times as, for instance, from 1840 on, when China was really powerless to resist the forces of oppression and exploitation by the foreign powers, they were not given up. The time has now arrived, as the leaders on the mainland believe, when they should be given a chance to prevail. There are three ideas that form the cornerstone of this edifice of political thinking. They are universal love or love for all, government of and for the people, and the kingly way or the way of virtue. The Chinese word for politics is *cheng,* which means correctness, rectitude, straightening what is crooked, being in the right direction, or being in conformity with what is just. It is the expression and embodiment of the moral law.* To be truly effective it is not concerned merely with one group of people or one race or even one nation as distinguished from other races and other nations, but with all people wherever and whatever they may be, for it is predicated on the proposition that "within the four seas all men are brothers."

With the exception of one thinker—Yang Chu (fourth century B.C.), who believed that he should not so much as pull out one hair for the benefit of others—all the philosophers spoke eloquently, though often from different points of view, on sharing the fruits of benevolence from an orderly government. Here are some remarks chosen at random that illustrate the trend of Chinese political thinking:

From the *Shu King* or the *Book of Poetry,* which is pre-Confucian, we learn "Heaven sees through the eyes of the people; Heaven hears through the ears of the people," which expounds in a few words the whole concept of popular sovereignty. The parallel between these remarks and the sentiment expressed in that part of the preamble of the Declaration of Independence which says, "Governments are instituted among men, deriving their just powers from the consent of the governed" is quite obvious. The leaders on the Chinese mainland have adapted this remark to the widely spread saying, "The eyes of the people are dazzlingly bright: their vision is unusually clear."

From Kuan Chung, the prime minister of the State of Chi, also pre-Confucian, came these remarks: "To love people, to give them the opportunity to fulfill themselves, to help them to live well, to protect and nourish them, to confer benefit on them with the utmost sincerity, and then to be loved by all the world—these constitute the best of virtues." "The love of people without being partial is the highest form of virtue, and virtue is the embodiment of Tao."

Confucius himself, of course, made any number of remarks on similar lines. Here are a few: One disciple asked him for the mean-

---

* *It is interesting to compare this Chinese word with the origin of the word "politics" or "political," derived from the Greek word* politikos, *which means "belonging to the citizen or state." It is purely a descriptive word without any moral connotation.*

ing of *jen*. His immediate reply was: "Love all fellow men." To another asking the same question he said, "Do not do to others what you do not wish that others do to you." This has often been considered as being negative and therefore inferior to the more aggressive and positive thought in the Christian religion, which is a typical missionary interpretation. It is obvious that in fact it is much nearer to the possibility of practical realization. Further, "The man who has cultivated *jen* is one who, wishing to perfect himself, seeks also to perfect others, and, wishing to develop himself, develops others. To be able to draw a parallel from himself for the treatment of others—this is the practice of *jen*."

Mencius, the great disciple of Confucius, who lived over a century later, was even more explicit. "From the love of one's kinsfolk one proceeds to the love of the people. From the love of the people one proceeds to the love of all created beings . . . The rulers of the past could not bear to see their people suffer. To conduct a government with such an attitude is to enable them to rule the world as easily as to turn the palm of your hand." For "when a ruler rejoices over the people's happiness, the people will also rejoice over his happiness. When a ruler feels sorrow for the misfortunes of the people, the people will also feel sorrow over his misfortunes. To be able to rejoice with the world and to feel sorrow with it—that is the way to make himself a perfect ruler."

Mo-tzu, a contemporary of Confucius, was an exponent of universal love, though he was the founder of utilitarian thought. He mourned over the many misfortunes and calamities with which the world was then beset, and asked himself what these were. "I say the attack of small states by large states, the disturbance of small houses by large houses, the oppression of the weak by the strong, the abuse of the few by the many, the deception of the simple by the cunning, the disdain of the humble by those who are more privileged—these are among the major misfortunes and calamities of the world. But how have these arisen? Have they arisen because people love each other? Definitely not. They have arisen out of mutual hatred and the desire to hurt others for one's own good. Therefore to hate and to be partial in love is evil, as it is the root of all our misfortunes and calamities." The remedy, according to

Mo-tzu, was simple. If we learn to be universal and not partial in
our love, all the calamities will disappear. "When every state regards other states as its own, who will start any attack? When
every ruler considers the capital of other states as his own capital,
who will start any invasion? When the owner of a property regards
the properties of others as his own, who will cause any disturbance? Now when states and rulers do not attack and invade each
other and property owners do not disturb one another, then is it
not true that the misfortunes and calamities of the world will disappear?" The emphasis is always on the suppression of the ego,
consideration for others by not doing to others what a person does
not wish others to do to him. Then as now if we only put into practice some of these simple observations, the world should be at
peace.

This trend of political thought, which grew out of the conviction
that the individual and the social and political organism must be
motivated by the identical moral values, grew in volume and in
power with all subsequent thinkers. The great idealist philosopher
of the Ming Dynasty, Wang Yang-ming (1472–1529), who like
Oyomei in Japan, exercised such profound influence on that country, said without hesitation that a princely man felt that he was
completely in harmony with the universe and all its creatures. "He
considers the world as one family and the state or nation as one
man." And he even extended this feeling of compassion and of
human-heartedness to the birds of the air, to the beasts and plants
of the earth, and even to inanimate objects. The Sung philosophers
before him had the same sentiment. Chang Tsai, who lived over
four centuries before him (1020–1077), used to say: "I call
Heaven my father, Earth my mother. All the people are my brothers and all the created beings my friends." And Huang Tsung-
hsi, a later philosopher (1610–1695), following similar lines of
thought, had the courage to criticize what is normally considered
an autocratic society, in the following words: "There used to be
ideal rulers who were neither interested in accumulating personal
wealth nor in inflicting personal injuries; what they were really interested in was enjoyment of the common good and the avoidance
of public evils for all the world." Then he went on to say: "But

our latter-day rulers found it gratifying only to make perverted use of their political power and did all they could ruthlessly to acquire benefit for themselves and allow the people to suffer in misery. For they regard selfish interests as the common good. At first they still felt a sense of shame, but it became so confirmed a habit that finally they put selfish interests above everything openly and without fear." These words became a clarion call to the young revolutionaries who brought on the downfall of the Manchu Dynasty in 1911–12, and must still ring in the ears of the man, then in his late teens, who is now the leader on the Chinese mainland. Always in the case of Mao Tse-tung it is essential to remember that his roots, his education, and his training are all authentically Chinese, having nothing to do with Marxism or any other aspect of the West. But, as he confessed in one of his recent poems, he was always in a hurry. "Ten thousand years—too long, I strive only for the morn and eve." He read Marxism furiously, in Chinese translations of course, and thought he had found in Marxism an effective instrument with which he could accomplish for China in a day what normally would perhaps take ten thousand years. May I invite the reader to revise rather drastically the ancient image held by the West of the Chinese as being a patient race? But then Mao comes from Hunan, a province in central China, where the people are not celebrated for their patience. They are passionately devoted to the hot pepper!

The account I have thus far given of the harmonization of political action with moral ideas in Chinese thought leads to the further thought that this should be a matter of concern not only for one nation, or one race, or for one section of the world, but for all humanity. This is nowhere so well expressed as by the great master Confucius himself. He was giving his views as to what would happen to the world, as the world was then known, if the moral concept which he insisted he inherited from the sages of old, and which he spent his life in explaining and amplifying, became a reality. The stage of development would then be when the Great Way prevailed, and the world would be in absolute peace. This was how he described it: "When the Great Way was in practice, the world was common to all the people. Men of talent, virtue, and ability were selected to be in the government. There was widespread sincerity, and friendly relations were cultivated everywhere. People did not only love their own parents, but regarded all elderly people as their parents; nor did they treat their own children as their sons and daughters, but others also as their children. Provisions were made for all the aged till the day of their death and for properly bringing up the young. There was employment for all the able-bodied people. Widows, orphans, people without children, and those who were incapacitated by disease were shown kindness, consideration, and compassion so that they were all adequately supported. Men were given the work they could perform and women were given homes to take care of. They did not like to see natural resources wasted or undeveloped, but neither did they monopolize wealth for their own exclusive use. They did not wish to stay idle, but neither did they wish to exert themselves for their own profit. Thus all selfish desires were curbed and had no opportunity to develop. Robbers, burglars, and traitors could not show themselves, and the doors were left wide open. This was the period of *Ta Tung*, the Great Commonwealth."

The political views of a race are but one expression of its general view of life. In this, China and the West are at variance with each other, because the Chinese view sees in God, nature, and man a sense of harmony and identity where in the West there is the principle of separation and bifurcation. This does not mean there are no thinkers in China who believe in the existence of evil that can be overcome by a system of regimentation. I have said that Yang Chu was a thinker who was so impressed by the amount of evil in the world that he would not think of pulling out one hair for the benefit of his fellow human beings. There was another philosopher, Hsün-tzu, who also believed that man by nature was evil, much as Machiavelli and Thomas Hobbes did, and thought that, in order to establish an orderly society, the only possible way was the rigid enforcement of laws to curb the tendency toward evil. His ideas were taken up and applied in the political sphere by Han Fei who succeeded in inducing the ruler of the State of Chin to conquer the remaining six states through military power. He thus became the first emperor of China, but neither Han Fei himself nor the empire of Shih Huang Ti lasted long. The empire was dissolved in a little more than ten years, and was taken over by Liu Pang who immediately revived the Confucian concepts and established an empire lasting four hundred years. As for Han Fei himself, the state of which he was a citizen was conquered by the King of Chin through the very ideas that he propagated; and when he was sent as an emissary to negotiate with Chin, he called on his fellow student Li Ssu who had become the king's trusted minister and was thrown into prison. Li Ssu advised the king that Han Fei was a dangerous man, and before he had an audience with the king, Li Ssu sent poison to the prison.

Since then, not another Han Fei has openly expressed expediency as a weapon that can ultimately succeed in achieving political ends or considered military power as being a lasting solution of differences between peoples. War remained, as Lao-tze reminded us earlier, an instrument of ill omen; and even if the urge to have recourse to such measures is strong, it must needs be covered with sanctimonious homilies. I do not believe that it is possible to find in the whole realm of Chinese thinking anyone who justified war, either on philosophical grounds or as being essential for expansion or national survival. And yet this is precisely what mainland China is today being accused of! In the gallery of China's national heroes there are no soldiers. No statues have been erected to the memory of a warrior like Alexander or Napoleon. Kuan Kung and Yueh Fei are respected not because they were good soldiers, but because they were superbly good men.

The unceasing and unflagging insistence on moral integration in China in all spheres of human action has had such a long history that, like dividends or compound interest in the bank which have become self-cumulative, it can always be drawn upon when there is a crisis. It is always there to help; it can never be eclipsed or made inoperative because of the popularity of a new ideology like Marxism. It is the moral content that more than any other single element has kept Chinese civilization going for these thousands of years and prevented it from collapsing, as it might very well have done when confronted with crises as serious as those which brought Rome down on her knees. That may sound too simple an explanation of the decline and fall of a mighty empire, which took

Gibbon a lifetime to write about, but I feel it is still the most satis-fying explanation because it is the most fundamental and nearest to the truth. As long, therefore, as China has faith in its ancient traditions—and there is nothing to indicate that it has not—we should have no fear that she would uphold war or the threat of war in the solution of human problems.

There were times when this tradition was understood by the Western world. We now talk of the balance of power as if it is an established law, but there were periods in relatively modern history when man had a more effective balance, that of culture. The West in the seventeenth and eighteenth centuries regarded the world with, on the whole, a more adequate sense of values. Not every-thing was appraised in the light of the West's technical, com-mercial, industrial, economic, or military superiority, which later completely upset the balance of culture. For all the lack of com-munication and physical contact between China and Europe, we are told that "China is better known [to Europeans] than some parts of Europe itself." The reasons are perfectly simple and just. Take Leibniz, for instance, who was among the first of the great modern thinkers of Europe. His concept of monadology and his binary theory were admitted by himself as being influenced by the *Yi King*. In 1695 he planned an expedition to China for the "propa-gation of light and wisdom." He suggested an academy in St. Petersburg to unite the East and West culturally. In 1700 he estab-lished a society in Berlin for the "interchange of civilizations be-tween China and Europe," which later became the Prussian Academy. He thought he found so much in China from which Eu-rope could learn, and in his *Novissima Sinica* he even suggested that "the Chinese should teach us the aim and practice of natural theology as we send missionaries [the Jesuits] to teach them re-vealed theology." And he was immensely impressed by the Con-fucian concept of *Ta Tung* or the Great Commonwealth.*

---

* *This is a typical view of Leibniz: "Even if we are equal to them [the Chinese] or if we surpass them in the theoretical sciences, it is certainly true (I am almost ashamed to admit it) that they surpass us in practical philosophy by which I mean the rules of ethics and politics that have been devised for the conduct and benefit of human life."*

Voltaire was even more emphatic and enthusiastic about what he learned, mostly from Grimaldi and the other Jesuits. "The Chinese," he said, "have perfected moral science, and that is the first of the sciences." He had reason to say so, considering the state of affairs in his own Europe. Here he was referring to precisely the trend of thought that I have been trying to discuss in this chapter. From the time that he was a young man till he died at the age of eighty-four there was no moment when he failed to convey to the people of Europe his knowledge of the beauty of Chinese culture. His play *L'Orphelin de la Chine* was adapted from Chinese to expound the morals of Confucius, about whom he said, "I have read his books with attention. I have made extracts from them: I have found that they spoke only of the purest morality . . . He appeals only to virtue, there is nothing in them of ridiculous allegory." And he was ashamed, like Leibniz, that "never have these people sent missionaries to Europe. We alone export our opinions as well as our merchandise to the ends of the earth. It is for us to admire and to blush, but above all to imitate." It was for this reason that he compiled the *Lettres philosophiques* and the *Essai sur les moeurs et l'esprit des nations,* which were filled from beginning to end with information on the moral as well as on the social and political accomplishments of China. "The constitution of their empire," he kept on saying, "is in truth the best that there is in the world . . . the only one in which a governor of a province is punished if, when he quits his post, he is not acclaimed by the people . . . Four thousand years ago, when we did not know how to read, they knew everything essentially useful of which we boast today."

These are but two out of many writers in Europe who acknowledged goodness when they found it. Then came the Physiocrats * and the Encyclopedists and a number of lesser writers who spoke in the same vein. Their combined efforts contributed enormously to what came to be known as the Enlightenment,† and then came

---

* *Quesnay, the leader of the Physiocrats, said that his "physiocracy was only a systematic account of Chinese doctrine, which deserves to be taken as a model for all states." See "Chinese Influences on the Physiocrats" by Lewis Adams Maverick,* Journal of Economic History, *February, 1938.*

† *Adolf Reichwein, the historian of the relations between China and Europe*

128   AMERICA AND CHINA

finally the French Revolution * itself with its call for equality, which had long been developed in the classless society of the Chinese through their civil service examination and their system of education. Benjamin Franklin † and Thomas Jefferson knew China and praised her. Professor Maverick went so far as to say, "Though precise influences may never be discovered, it is not unlikely that Descartes, Spinoza, Hobbes, Locke, Berkeley came under Chinese influences." China for the Europeans in the eighteenth century was truly a magnificent spectacle. She was an empire far larger than anything Europe had seen since the days of Rome, not through an elaborate system of laws or a complicated political ma-

in the eighteenth century, said that the philosophers of the Enlightenment "discovered, to their astonishment, that more than 2,000 years ago in China . . . Confucius had thought the same thoughts in the same manner, and fought the same battles . . . Thus Confucius became the patron saint of eighteenth-century Enlightenment."

* The National Convention of the French Revolution, for instance, proclaimed, "When government violates the rights of the people, insurrection is for the people and for every portion of the people, the most sacred right and the most indispensable of duties," which is another version of the right of revolution so powerfully espoused by Mencius. Here we begin to see the shift of the earlier divine right of kings to the divine right of the people. The right to rebel appealed earlier to Benjamin Franklin, who proposed the motto "Rebellion to tyrants in obedience to God" as the seal for the new United States in 1776. Jefferson was enraptured with these words, adopted them, and put them on the state seal of Virginia. The extent to which this idea of the right to rebel had penetrated the thinking of the great minds of this country can be seen in the Declaration of Independence itself, where it says, "That whenever any form of government becomes destructive of these ends [to secure the rights of life, liberty, and the pursuit of happiness], it is the right of the people to alter or to abolish it, and to institute new government . . ." I am not sufficiently familiar with the intellectual atmosphere of America in the pre-independence years, but it would be interesting to find out where some of the major ideas came from. As far as I am aware, neither the concept of equality nor the concept of the right to rebel could have existed in a society where inequality had been more or less taken for granted and where the divine right of kings was so firmly established that any thought of rebellion would constitute treason of the most unqualified sort. Scholars in the future may yet discover that the relations between China and the founding of this great republic were more intimate than we are willing to acknowledge.

† In his letter to Mrs. Sarah Bache, dated January 26, 1784, Franklin spoke about "the Chinese [as] the most ancient, and from long Experience the wisest of Nations." Quoted in The World of the Founding Fathers *by Saul K. Padover, p. 160.*

THE UNITED STATES AND CHINA: 2

chinery, but through examples of moral rectitude, starting from the emperor himself to the local magistrate. John Locke, for instance, who made such an impact on early American history, said, "All power given with trust for attaining an end, being limited by that end, whenever that end is manifestly neglected or opposed, that trust must necessarily be forfeited," which is another version of the Chinese concept of the "mandate of heaven."

Then came the nineteenth century: never in the history of opinion of one part of the world toward another has there been another case of a change so drastic, so complete, and so thorough. From that time on, all that counted was commerce, economic privileges, political domination, the gunboat policy, power, and more physical power; and China, brought up for thousands of years to appreciate the values of the mind and of the heart, could offer no resistance and fell asunder. She was at the mercy of the West. Europe had become "superior"; and for her to continue to study the virtues of the Chinese became unthinkable. All that had been written about China was forgotten. Latter-day scholars like Gustave Lanson, Elie Halevy, Paul Hazard, or Daniel Mornet, all "specialists" of the *"situation intellectuelle"* of pre-revolutionary Europe, even they, who knew enough to sustain intellectual honesty, refused to admit that there was any such influence so eloquently expressed in the works of Leibniz, Voltaire, Christian Wolff,* Lecomte, Quesnay, Diderot, the Marquis d'Argens and their collaborators.

The Chinese tradition has survived to this day, regardless of what the Westerners may think, and to say that the Chinese have become warlike, aggressive, expansionist, imperialist, colonial-minded, is to argue against the spirit of that tradition. But then it is said the Chinese Communist is no longer Chinese. He is a changed man with a new set of beliefs. Is this an accurate observation? Where did he get these new beliefs? From the West? One way or the other, the Western world is caught in a dilemma. It does not wish to believe that the new Chinese have faith in the old ideas, and yet it refuses to admit that the new ideas have come from the West.

---

* *Christian Wolff, by saying "In the art of governing, this nation [China] has ever surpassed all others without exception" and by making remarks along similar lines, got himself into trouble and was dismissed from his university.*

The truth is perhaps to be found in a combination of the two. As long as the West dominates the rest of the world with physical force, the Chinese have no alternative but to meet the West on its own ground. No one can expect them to submit and go through the bitter experiences they knew during the last hundred and twenty-five years. Do they then seek reprisals? I can emphatically say that no thought is more alien to the Chinese than the thought of reprisal. Like the Americans, the Chinese are a big race, big in their territory, big in their population, but bigger still in their heart. They can sometimes be big to the extent of being over-generous. Mao Tse-tung in one of his well-known poems said that he wished he had a sword—a sort of super Excalibur—with which to hack China's highest and longest mountain range, the Kunlun, into three equal parts—one to be given as a gift to Europe, one to the United States, and the third to be kept at home—if that would help in achieving world peace. These do not sound much like the words of an aggressor. How can the idea of reprisal ever be made compatible with the noble traditions of their culture? Reprisal is pettiness of soul, and neither Confucius nor any other thinker believes that pettiness of soul is a virtue to be cultivated. I hope it is not this fear of reprisal that has led the Western world to be so uncompromisingly antagonistic to China. China does not look back to the past but to the future, and all that she asks at present is for a modicum of justice and consideration.

Let us take an example of the denial of this justice. The island of Taiwan is an integral part of China. It has been as much a part of China as the Isle of Wight or the Isle of Man is of Britain. For half a century it was wrested from China by Japan through *force majeure*. During World War II it was agreed that it should be returned to China at the conclusion of the war. This has not been done. The United States deliberately shields it by supporting a government that under normal circumstances should have faded away long ago. Then it tries to put into practice a "two Chinas" policy. Not making much headway with that policy it tries now to create an "independent" Taiwan. In one way or another it attempts to detach the island from the mainland. Is this just?

Further, the way in which America treats the Taiwan question is a deliberate violation of China's territorial integrity and endangers her security, because the American presence on the island poses a direct military threat to her very existence. Mr. Stanley Spector offers a comparison to this American involvement in Taiwan that is interesting. "The position," he said, "is comparable to what would have been the case had Great Britain, during the American Civil War, evacuated the Confederate Government to Puerto Rico (assuming it was then American territory), proceeded to arm it, placed the British fleet between the islands and the American mainland, permitted Jefferson Davis to call for and encourage a general uprising in the United States and to declare that he would reoccupy America within five years, and then to call the government in Washington aggressive and irresponsible because it had announced its intention to recover the island and eliminate the Confederate Government." *

It is relevant to bear in mind also that in an interview in Tokyo on March 2, 1949, General Douglas MacArthur defined the defense perimeter of the United States in the Pacific in these words: "It starts from the Philippines and continues through the Ryukyu Archipelago, which includes its main bastion, Okinawa. Then it bends back through Japan and the Aleutian island chain to Alaska." Mr. Dean Acheson, when he was Secretary of State, as I recall, spoke in the same manner on two or three occasions. Neither Taiwan nor Vietnam was included in this "line." It could not have been a slip of the memory.

Tibet has been a part of China since the T'ang Dynasty (618–907) and has been internationally recognized as such by all the powers, including the United States. It has enjoyed a large measure of local autonomy, even when the Communists came in, but through external stimulus it began to abuse that autonomy. The Chinese government then began to send in troops, and at once the act was considered as an "invasion" of an "independent" country? Is that just? Would the dispatch of Federal troops to, let us say, Alabama or Mississippi likewise be considered as "invasion"?

Then came the demarcation of the boundary between the Tibet

---

* The Nation, *January 28, 1961.*

region and India, which runs for hundreds of miles. Throughout history it has been more of a frontier than a boundary. It consists of high mountainous terrain where only a few shepherds live. When the time for actual demarcation came, differences of opinion were bound to arise, but there was no reason at all why these differences could not be straightened out if both sides assumed a conciliatory attitude. It is on record that China repeatedly asked for settlement of these differences with India through conference and negotiation. She was prepared to follow a policy of give and take, which all negotiations must entail. Conciliation worked with Burma, Nepal, Sikkim, Bhutan, and all the other neighbors having common boundaries with China. But not India. She insists on the right to do all the taking but not the giving. The negotiations broke down, till on October 20, 1962, Mr. Nehru openly declared that India would drive out by force every single Chinese soldier who was believed to have occupied what he considered to be Indian territory. War ensued. What could be more natural? The Chinese troops went over the Himalayas, reached the foothills, and in another couple of days would have cut off all of Assam from India. Assam where all the tea plantations are, is the source of India's foreign exchange. But true to her word of wanting to settle the question through negotiation and not desiring one inch of Indian soil, China withdrew her troops to the original line from which they started, thus setting an example, nowhere to be found in the history of man, ancient or modern, of voluntarily giving up deliberately the fruits of military victory. But still she is accused of wanting to conquer India. Is this just?

Then comes Southeast Asia, about which millions of words have been written in news dispatches, magazine articles, and books, or spoken on radio and television; and a few more words are not going to make the situation any clearer. But this much must be said. All the talk about China wanting to create a huge Communist empire under her control, with the inclusion of all Southeast Asia as the first stage of conquest, to be followed by the inclusion of Australia and New Zealand as the second stage, is purely a figment of a diseased imagination. Even if she had the weapons, I hope I have made it abundantly clear that China has never been in the habit of conquering foreign territory, nor is there any likelihood that she will do so in the future. But no one can deny that she is entitled to feel sure that the land over the border will not be used to threaten her security. Even so, in the presence of the threat that she believes to exist, she has been extremely cautious. There should be no difficulty in working out a plan whereby China will feel secure and Southeast Asia will remain free and independent. De Gaulle's neutralization is one such plan, which at least should be looked into and not just rejected automatically. Chou En-lai's non-aggression pact is another. If both are unsatisfactory, others may be suggested so that finally something is worked out and foreign troops are withdrawn from that area. By continuing a war of nerves with China we do not reduce the possibility of conflict but increase it. And when war does break out, China will be made to shoulder the responsibility, even though to this day, as Ambassador Lodge and Senator Morse testified, not one Chinese soldier has been found dead or alive in South Vietnam. Secretary of State Dean Rusk has been saying repeatedly, but rather naïvely, that South Vietnam should be left alone, but it is the United States that has over one hundred thousand "advisers" there.* I reiterate that I do not see how China can welcome a confrontation of war with the United States when she has no means to conduct such a war, particularly when her relations with Russia are as bad as they are.† And yet so many, even in responsible positions, are quite sure that the situation in Vietnam is worth risking a war with China.‡ The reason why such a war is contemplated is perhaps re-

---

* As of October 1965 the number has increased to over 140,000. They are now openly in combat duty along with the soldiers of the South Vietnamese government.

† Mr. Hanson Baldwin, the military expert of the New York Times, in an article on China's military power published on June 29, 1964, says, among other things: "Communist China's military forces . . . have very major weaknesses." "Chinese military operations in Southeast Asia, or anywhere near the land frontiers, could be formidable in numbers but not in much else," and "China's greatest strength is in manpower—'cannon fodder' is what the country's mass army, undertrained and poorly equipped, has been called." No country, it is obvious, hankers after war under such circumstances.

† It was Admiral Felt who started this loose talk of war. He was followed by General Paul D. Harkins. And then President Johnson, in his famous speech at Minneapolis, referred to in the New York Times editorial for July

vealed in a letter to the New York *Times* on June 28, 1964, by Mr. Robert W. Harper, who at one time served as a Foreign Service staff officer in Indonesia. The letter is worth quoting at some length, because it seems to confirm my own personal fears, which I feel but do not wish to express publicly:

> The Americans tell themselves [Mr. Harper began] that they can succeed where the British, Dutch, and French failed. Our egotism has now led us face to face with China (there is only one China plus an American-sponsored protectorate over Formosa) and we think the problems of the 1960's with China can be solved as the Taiping Rebellion was solved by the West a hundred years ago.
>
> What the West is really reaping is a just reward for its rape of China beginning with the cruel Opium War of 1839–42 through the Boxer Rebellion. Indeed, the Chinese melon was sliced nicely, and once-proud China reduced to indignities, indemnities and the whims of Western economic interests.
>
> Despite the implied wisdom of Admiral Felt [who said it was worth risking a war with China], it can be seriously doubted that China wishes to take over Southeast Asia. The New York *Times* will rue the day it approved "the use of additional American military and economic resources to misabuse Mao Tse-tung and Ho Chi Minh . . . Indeed we have become virtual slaves of the bogeymen called Communism and we see the evil hand of the Communists everywhere, especially in those places where the American God-playing image is challenged.
>
> We have extended the Monroe Doctrine to every corner of the globe and the rationale for such behavior is the so-called threat of Communism. Our national security requires us to become the saviors of the world. Let us hope there is both time and wisdom enough left for us to succeed.

3, 1964, is alleged to have said, "If a nation is to keep its freedom, it must be prepared to risk war. When necessary we will take this risk." The atmosphere during those days was rather tense, until, fortunately, Secretary Dean Rusk came out with the statement that the time has come for a moratorium on this kind of threat mongering and all this talk "blithely to threaten large scale war with Communist China." But the danger of war remains.

In other words, it seems to Mr. Harper that the issue of Communism is not the real issue between China and the United States. What is at stake is that China is again standing on its feet, and that she is considered a source of potential danger that must be eliminated. America is now doing to China what the Western world did to her in the previous century.

The Taiping Rebellion in the 1860's was an effort on the part of the Chinese people to overthrow the then incompetent government. But the West did not welcome it, because a new and better government might upset its vested interests in China, and so it did everything financially and militarily to keep the tottering government from falling and to crush the revolution, which it did. For forty years afterward the West continued its exploitation of the country whose government now depended on foreign assistance for survival, until the people could not suffer the humiliations and indignities any longer. Then they started another revolution, which is called the Boxer Rebellion of 1900. That again was squashed with the occupation of Peking by the combined forces of eight nations. Every subsequent effort to put the Chinese house in order met with the same fate. Today the drama, as Mr. Harper correctly observes, is being repeated. It is the United States that is playing the major role.

I have raised a number of issues to which I have applied the query, "Is it just?" Is it just for the United States to treat the present revolution in China as another Taiping Rebellion? She has also persistently prevented China from becoming a member of the United Nations, regardless of the fact that the action is a travesty of the world organization, when one-quarter of humanity is being excluded from it. It is part of the same game to give no position, recognition, or prestige to the new government, and to embarrass and weaken it as much as possible.

For all that, dark as the picture is for the moment, I am willing to predict that the present confrontation will ultimately yield to a policy of conciliation and accommodation from both sides, even though that may be slow in coming. The confrontation will not lead to war, because such a war would be completely one-sided, a fight between sheer manpower and overwhelming nuclear power.

To speak of nothing else, the very instincts of the American people will find such a war revolting. It is not like the Cuban crisis. Then the whole nation was assumed to be in imminent danger, when two equal powers, the United States and the Soviet Union, challenged each other. Then the nation's security was at stake.

But how can the security of a mighty nation be at stake because the local population of Vietnam does not give sympathetic support to its government, which therefore finds it increasingly difficult to cope with the guerrillas? In an interview given by Mr. Henry Cabot Lodge on his return from South Vietnam after resigning from the ambassadorship there, he was asked what he thought were the intentions of the Chinese Communists and "their capabilities as applied to Southeast Asia." Mr. Lodge's answer was, "Well, we have never captured a Red Chinese in Vietnam that I know of, we have never found a body of a Red Chinese," and he then cautiously and slowly spelled out: "I think the reasonable thing to conclude is that Communist China is back—is supporting what the North Vietnamese are doing," as if he were not too sure of the involvement of Communist China even to that small extent. Senator Wayne Morse likewise said, "There are no Chinese soldiers fighting in Vietnam; there are no Russian soldiers. The only foreign troops are American . . . the unilateral war being conducted by the United States in Vietnam must be stopped, and the only force that can stop it is American public opinion." And yet there are people who think that it is worth risking war with Communist China, or that it is time to "begin an exercise in brinkmanship that could conceivably end in war between the United States and Communist China, or to say that "the danger of a global conflict seems to be advancing with fearful speed." * Where are the indications of "Communist China's military expansion and subversion in Southeast Asia," over which Representative Gerald H. Ford and his Committee of Thirteen Republicans are so much exercised? Somehow there is an air of unreality about this excitement. Along with the voices counseling war there are also voices advising the United States to pull out of Southeast Asia entirely or "lead the way to

---

* *New York* Times *editorial, June 21, 1964.*

bring China into the United Nations [so that] all freedom-loving peoples can negotiate with China politically and economically through United Nations channels." * A war with China is not likely to have wide popular support, for all the propaganda against her. For what boots it to pulverize her and to see millions of innocent Chinese dead and mutilated in their cities and on their fields, with all their towns and houses destroyed and reduced to radioactive ashes, simply because they may have sent probably some food and some simple crude munitions to the North Vietnamese, even though they in turn transmit them to the guerrillas in South Vietnam? President Eisenhower in his Farewell Address as he stepped out of the White House warned that the United States seems to be increasingly dominated by a military-industrial combine. And now less than four years later, he writes an article in *The Saturday Evening Post* that confirms his earlier views. "We are headed," he said, "toward the intense consolidation of power . . . in the hands of a few politicians." It is these few who desire the expansion of the war even though there is no or hardly any excuse for it. As Senator Morse said in a Senate debate, "There are those who wish to escalate the war. There are those who wish to start using nuclear power in North Vietnam." † And then he continued: "There is a great deal of monkey business in South Vietnam that the public does not know about. It is about time that the Congress proceeded to find out all the facts and disclose them to the American people, because the sons of American mothers and fathers are dying in South Vietnam and, in my judgment, that cannot be justified . . . I was against going in [South Vietnam]; I have been against staying in. I am for getting out immediately."

And then came the letter from the grand old man Norman Thomas (New York *Times* July 1, 1964), who believes as Senator Morse does, that "in the State Department and Pentagon are men who think Red China will never be weaker than she is at the pres-

---

* *Letter by Everett R. Clinchy, New York* Times, *May 29, 1964.*
† *If the United States should drop a nuclear bomb on North Vietnam or China, that would be the second consecutive time when such power was used against a non-Caucasian race. The image of racial genocide thus created would go down the corridor of time indefinitely. Like Lady Macbeth, the United States would never be able to wash her hands clean again.*

ent time, and therefore now is the time to finish her off if she resists a United States takeover in Southeast Asia." Mr. Thomas thinks that all this thinking is dangerous and wrong, for "even in the name of the most righteous anti-Communism, it is madness for us to embark on a course that may lead to world war. The world in general would not think us champions of righteousness but of neo-imperialism, and even if we could or should crush China in a military sense, we would lose."

But more than this, the United States, even if she crushes China through physical force, will start going down the road which must ultimately lead to her own destruction. The image of a merciless and inhuman America will so horrify the rest of mankind that she will always be living in a hostile world. Further, even if China is crushed in a military way, her spirit will survive stronger and longer than ever, and nurse a hatred, if need be, for another 4,000 years against the American people, if they should live that long. I think if statesmanship means anything, it is to take a long-range view of things and to consider even one's worst enemy as though one day one may need his friendship, and not to take an ultimate step and cut everything behind one.*

---

* It may be interesting at this point to see how some people in Japan regard the situation in South Vietnam. American action there is often compared to Japanese action toward China a generation ago. One writer said: "When President Johnson was saying 'We do not seek a wider war,' before the words were out of earshot, the war in Vietnam was already extended. That was exactly what Japan did in 1937. When Japan attacked at Loukouchiao (Marco Polo Bridge) on July 7 of that year, the Japanese government made the identical statement: 'We do not seek any wider war,' but at once the war was brought to other parts of China. One Japanese lieutenant-general (Eisaku) who had personal experience in the Sino-Japanese hostilities said the present U.S. attempt to cut the Ho Chi Minh trail is similar to the Japanese attempt to cut the Burma Road. China did not capitulate, nor are the Vietcong doing so. Also a three-man mission, consisting of a member of the Japanese Diet from the Liberal-Democratic Party, Matsumoto Shun-ichi, author Ken Kaiko, and Professor Tokumatsu Sakamoto, recently went to Vietnam to make a study on the spot. On their return they made separate reports to the Foreign Affairs Committee of the Diet. Mr. Matsumoto said he was told by some Americans in Vietnam that while they cannot win a military victory, they cannot suffer a political defeat. Between these two ends he felt that the United States is getting bogged down. Author Ken said that those among the American forces who had gone through the Korean experience know that they cannot blame the peasants from going over to the Vietcong. There is much defection going

The *Yi King* or *Book of Changes,* followed by Lao-tze later on and the other Chinese thinkers, said thousands of years ago that when events, both human and natural, reach the extreme point—Chinese-American relations have now reached such a point—the principle of reversion begins to be operative, and they begin to seek their own level again. We shall then start another cycle, with a realignment of forces, leading to the formation of a new pattern of life. I cannot help thinking that the two great nations facing the Pacific, one very old and the other very young; one representing all that is good and beautiful in the Eastern world, the other having become the repository of Western energy and technology; have been cast not to annihilate each other, but to contribute the best in each to the building of a higher and nobler civilization for all. As long as China was weak, the fullness of her strength and beauty lay dormant, but when, as previously in her long life, she continues to go through the cycles of her inner transformation until she reaches a moment when somehow the primordial forces converge to produce the spark, then the latent energy will blossom forth again with a brilliant iridescence. The moment has now arrived. All true-born Chinese feel it; they are aware that it tingles in their blood. It is an indefinable experience. When hundreds of millions of Chinese know that something vital is again coursing through their veins, then the stage is being set for another great drama. A new period of creativity and productiveness, bursting forth from the age-old concept of cosmological harmony, is near at hand.

There was a strange prediction made, nearly a hundred years ago, by a Congressman at a time when Alaska was being pur-

---

on; *the Vietcong stand a good chance of winning the war. Finally, Professor Tokumatsu said that the four principles for negotiations passed by the North Vietnamese Government on April 10 of this year, even though it is difficult to carry them out at once, will sooner or later have to serve as a basis for eventual peace. The* Yomiuri Shimbun *in its editorial said that there is no military solution for the United States except through total war, but that will be followed by incalculable difficulties. The* Tokyo Shimbun's *Saigon correspondent said in his dispatch that not only are the Vietcong now in a position of large-scale war, but they are also free to move about in the larger cities, where their currency is already being widely used. U.S. defeat is almost certain: it is about what the situation was when the Japanese were confronted by the Chinese Eighth Route Army in those days.*

140

AMERICA AND CHINA

chased by the United States from Russia. The date was July 22,
1868. The speech was made on the floor of the Congress, and the
man who spoke those uncanny words was Representative Nathan-
iel Prentiss Banks. Somehow he felt that for the United States,
from then on, to be separated from Asia by a few miles of the
Bering Strait would mean that his country would be forever cast
for a new and unpredictable role. This was what he said: *

> The Pacific Ocean will be the theatre of the triumphs of the
> civilizations of the future. The battles of tomorrow will be fought
> there, the world's institutions of the future will be forged on its
> anvils, the world's destiny will be decided there. Then there will
> be no more talk of "European civilization" or "European destiny."
> We shall see born a higher civilization, a nobler destiny.

These are the most prophetic words ever uttered. They came not
necessarily from reason, but from something much deeper, from
the depths of one's unconscious being. Not even Banks himself
could have dreamed that every one of his words is being transformed by events and actions that are occurring daily in front of
our eyes or have occurred in the immediate past. First, the ravages
that were perpetrated on the huge and amorphous body of a helpless China, every one of which was the embodiment of the utmost
cruelty, and yet I believe that somehow the perpetrators felt a
sense of guilt in these acts. The United States was among these nations. She would not allow herself to be left behind when others
were getting away with their booty. So she obtained her first re-
ward in the Wanghsia Treaty of 1844, following closely on the
Nanking Treaty forced on a prostrate China by Britain two years
earlier. The spot where this first treaty of the United States was
signed with China remains idyllic after a hundred and twenty
years. It lies in the left inner courtyard of a temple in Macao dedi-

* Representative Banks was born in 1816 and died in 1894. He was entirely
self-taught and became the editor of a weekly paper. He read law, was
admitted to the bar, and then entered politics. He was elected to the Massachusetts Legislature in 1849 and served as its speaker 1851–52. In 1853 he
was elected to the Congress, where he became Speaker of the House in 1856.
None of his decisions while Speaker was ever reversed by the House. He
was Governor of Massachusetts 1857–59.

cated to the worship of Avalokiteshvara, the Goddess of Mercy, surrounded by blossoming trees, and in the middle of the court-yard stands a round, rough-hewn stone table some five feet in diameter on which the signatures for one of the early unequal treaties between China and the United States were affixed.

Then came a succession of these acts of spoliation, with Britain always in the vanguard, followed by all the nations of Europe, including the Russians from the wilderness of the north; and the bleeding body of the venerable and ancient nation of China was beginning to ebb out, its pulse low, until it made a last desperate effort, with the Boxer Rebellion, to shake off the yoke of sixty years. That was an eruption of madness in the midsummer of 1900.* The conscience of America was stirred. She announced the Open Door policy. She championed China's territorial integrity. She defended China's national sovereignty. She returned a portion of the Boxer indemnity for the education of China's youth along modern lines. Even though the results were meager, it was now apparent that a national catastrophe of immense proportions had been averted. Those sixty years constituted the first act of a tremendous drama.

The second act of what still portended to be a tragedy was more restricted. Japan became the principal, but the action became more concentrated. That China should now suffer, as it were, from one of her own children was unthinkable, for has not Japan for over a thousand years, from the time of Shotoku Taishi, derived all the essentials of her civilization from her great neighbor? Japan could not be the equal of China any more than the moon can be the equal of the sun. But the principle of gratitude does not function in international relations. And so Japan cut more and more deeply into the body of her mother, though she could never reach her heart. China suffered as no other nation suffered in the recorded history of civilized mankind. But out of this suffering was born a noble resolve. Out of the purification of her soul, out of this catharsis, came inner strength; today China seeks to repair the ravages of time. How can she therefore welcome war or destruction in

---

* *See my novel* The Fabulous Concubine.

142 AMERICA AND CHINA

any shape or form when the tasks of reconstruction and rehabilitation are everywhere around her, demanding, as all foreign visitors observed, at least a century of concentrated and unremitting effort? There is no doubt that what the present government of China wants more than anything else is a long period of uninterrupted peace, especially with the great country on the opposite side of the Pacific. But it must be a peace with self-respect, and that self-respect involves two basic conditions: she has a right to know what her territorial limits are and she must have a sense of complete national security. This is where the United States can help China to obtain her assurances. When Mr. Chou En-lai in his interview with Reuters on October 13, 1963, said, "We are willing to be friendly with all peoples throughout the world," we can be sure that he was speaking, with the United States in mind, about the most essential condition for the stability of the government of which he is prime minister. This statement was followed by another, again with the United States in mind, in which he said, "But China could not be friendly with any country that invades us, commits aggression against us, or interferes in our internal affairs."

Somewhere in the evolution of these vast historical forces I feel that these conditions which Mr. Chou En-lai so anxiously desires will be eventually fulfilled. China will avoid war. Even if she is brought to the brink of this precipice, she will not jump into the vast abyss below. Then will ensue a new equilibrium of forces. The cosmos will then revert to its original form, and a new cycle will begin, as the *Yi King* predicted. So will China and the United States, then fully aware of each other's strength, put their shoulders together in the building of a "higher civilization, a nobler destiny," which Representative Banks prophesied something like a century ago. The problems now besetting us will become so trivial that we shall wonder how they could have occupied so much of our attention. The Chinese-Indian border question will be of little consequence. China and India will again be the best of friends as in earlier history. The Southeast Asian problem will likewise be a matter of no importance. The small countries there will live in freedom and independence, unmolested by the scourge of war, which has now become a habit of life for a generation for many of them. All this can happen if the United States lends a helping hand. Can she? Will she? It is important for the United States to know that some 1,200 or 1,300 years ago, during the T'ang Dynasty (618–906), with Buddhism as the binding force, the people in that enormous expanse of Asia were members of a spiritual commonwealth. Ennin went to China and could feel as much at home as in his native land of Japan. Hsüan Tsang could brave the burning sand of the deserts and the high mountains of central Asia and live in the Nalanda monastery, sustaining long discussions with the venerable master Silabhadra and receiving honors and respect from the Indian Buddhist scholars. And Bodhidharma earlier had gone into China and became the initiator of Zen Buddhism. The spirit transcended national boundaries and national interests, as it should. Today with the easy mingling of peoples our task should be much simpler. Actually it is getting more and more difficult. What is lacking is a spiritual force of cohesion. That will never come out of national prejudice or out of war. If we cannot create that cohesion out of religion, with its clash of dogmas and theologies, we should certainly be able to find it from a humanistic source where, since we are all human, there is a large area of identity. But wherever we find it, the role that the United States can play as the major representative of the West will be decisive. The major countries of Asia will have to re-establish their historic relationship. It is best that America help in this noble task, and not render them asunder through the injudicious use of the worn-out Roman principle of divide and rule.

When that day comes, not the least of the beneficiaries will be the United States herself and with her the entire Western world. For then all that incentive for war will be reduced to the minimum. There will be no need for the United States "to fill every vacuum, everywhere," for she will be bringing peoples together, instead of dividing them and then trying to control them. She now enjoys and will continue to enjoy an economic affluence unknown in the history of man. But she will realize also that in the last analysis economic prosperity or the struggle for economic prosperity, important as it is, is not the only aim of the good life. It is even possible that there may be lurking in it invisible forces which are destructive of that life. For consider the history of the West within the last half-century. It has gone through a period of unparalleled prosperity but also experiences of unspeakable horror: the carnage of the First World War, the exhaustion of the years of depression, the frightful inhumanities of the Fascist nightmare, the culminating fury of the Second World War, and finally the uncertainties and possibilities of complete annihilation of life itself on the planet.

Western observers themselves frankly speak out on the sickness of our society. Mr. Arnold Toynbee, in an article "Why I Dislike Western Civilization," published in the New York *Times Magazine* on May 10, 1964, fearlessly said, "Since I have grown up . . . the West has produced two world wars; it has produced communism, fascism, and national socialism; it has produced Mussolini and Hitler and McCarthy. These Western enormities make me, as a Westerner, feel insecure. Now that my German fellow Westerners have murdered 6,000,000 Jews, how can I be certain that my English fellow countrymen might not do something equally criminal? . . . What might I not be capable of doing myself, if this contemporary Western criminal lunacy were to waylay me. I shiver and shake. Old-fashioned Christian humility, please come to my rescue. Please save me from contemporary post-Christian Western self-complacent sinfulness." Mr. Toynbee goes on to deplore "the lengths to which contemporary Western civilization has gone. The contemporary West is callous toward the aged. This is, I believe, the first civilization so far, in which the aged have not had a place, as a matter of course, in their adult children's homes. Looking at this Western callousness with de-Westernized eyes, I find it shocking." Mr. Toynbee also finds the contemporary advertising business "an ugly aspect of the affluent society; and, if I am told that advertising is the price of affluence, I reply, without hesitation, that affluence has been bought too dear," because "it rams unwanted material goods down surfeited throats." Affluence consists in the incessant satisfaction of physical desires and the creation of new desires as they are being satisfied. All religions of old have taught the curbing of desires or even their elimination as being essential to the good life. Our contemporary society teaches us the very opposite. It wants us furiously to multiply our desires so that we may never stop thirsting and panting for them. But the most frightening side, according to Mr. Toynbee, of the irrational contemporary Western society is "our blind adulation of speed for speed's sake," which has invaded even the realm of innocent children. "We force their growth as if they were chicks in a pullet factory. We drive them into a premature awareness of sex even before physical puberty has overtaken them. In fact, we deprive our children of the human right of having a childhood. The forcing of sex-consciousness started in the United States; it has spread to Britain; who knows how many other Western countries this perverse system of miseducation is going to invade and demoralize?"

"Our whole present policy," continued Mr. Toynbee, "in the upbringing of the young is paradoxical. While we are lowering the age of sexual awareness—and frequently the age of sexual experience, too—to a veritably Hindu degree, we are at the same time prolonging the length of education. We force our boys and girls to become sex-conscious at 12 or 13, and then we ask them to prolong their postgraduate studies till they are nearly 30. How are they to be expected to give their minds to education during those last 16 or 17 sex-haunted years?"

These are words of anguish from the mouth of a scholar who has studied and who loves all that is good and beautiful in societies both ancient and modern, both Eastern and Western. In the presence of these serious defects a man must be brave and conceited indeed who still has the audacity to think or feel that the world simply aspires to be what Western society is.

Let us now turn to an American observer, a man who commands the respect of all Americans regardless of their political beliefs and affiliations. In a convention speech given on July 25, 1960, ex-President Herbert Hoover integrated the political campaign with the moral issues of our day. This was what he said: "Today America is in the midst of a frightening moral slump. During the fourteen years following the end of the Second World War, our statistics show that major crimes in most of these years have increased about three times as fast as the population . . . Our cities have become increasingly infested with teen-age gangs with criminal intent. In a recent year, 740,000 of these youngsters were arrested by the police. But beyond the terrifying warnings of statistics we can hardly believe that integrity and moral steadfastness are increasing when we witness the constant exposure of state and municipal corruption, and when we daily read blazoned headlines in the press exposing corrupt practices in some of our nationwide services and the fraudulent practices of some of the distributors of our daily necessities . . . The nation needs a rebirth of a great spiritual force, which has been impaired by cynicism . . ." Then, in his final words, Mr. Hoover said that he would not have the people "believe that our nation is in its decline and fall," but "my friends, you are convened here not alone to nominate a President and a Vice-President, but to declare anew the principles which must guide our country."

Less than two months previous to this extraordinary speech of Mr. Herbert Hoover, there was a survey, in the New York *Times,* among some of the leading Americans on the subject of national purpose.* Here are some of these views. Mr. Adlai E. Stevenson raised the questions: "Why are many Americans fearful that we have lost our sense of national purpose?" and "Why is there a slackness about public problems and a wholesale retreat to the joys of private life?" While he gave no specific answers, the implications seemed to be clear enough. Mr. William Faulkner likewise raised a question: "What has happened to the American dream?" His answer was forthright. "We dozed, slept, and it abandoned us. There no longer sounds a unifying voice speaking our mutual hope and will." The words seem to have been corroborated by Dr. Grayson Kirk in his speech during the commencement exercises at Columbia University in June of 1964.

Here is a more lengthy comment by Mr. Walter Lippmann. "The critical weakness of our society is that for the time being our people do not have great purposes which they are united in wanting to achieve. The public mood of the country is defensive, to hold on and to conserve, not to push forward and to create. We talk about ourselves as if we were a completed society, one which

---

* *Article by John K. Jessup, May 19, 1960.*

has achieved its purposes, and has no further great business to transact. . . ."

What a contrast there is in the mood that these seasoned observers of the American scene have described with that of a man like George Bancroft, who, scarcely a hundred years ago, could say, "In the fullness of time a republic arose in the wilderness of America. Thousands of years had passed away before this child of the ages could be born . . . from her the human race drew hope." There is in this a note of affirmation, which, as Goethe noticed long ago, has to do with the rise of nations, while negation is a prologue to their decline.

I am sure there are people who will take exception to the quotations that I have given, but they are all utterances from men who are not known as prophets of doom, but keen and experienced observers who begin to despair at the spectacle of a prodigal son drawing heavily upon the spiritual and moral capital so richly built up in the generation of the Founding Fathers without the ability of adding to it. Or to change the metaphor, the fertility of the soil seems to be getting so dangerously thin that a further relatively short period of erosion, without the instant effort to enrich it, can transform it into a kind of wasteland unfit for cultivation. When people think only of their immediate selfish interests, become narrowly patriotic and chauvinistic, and can blandly talk of dropping nuclear bombs which bring death and destruction to millions of human beings without so much compunction as the killing of a few flies; when people have lost that passionate concern for the future or that sense of responsibility, so characteristic of the Washington-Jefferson era, for "our descendants to the thousandth and thousandth generation"; when people are neither interested in nor capable of spacious and tolerant ideas nor wish "to think the unthinkable"; when, in other words, men are no longer men with profound moral convictions upon which they can build character and personality and are merely interested in becoming technicians and managers of advertising corporations, then indeed it is time to pull back the horses before they reach the brink of the precipice.

How the Western world has come to such a pass is a long and

complicated story. Dr. Reinhold Niebuhr has described it as "the tragedy of the human spirit," which consists basically in the inability of the individual to help collective life to conform to the principles and ideals that are deemed essential for his daily life. As a social and political animal, Dr. Niebuhr has found that man is quite willing to sacrifice "his individual morality to the egoism that is the accomplishment of the social life" * But that distinction need not be made and could have been avoided. Certainly Aristotle was not making any such distinction when he was talking about man being a political animal. Neither did Plato, whose view of the state was the human personality writ large so that whatever principle makes for justice in the state must also be the principle making for righteousness in the individual. The Middle Ages, with its passionate devotion to the Christian ideals, erred least of all in this respect.† But since the Renaissance the views on the relationship between man and society have been revolutionized, and unless somehow the Western man finds his way to recapture the spirit that prevailed in pre-Renaissance Europe, this dangerous dichotomy and the application of a divided standard on man's conduct as an individual and as being a part of organized society will continue to be a source of profound harassment, and, in our age of nuclear capability, it is needless to say, may bring an end of all civilization.

---

* Moral Man and Immoral Society, *quoted by Alfred Cobban in* In Search of Humanity, *p. 25*

† *See A. L. Smith in* Church and State in the Middle Ages, *Oxford, 1913, p. 135–6. "Christendom was destined to break up into the nations of Europe. If any one says that this disruption was all for the best—that what had to be is that which ought to be—I would not quarrel with what I cannot presume either to affirm or to deny. But if we reflect on the beauty, on the majesty, the potentialities of that which the word 'Christendom' embodied; if we realise that the conception of a reign of God upon earth was the ideal to which men [Western men] did homage in their hearts—however much their conduct fell short of their ideal, as conduct now falls short and will do so in all ages—then we may turn and meet the problem whether it has been for the mankind [Western mankind] that the Reformation which had to come should come as a revolution, that the church of saints and martyrs, of missioners and crusades, should be dragged through the mire of Avignon and bound to the chariot wheels of contemptible Italian dynasties, should become 'an example of all the shames and infamies in the world,' as one of its greatest servants called it."*

Even without nuclear destruction, life without a moral purpose becomes practically meaningless. For so long as the bifurcation of
the human personality persists, the allegiance to one source of authority will ultimately inflict incalculable damage on the other,
with results that are already quite manifest, as the quotations given
above amply testify. There are people who will argue that this
pessimistic view is uncalled for, that for all our defects, this is the
best of all possible worlds. All that I can say is that I am not
among them. I have known this wonderful country, as I have said
before, for close to half a century, and in my years of maturity I
cannot say that in any dispassionate appraisal of its moral situation I can gladly join their ranks, much as I wish to. There are
others who will argue that in any case it is neither possible nor desirable for the Western man to attempt to reabsorb an earlier
spirit, whether it be the classical Greek spirit or the medieval
Christian spirit, for time marches inexorably on, and Western man
must meet his problems head on with whatever spiritual resources
he may have at his command. But unfortunately these resources
are wearing down and becoming depleted through a continual
process of erosion and attrition.

Shortly after the conclusion of the First World War, Bertrand
Russell was on a lecture tour in China, and some of the words that
he then uttered may still be worth our serious attention. "Our
Western civilization," he said, "is built upon assumptions which,
to a psychologist, are rationalizings of excessive energy: our indus-
trialism, our militarism, our love of progress, our passion for dominating and organizing, all spring from a superflux of the itch for
activity. The creed for efficiency for its own sake, without regard
for the ends to which it is directed, has become somewhat discred-
ited in Europe since the war. But in America this creed is still almost universally accepted . . . this belief that Western push and
hustle are the most desirable things on earth. I cannot now take
this view." Then Lord Russell went on to say: "The evils produced
in China by indolence [sic] seem to me far less disastrous, from
the point of view of mankind at large, than those produced
throughout the world by the domineering cocksureness of Europe
and America. The Great War showed that something is wrong with

our civilization . . . The Chinese have discovered, and have practiced for many centuries, a way of life which, if it could be adopted by the world, would make all the world happy. We Europeans have not. Our way of life demands strife, exploitation, restless change, discontent, and destruction. Efficiency directed to destruction can only end in annihilation, and it is to this consummation that our civilization is tending, if it cannot learn some of that wisdom for which it despises the East." *

I am inclined to believe that these words are truer now, after the Second World War, than ever before. Senator Barry Goldwater apparently does not agree, for he believes that he is in the vanguard of "a struggle between godless people and people of God," † unknowing that the godless people, at least in China, have for centuries been godless but are deeply attached to moral ideals that have strongly influenced every phase of their life, while the people of God have all too easily and frequently deserted their God for the worship of Mammon. Or, as the veteran architect Edward D. Stone cried out recently in a fit of frenzy, "Everything betrays us as a bunch of catch-penny materialists devoted to a blatant, screeching insistence on commercialism." And then he added, "If you look around you, and you give a damn, it makes you want to commit suicide." It is not the best advice to go to such excesses. I

---

* The Problem of China, pp. 11–12.

† In this connection it may be interesting to recall the words of the publisher of the Atlantic Monthly, Mr. Donald B. Snyder, who, in his letter which appeared in the New York Times for August 22, 1964, does not seem to think very highly of the Senator, from the moral or any other point of view. ". . . the methods and political strategy," said Mr. Snyder, "by which he [Senator Goldwater] rode to power were inherently immoral." Strong words these! "Senator Goldwater built his delegate strength by proclaiming doctrines that betrayed Republican party principles going all the way back to Abraham Lincoln." "Extremist votes of the John Birch Society in Los Angeles County gave Senator Goldwater the paper-thin margin by which he captured California's 86 votes." And then toward the end of his letter Mr. Snyder merely raised a couple of questions concerning the Senator's political tactics and conduct. "When, if ever," he asked, "has the democratic principle of 'one man, one vote' sustained a more vicious assault? When, if ever, has the belief in 'government of the people, by the people, and for the people' been more cruelly betrayed?"

much rather prefer Mr. Herbert Hoover using his efforts to help in the "rebirth of a great spiritual force" in the United States. And in this new Renaissance he may with confidence look toward a country which he knew as a young man and which, for all its communism, still believes in Confucius, when he said, "There is no place in the highest heavens above nor in the deepest waters below where the moral law does not reign." It was Confucius also who said, "The art of government depends upon the proper choice of men. This choice depends on their character. The development of character depends on the observance of the moral law. The expression of this moral law is in their love of humanity." Or again: "Only he who knows how to develop his character will know how to rule over men. Only he who knows how to rule over men will know how to rule over nations and the world at large." This moral law, in the words of Immanuel Kant, must be an absolute, a categorical imperative. It is coeval with the universe, for did he not say that there are two things that impressed him most, the immensity of the heavens without, and the power of the moral law within us. For the categorical imperative within us is the unconditional command of our conscience to "act as if the maxim of our action were to become by our will a universal law of nature." *

Someday there will be another Leibniz, let us hope from the United States, who can say as that German philosopher said in a letter from Hanover in December of 1691 to one of his Jesuit friends: "I besought Grimaldi not to worry so much about getting things European to the Chinese, but rather about getting remarkable Chinese ideas to us" for the reason that "they [the Chinese] despise everything which creates or nourishes ferocity in men, and almost in emulation of the higher teachings of Christ . . . they are averse to war." Or as he said in his *Novissima Sinica* (1697): "Certe talis nostrarum rerum mihi videtur esse conditio, gliscentibus in immensum corruptelis, ut propemodum necessarium videatur missionarios Sinensium ad nos mitti . . ." (Certainly the condition of our affairs, slipping as we are into ever greater corruption, seems to me such that we need missionaries from the Chinese

---

* Critique of Practical Reason, *London, 1909, p. 139.*

who might teach us the use and practice of natural religion . . .)

The Chinese, with all their rich heritage, have still much to contribute to a sane and happier world order. Are they to be destroyed or sustained?

VI THE UNITED STATES AND INDIA

I T IS obvious that United States policy toward other parts of Asia
is determined only by her attitude toward China. The fact that
China is at once Communist and a rapidly developing country is a
source of uneasiness and discomfort to the United States. Given her
immense resources,* the extent of her territory, the industry and intelligence of her people, and her unique history, the American government is under no illusion that China will not very soon become
a first-rate power by any standards. She is already upsetting the
"balance of power" in the world. To prevent this from happening,
the only clear course of action, as conceived earlier by John Foster
Dulles, is to marshal all the forces of opposition against China, especially along her borders. It was from this that the policy of containment grew.† My own belief is that it is a shortsighted policy;

---

* For over half a century, when China's own technical and scientific ability
of the modern type remained relatively undeveloped, the world was given to
understand that her resources were limited and that she had little opportunity
of becoming a first-class industrial power. The surveys, for what they were
worth, were made by Westerners. Whether they were accurate, or made to
create a certain impression for an undefined reason, is a matter for speculation. But the surveys conducted by China's own experts within the last
fifteen years give no ground to believe that nature should be so parsimonious
in apportioning these resources to China and so bountiful and generous to
other countries. The presence of oil, which is so essential for the modern
economy, in the northeastern provinces and in Sinkiang seems now to be
well established and is adequate for many schemes that China has chosen
to embark upon. For a long time it was believed that there was practically
no oil in China.
† But as Dr. Hans Morgenthau pointed out in his article "War with
China?" New Republic, April 3, 1965, while the policy of containment might
conceivably be successful with the USSR, it cannot succeed with China for
the simple reason that on this side of the line of containment there are also
large numbers of Chinese all over Southeast Asia who traditionally have

and as long as it is being practiced, it is impossible for China to respond in a conciliatory manner.

If we keep this in mind, then what is happening in Asia becomes intelligible. There is no event in that part of the world that is an isolated event. It is all part of an integrated plan. Shortly after the outbreak of the Korean War, protection was given and is still being given to the exiled government in Taiwan. The massive military and financial support that accompanies that protection is designed to make China divided. That was the first major step taken to create a serious obstacle for mainland China. Up till then there was no such thing as mainland China. China was China. But from then on, there was to be a mainland China as distinguished from another China on an island.

Next came the rapid rehabilitation of defeated Japan and the conversion of China's former aggressor into a United States friend and ally. She is to become strong enough to be the enemy of China again and the first line of defense against any attempt of Chinese "expansionism." The aim is to make it difficult for Japan to establish rapprochement with the Chinese mainland. The kind of adulation that has been going on for Japan in the United States has quite obvious reasons. Nothing now seems good enough for the Japanese. The gates are wide open for the influx of Japanese goods, very often against the protests of native manufacturers. Porcelains, toys, a large assortment of household articles, cameras, television sets, and, when the time comes, even automobiles—whatever, in short, the Japanese can turn out finds now a ready and welcome market in this country. In addition to these products of Japanese technology (which is admittedly well developed) there is also an organized effort to spread the knowledge of Japanese culture, with its Zen Buddhism, haikus, samisens, gagakus, kabukis, flower arrangements, architecture, cinemas, etc.—just so long as Japan agrees to stand with America in preventing any rapprochement with the Chinese. Students in high schools and colleges are even being taught that Japanese culture is quite independent of Chinese culture, is superior in fact, and is even more ancient, so that, if

---

been on a higher cultural level than the people among whom they live. The line of containment therefore cannot do any containing.

THE UNITED STATES AND INDIA

there is any relation at all between the two, it was the Chinese who derived their civilization from the Japanese, rather than the reverse!

The Japanese themselves, of course, know better. No one can blame them for striking when the iron is hot or for reaping a good harvest while the crop is abundant. But if the United States feels that by so doing she has succeeded in making Japan a tool or instrument to be used against China, she is sadly mistaken. There are indications already that not everything is turning out as it was planned. But for the moment this is an integral part of the sacrosanct policy of *divide et impera,* which the United States believes, along with other Western nations, to be infallible from time immemorial.

Next comes the situation in Vietnam and Southeast Asia, where, after the French debacle of Dienbienphu in 1954, a solution could have been worked out under American initiative. But instead of that, the United States decided to plunge in, confident that with her superior military power and enormous financial resources she was sure to succeed, in a short time, in converting the territory into the kind of area she desires, so that the extension of Communist influence from the north could be stayed. But why were we so sure that the Communists in the north were determined to seize all of Southeast Asia? They were then relatively weak, much weaker than they are today, and they might have been amenable to a scheme for real freedom and independence, so long as it was not prejudicial to their interests. A guaranteed form of neutralization might then have worked.

General Maxwell Taylor and his collaborators are belatedly beginning to realize that, in order to achieve military success, one very important condition is essential, and that is political stability. Such a consideration was entirely unnecessary in an earlier century. The fact that the United States must now support one government, now another, first the Diems, then Minh, then Khanh, then someone else, and then back again to Khanh, shows that with all the money and military support in the world there are disturbing human forces that resist control.

Nowhere was this better shown than in the interview that General Taylor gave on September 9, 1964, on leaving the White House when he submitted his first report to President Johnson after assuming the ambassadorship in Saigon. He gave a threefold appraisal of the situation—military, economic, and political—and admitted that it was the uncertainty in the political life of South Vietnam that made it difficult to be sure of anything. The American authorities should have known this earlier, but they didn't, and that is why South Vietnam through the years is such a kaleidoscope of confusion. Where before there was optimism buttressed only by an abundance of military hardware and financial aid, there is now caution in any assessment of the situation. Perhaps it is all to the good. This maturity may hopefully have benefits, not only in South Vietnam, but in other parts of the world as well.

We have had the lesson of China, where literally millions of people turned over to the Communists for the simple reason that they thought any change would be for the better, and it has become a trite observation that we have not learned anything from that lesson. There is little reason to feel confident that the people in South Vietnam and the United States government see eye to eye on the subject of Communism. The proposition that Americans are helping the Vietnamese to help themselves is true only with a fraction of the population. The fighting, in any case, is a domestic affair; and as Professor Quincy Wright pointed out, neither according to the Charter of the United Nations nor to international law should any foreign power answer the call for assistance from either side in the conflict. Besides, the military situation in Vietnam is even more difficult than it was in Korea. Victory there is essentially victory on land, and that is virtually an impossibility; air and naval power can destroy, but they cannot occupy territory.

As to the political situation in Vietnam, we have found to our sorrow that the Vietnamese are impervious to any influence, persuasion, or pressure. There is even less stability than in the Chiang Kai-shek regime on mainland China between 1945 and 1949. For all its corruption, nepotism, incompetence, and immorality, there was not in China then the rivalry for power that has made the South Vietnamese regime a tragic circus. Yet, despite the combination of such unfavorable circumstances, we are asked to believe that stability will somehow come about, and with it victory. "Optimism is the madness of maintaining that everything is right when it is wrong."

Now the United States seems constrained to consider or even to accept a solution less favorable than she might have had from the very beginning in 1954, when the French surrendered at Dienbienphu. A few senators saw the picture quite clearly, but theirs has been a cry in the wilderness. They have been up against those in power who insist upon building the ramparts against Communism with steel rather than with understanding and thought. The belief that Easterners only understand force is one of the most tragic misunderstandings in all history. Exactly the reverse is true. The results so far, morally speaking, of this policy of force have been negligible. All that we have is the dubious satisfaction of seeing the principle of divide and rule in full operation. Thus we have one part of Vietnam fighting against another part of Vietnam, one part of Southeast Asia antagonistically arrayed against another part of Southeast Asia, or all of Southeast Asia against Asia north of that area. But the methods of ancient imperialism do not work any more. Prince Norodom Sihanouk can openly say in Phnom Penh, "The enemy number one, the United States and especially its lackey, must now realize that little, non-Communist Cambodia is capable of surviving freely and even progressively without a single injection of dollars and without [their] protective umbrella." The Prince is among the most intelligent young rulers in the world: he is just, courageous, intensely patriotic and knows exactly what he does and says. These words would have been quite inconceivable in an earlier period of imperialism. The change in mood and attitude has been phenomenal.

The builders of this rampart of steel are also behind the creation of Malaysia. But that again, I am afraid, will go down in history as another example of ill-conceived imperialism. No real nation can emerge out of such an obvious contrivance: for a nation is a living organism. It must have a soul in order to survive, to grow, and to develop. In the case of Malaysia, what is there but the unrelated parts of a jigsaw puzzle, put together to serve the purposes of an alien power? How can it survive? It is understandable that Britain wishes to salvage what remains of her empire in that part of the

world and to give protection to Australasia, but why should the
United States see in this another rampart to stem the Communist
tide? The result so far has been to alienate the Indonesians, who
have no wish to be friendly with the Communists, but who are now
driven to co-operate with them and to declare openly that they will
not rest until the new "nation" of Malaysia is dismembered.

In this nuclear age the policies of "balance of power" and "divide and rule" are obsolete. They should be discarded. Nations
have become much too independent for their effective application.
Even Lecky, in his day, was of the opinion that the concept of the
balance of power had done more harm than good to Europe. In his
History of England in the Eighteenth Century (1893, Vol. vi, p.
95–6), he acknowledged that the balance of power "has done more
to subvert than to promote the security of Europe and it has produced far more warfare than it has prevented." The reason, he
thought, was obvious: the effectiveness of the balance of power
depended not on justice but on force and expediency.

Another view in support of Lecky is that of Eyre Crowe, who in
a secret memoir to Sir Edward Grey dated January 1, 1907, stated
that in order to be effective, the balance of power must presume
the existence of static conditions; but, he continued, "nations are
never static" so that "balance of power never achieved a satisfactory equilibrium long and failed in preserving peace." Today, when
the entire world is going through massive revolutionary movements, stability becomes possible only when there is a total peace
founded not on force but on justice. The same observations can be
applied to the concept of divide and rule, which has become irrele-
vant to our current problems. That is why in Taiwan, Southeast
Asia, Malaysia, and in India—to single out those areas of Asia in
which American policy is so deeply involved and where those two
antiquated principles are in full operation—the results have been
and will continue to be disappointing.

I have pleaded for a more friendly approach toward China. I believe that the immense resources of the United States, when they
are used to sponsor a new approach, not only toward China, but
toward all of Asia, will be productive of far more good than the
present policy. As it is, these resources are being used to antago-

nize China and to build up the surrounding areas for the purpose of strengthening that antagonism. The new approach would require a reversal of that policy: it would stimulate friendly relations, through the American intermediary, between China and the rest of Asia. One of the most fruitful and promising areas, I believe firmly, is the relationship between China and India.

By virtue of her strategic position, the United States can help to bring together the two most populous countries in the world, comprising over a billion people, in a manner that will contribute enormously to the advancement of those countries. But also it will add immensely to the prestige and moral leadership of the United States and lay the foundations of a long and lasting peace of the world. India is not in a position to successfully wage war. This is not to say that she is therefore not an important nation. Quite the contrary: to be able to wage war successfully should not be the criterion of a great nation. But unfortunately it has become the one true measure of national stature. For India to attain that stature the problems are not only immense; they are staggering and overwhelming. It is a pity, therefore, that she should even think of embarking, at this period of her history, on any course of action that can bring nothing but ruin and disgrace upon her.

India is unique among the nations of the world. She is unique not only from the Western point of view, but is so considered even by the Eastern peoples to whom she belongs. There are thinkers in the West who feel that the magnificent metaphysical systems of the Hindus and their profound religious beliefs are too esoteric to be of value, and represent a corpus of inane and feckless effort which could have been used more profitably in other areas. But the majority of them deem otherwise, and they are, I think, right. The elaborate intricacies of the Indian mind, from the days of the Upanishads down to the present, with its utter disregard of the immediate and practical ends of life, are a monument of the supreme intellectual accomplishment of which the human mind is capable. With the possible exception of the Germans, who have the same flair, there is hardly another race that is equal to the task. Certainly the Chinese have nothing comparable to show in their long history. Least of all do the Japanese, who have not produced any great thinkers, in the same class as a Sankara or a Ramanuja or even a Radhakrishnan.

Max Müller, the renowned Indologist, used to say, "If I were to ask myself, from what literature we here in Europe—who have been nurtured almost exclusively on the thought of the Greeks and Romans, and of one Semitic race, the Jewish—may draw that corrective which is most wanted in order to make our inner life more perfect, more comprehensive, more universal in fact, more truly human, a life, not for this life alone, but a transfigured and eternal life, . . . I should point to India." Another scholar, W. J. Grant also used to say, "India indeed has a preciousness which a materialistic age is in danger of missing. Someday the fragrance of her thought will win the hearts of men. This grim chase after our own tails which makes the present age cannot continue forever. The future contains a new human urge towards the real beauty and holiness of life. When it comes, India will be searched by loving eyes and defended by knightly hands." *

And Hermann Keyserling, himself one of the most penetrating of contemporary European philosophers, spoke glowingly also throughout the pages of his *Reisetagebuch* of the noble accomplishments of the Hindu mind. "Indian wisdom," he said, "is the profoundest which exists."† "What impresses me so much," he further said, "is the existence of a state of consciousness which permits them [the Hindus] to perceive reality which is quite beyond the average Westerner." ‡ Or again: "The Indians have overcome the static concept of truth and replaced it by a dynamic one which transfigures its meaning: we too will do this sooner or later. We too will realize one day that recognition of being cannot be attained even by the far-reaching perfection of our conceptual apparatus, not by the most exhaustive exploration of our consciousness as it is, but only by the acquisition of a new and higher form of consciousness . . . [Man] must grow beyond his present gauge; his consciousness must, instead of cleaving to the surface, learn to reflect the spirit of profundity which is the primary cause

---

* The Spirit of India, *1933, p. vi.*
† Travel Diary of a Philosopher, *I, p. 265.*
‡ Ibid., *I, p. 92.*

of his being. This higher development has begun in India; hence the miracle of India's recognition of being and its wisdom of life." *

No one who has had the opportunity of working through the labyrinth of Indian thought can, I believe, take exception to the sentiments expressed by these writers. All three of them were thinkers who commanded great respect in the scholarly world, and the tribute that they paid to the Indian genius was not lightly given. But the Indians, for their part, should accept this tribute, which they richly deserve, with humility and with an awareness that there is much in the modern world in which they are still profoundly deficient; and until these deficiencies, even though they fall within the realm of practical realities, are properly remedied, they will continue to limp behind other nations. Keyserling spoke of the existence of a state of consciousness that enables the Indian to perceive reality with unusual clarity, but neither he nor any modern Indian will deny that the world of immediate phenonema has long been conceived in India as being an illusion, or maya. That is the central theme of Indian philosophical or religious thinking. The task of the modern creative thinker must certainly attempt to regard the universe as being essentially a profound unity in which the transcendental value, the "higher consciousness" of Keyserling, and the world of practical affairs are manifestations of an identical spirit. This sense of harmony, of reconciliation of two realities that do not stand opposed to each other, has been the burden of Chinese thinking. Dr. Sarvepalli Radhakrishnan, the philosopher-statesman of India, is trying to do precisely what has become an accomplished fact in China. But it will take generations of creative effort before there will be any substantial result. For he is battling beliefs and prejudices that have become too deeply ingrained.

In his Upton Lectures delivered at Oxford in 1926, which were published under the title *The Hindu View of Life,* Dr. Radhakrishnan admitted that the concept of maya has been one of the chief obstacles to India's becoming a truly modern nation. "The doctrine of maya," he said, "is supposed to repudiate the reality of the world and thus make all ethical relations meaningless. The world

* Ibid., *I, pp. 264–65.*

of nature is said to be unreal and human history illusory. There is no meaning in time and no significance in life. To be delivered from this illusion, which has somehow come to dominate the race of man, is the end of all endeavor." The implication is that this doctrine of maya has been wrongly interpreted. It is important for Dr. Radhakrishnan to make this assertion, because it is a necessary part of the work of reconstruction and of revamping Indian philosophy so that it may serve the purposes of the modern world. And yet, who can deny that the accusations are just, for generations of scholars could not have made the same mistake. The Indians, for instance, have no concept of history as the Western peoples or the Chinese understand it. The very existence of their most distinguished ruler, Asoka, in the third century B.C., was not known, according to Vincent Smith, until he was revealed to them by accident through the findings of alien archeologists. The very material upon which to base the writing of Indian history does not exist in India, for the Brahmans, the principal literary class, "certainly had not the taste for writing histories, their interest being engaged in other pursuits." They "cared little for historical composition as a form of literature." * Historians therefore have to rely on material largely of foreign provenance. Megasthenes, the Greek ambassador from Seleucos Nicator to Chandragupta Maurya, gave a valuable account of early India, but the principal sources of information are the Chinese pilgrims between A.D. 400 and 700, who visited India for the quest of Buddhist lore. Fa Hsien gave one account, followed by the learned Hsüan Tsang, who supplied full and interesting descriptions covering many parts of India. Then came Yi Tsing and sixty other pilgrims without whose travel books, which are full of vivid and accurate details, it would be virtually impossible to write the early history of India.

A people who shows scant interest in its own history is, I think, a people that does not regard what happens to the empirical world as a matter of especial concern. Dr. Radhakrishnan, therefore, has finally to admit that Sankara, who perhaps more than any other single thinker helped to shape and mold Indian thought, was of the

---

* Vincent A. Smith, The Oxford History of India, 1919, p. xviii.

opinion that time and space cannot be "rounded in a systematic whole," and are thus "imperfect and unreal," for "the real must be exempt from all change and persist for all time." *

The work that Dr. Radhakrishnan is doing in reconditioning Indian thought needs desperately to be done, and when results begin to show, then and then only can we feel confident that India is moving in the right direction to become a modern nation. This work of reconditioning was done before in China (and later in Japan) when Buddhism was introduced into those countries. "The only useful work," Dr. Radhakrishnan says further,† "which the liberated souls do is to help struggling humanity. So long as there are individuals who are unredeemed, and so stand in need of saving, the liberated have some work to do." This is his plea for the integration of the universal and the particular, for the integration of the infinite and finite. This is not the traditional Indian view either in Hinduism or in Buddhism. But that was what Buddhism came to be when it was transformed by the practical-minded Chinese into what has come to be known as Mahayana Buddhism. Rather than saying, therefore, as Dr. Radhakrishnan has often said, that "In Asia all roads lead to India" or that "Half the world moves on independent foundations which Hinduism supplied. China, Japan, Tibet and Siam, Burma and Ceylon, look to India as their spiritual home," ‡ it is perhaps more correct to say that Buddhism, which has virtually become extinct in India itself since the time of Harsha, should be revived in India along the lines suggested by its evolution in China and Japan.

For the difference between the Buddhism as it existed in India for a thousand years and the Buddhism that developed in China and Japan has created two entirely different worlds. We are in the habit of lumping them together as Oriental countries, thinking that they are animated by the same spirit. Actually the gulf separating India from China and Japan is as wide as between Judaism and Christianity. China and Japan constitute a world of their own: they are indeed the real Orient. This is not to deny that the impact

---

* The Hindu View of Life, *p. 64.*
† Ibid., *p. 12.*
‡ *Ibid., p. 12.*

of Indian influence on those two countries was not extensive and long-lasting. But in the arts, in painting, sculpture, architecture, as well as in Buddhism itself, the influence had, as it were, to go through a sieve so that every particle that did not respond to the needs and demands of the Chinese soul had to be rejected; what finally emerged became something quite alien to the Indians.

Zen Buddhism, for instance, which is derived from Ch'an Buddhism in China * is in essence a revolt against the Buddhism that was practiced in India. To put it in the simplest possible form, the image of a Buddhist in India was that of "a rhinoceros wandering alone in the wilderness" on his way to nirvana, but the image of a Buddhist in China and Japan is to this day that of a bodhisattva who, arriving on the threshold of the western paradise, refuses to enter the realm of eternal bliss and turns around to face the teeming multitude of living forms who need his assistance, so that they too in time may share in the supreme bliss. The goddess of mercy or Avalokiteshvara insists that "wherever the gnat cries, there am I." The implication is that of a social responsibility that is not of Indian but of Sinitic origin. Buddhism reached China, where a unique civilization had already been in existence for two millenniums, and where the instinct for social responsibility had become so highly developed that the concept of maya had real difficulty in making any inroad into the Chinese consciousness. Buddhism in China had to reckon with Confucian thought, which stood for unity and harmony, not with the ultimate transcendent reality, but with all human beings wherever they might come from and with all other forms of life. It was a society that knew no caste, as it was essentially an egalitarian society in which divisiveness had been reduced to the minimum. This is the kind of society that Dr. Radhakrishnan seemingly desires to create for India; and unless it *is* created, involving as it does, the undoing of traditional Hindu thought of many millenniums, India will continue to have a tremendous diversity of castes, of peoples who refuse to be merged, and of rival languages. No nation like this can discharge the functions of a modern society.

---

* The Japanese word "zen" is the same Chinese word "ch'an," but pronounced differently.

But while the concept of maya in the traditional thought of India exercises a profound influence over the Indian mind, the fact remains that the world of the immediate neighborhood, as Kirkegaard calls it, cannot be ignored without dire consequences. Two developments in India became inevitable. One was that when the impact of force from without reached her threshold, there would not be sufficient cohesion from within to resist, much less to overcome it. That is why, from the days of the Mohenjo-Daro civilization, over four thousand years ago, till now, the Indians have been unable to resist a determined aggressor. The Aryan invasion from the north, which brought an end to the Indus Valley civilization, was followed by Darius, who came into the Punjab in 516 B.C. That was followed by Alexander, who was in northern India in 327 B.C. Then the Indo-Greeks and Indo-Parthians established their ascendancy in the Punjab in 250 B.C., to be succeeded by the Saka or Kushan invasion of 150 B.C. The Huns invaded India in A.D. 450. And then soon afterward in 712 came the Arab conquest of the Sindh. The Moslem conquest of Delhi and Bengal took place in 1199. Amir Timur sacked Delhi in 1398, and he in turn was followed by the Mogul Dynasty in 1528–1707. Finally the British made India a part of their empire in 1858. The Indians have long been a conquered race. It is often said that the Indians are a peace-loving people. But are they really, or is it simply their geographical position and their own lack of unity that has made them subject to foreign invasions? Asoka, the most distinguished of the Indian rulers, killed two hundred thousand Kalingas before he turned to Buddhism. This is hardly an example of the peace-loving mind.

Of course, if the entire world succeeds in making war a thing of the past, then India stands a very good chance of being perhaps the most influential nation on the face of the earth. There is no denying that she has evolved a profoundly rich spiritual heritage, though some of its values need to be reassessed, even in a warless world. A culture that has consistently taught man to look *within* himself, rather than *around* himself, to have his attention riveted on the heavens beyond, rather than on the here and now, to be absorbed in contemplation of a "world without space and yet more spacious; without gold and dominions and none the less richer;

without conquests but yet in possession of greater safety; without tangible form but not therefore less real than the . . . conquered territorial globe" * will always win the respect and admiration of the world, even though it is beyond its reach. India has developed a culture such as few other nations have. It would seem to me wiser for her not to become involved in power politics.

The second consequence of this inability to integrate the world of spiritual values with the world of practical reality, was that Indian political life became a matter of *Realpolitik,* serving its own end without reference to any higher considerations. I doubt there is any thinker even in the Western world as utterly ruthless and cynical as some of India's political thinkers. This ruthlessness and cynicism are all the more striking when we realize that they come from people who are popularly thought to be devoted to the doctrine of non-violence or ahimsa and who throughout history have been dedicated to the spiritual life. And yet out of this people has emerged the thinking of a man like Kautilya, the author of that extraordinary book called the *Arthasastra.* It is important to know something about this adviser to Chandragupta, the powerful king of the Maurya Dynasty, as without such knowledge it is difficult to understand much of the foreign policy of present-day India either in the Kashmir or in the border conflict with China, or in her relations with all of her immediate neighbors. The fact that India is not on good and friendly relations with any of her neighbors is, I think, a significant comment on India's national policy.

The rule under the Mauryas in the fourth century B.C., with its "heedlessness of adventitious moral and religious standards," † as the Indians themselves admitted, was completely autocratic and bore striking resemblance to the police state of today. "It was a rule of mutual suspicion and general treachery," ‡ and Kautilya did everything to encourage it. He advocated a diplomacy of cold and cynical realism, of unqualified expediency. Nothing was not permissible for the sake of conquest and aggression. Dissension,

---

* *René Fülöp-Miller,* The Saints That Moved the World, *p. 350.*
† *Rangaswami Aiyangar.*
‡ A History of Asia *by Woodbridge Bingham, Hilary Conroy, and Frank W. Iklé, p. 153.*

seduction, the use of poison and arson, even the recruitment of beggars and intoxicated persons as sources of information, were all freely resorted to as long as they served the purposes of the expansion of power. The *Arthasastra* has often been compared to *The Prince,* but more than that many Indians feel proud that it might very well have inspired the Florentine thinker.*

One would think it inconceivable that a people so dedicated to the life of the mind and spirit could have given birth to a political treatise so utterly innocent of moral or ethical consideration and so completely cynical in its approach to human problems. And yet this is precisely what happens when there is a dichotomy between what one believes to be the world of ultimate truth and reality and the world of maya, which, unfortunately, cannot very well be ignored. The type of political thinking exemplified by Kautilya, which regards physical force, expediency, complete selfishness, aggression, as being the foundation of political action, could have very well ruined India with her unceasing conflicts, were it not for the fact that periodically an alien power intervened to impose its will and established a semblance of relative peace. Those conflicts would certainly have been increased by all the divisive forces that are a permanent feature of Indian life and show no signs of diminishing.

Prime Minister Jawaharlal Nehru, till the day of his death, was profoundly conscious of these divisive forces that prevent India from being a united or modern nation. At the time of the separatist movements in Assam and among the Sikhs in August of 1960, he said, "The time has come when every Indian will have to realize where he stands in relation to his country. Does he stand by his country, or his group, or religion, or state?" (New York *Times* August 16, 1960.) He deplored that "the real danger to India's unity and integrity came from internal conflicts over language, caste, religion, and province." Early, in his *Discovery of India* (p. 365, Doubleday Anchor Books), he had said, "It should be remembered that there are over 600 such states in India, some major ones and the greatest majority tiny enclaves." This is about what conditions were before the time of Confucius in China. The great diver-

* Indian Political Thought from Manu to Gandhi *by D. Mackenzie Brown,* p. 50.

sity that is India has always impressed the non-Indian. Thus, over half a century ago, George William Knox in *The Spirit of the Orient* (1905) said, "If India is continental in size, it is more than continental in the variety of inhabitants, and never from the earliest dawn of its history has it produced even a temporary unity or any consciousness of solidarity . . . It is a wilderness of peoples, languages, religions, and customs."

How different is the picture of China that Professor R. H. Tawney has painted for us. He was impressed by the fact that China lives "as a human being." She "exists as a single organism" —these are appropriate words to use, for the unity of China is a unity of the soul created out of a living and identical culture on a massive scale.

As early as the eleventh century, the eminent neo-Confucian thinker Cheng Hao (1032–1085), in his criticism of the Buddhists, said, "When they strive only to 'understand the high' without 'studying the low,' how can their understanding of the high be right?" * In other words, in the mind of the Chinese, the universe is all one piece. The differentiation of "high" and "low" is at best one of convenience, of nomenclature. They are different aspects of a basically identical substance. Any cleavage is harmful to unity and to each of the separated parts.

There is thus in the Indian and Chinese views of life and the universe quite a basic difference of approach, for which there is hardly room for reconciliation. The Chinese regard the Indians as being in every respect overwhelming and excessive. It may be that India's physical and natural environment is conducive to the development of those peculiar characteristics, for, as Mr. C. M. Bowra said of the ancient Greeks, "A people lives by its geography. What nature provides as a home and a background is the most enduring element in any national history." † Nowhere is this more true than it is in India. The impact of the heat, both in

---

* *It is significant that Cheng Hao quoted Confucius* (Analects, *XIV, 37*) *in support of his view. Confucianism is the very embodiment of the sense of harmony, moderation, centrality, proportion. It abhors excessiveness in any shape and form, and calls for restraint and ubanity.*
† **The Greek Experience,** *p. 2.*

its intensity and its quality, is so overpowering that the traveler loses his balance. Its fauna and flora are overwhelming in their luxuriance, and nothing seems comprehensible except from the botanical point of view. This experience has called forth a number of interesting observations from Hermann Keyserling. The whole of life, he said, turned into a process of vegetation. "Vegetating signifies a form of existence which proceeds without effort, but then effort is superfluous here: everything succeeds without it." "Thousands of gods sprang from the fruitful soil like mushrooms after rain. Hinduism in its boundless richness can only be understood as a vegetable process." "It is not I any longer who think, but something thinks in me; it is not I who wish, but something wishes in me." The process of growth is so rapid, so rich, luxuriant and unlimited that only one form of longing is possible, "the longing to escape from all superfluity and all abundance," for "abundance becomes an obstacle to energetic action, it weakens our sense of life and threatens to strangle self-consciousness." "Spirit seems powerful here only in so far as it tries not to create reality, but to deny it." *

These remarks are interesting and, I think, quite just, because in India, more than in any other area where civilization has flourished, man seems to have been completely taken over by the exuberance, the vitality, and the prolific energy of the natural environment. The exercise of the human will becomes no longer possible. The problem of the will did constitute an important part of the Buddhist metaphysics, as Mrs. Rhys Davids has clearly shown, but it seems to have been swept out of existence long ago along with Buddhism itself. Whatever the differences may be between the religions and philosophies in India—for Hinduism the goal is moksha, for Jainism Siddhahood, for Buddhism nirvana—the ultimate aim of human life is identical. It is release from an existence that is inexorably under the government of the iron laws of cause and effect. It is to bring to an end the continually revolving cycle of birth, old age, death, and then rebirth, old age, death all over again, ad infinitum.

---

* Travel Diary of a Philosopher, *Vol. I, pp. 39–45* passim.

Now India has been thrown into the modern world, with all its
complex problems, which expects her to play an important
and even a decisive role. Is this possible? For these problems,
which are essentially problems of human adjustment of social
relationship, of political adaptation, of mutual accommodation
between man and man, between nation and nation, are all an in-
trinsic part of this mundane world which has been consistently repudiated by the mind of India. As Mrs. Rhys Davids, the great authority on Buddhism, again correctly pointed out, the Buddhist in
India, in so far as he relied upon *ni-bbana* (nirvana) or extinction
of life itself as the ultimate form of salvation, the concept of a perfect state, either earthly or heavenly, was impossible, since that
presupposes the existence of life in some shape or form. This is
true also of Hinduism, of Jainism, or any other religion in India.
And yet without any preparation whatever, without any prelimi-
nary work being done to change a view of life of negation to one of
affirmation, we are already saying that India is a great democracy.
Are we not in too much haste? Or are we deliberately creating an
illusion?

The world of reality, finite as it may be, which the Western
world and the Sinitic world of China, Japan, Korea and parts
of Southeast Asia have been taught to observe and master, has little interest for the Indians. That is why when they did take an interest in it, they lost all sense of direction. Hence the *Arthasastra,*
with its lack of moral restraint or responsibility. Until there has
been an adequate period of training, following a drastic change of
Lebensanschauung, it is unsafe to entrust major political decisions
to the judgment of the Hindu mind. The sense of balance, of measure, of proportion, of where and how to stop, requires a degree of
finesse that, with due respect to the Hindu, he does not possess. He
may have extraordinary visions of the infinite, of prajna or intuition, and he may feel at home in sunyata. But when it comes to the
matter of worldly affairs, of the likes and dislikes of man, of his
foibles and prejudices, of his emotions, feelings, pride, greed,
avarice, to which unfortunately our political and international life
belongs, a much surer and reliable guide would be Confucius, Lao-
tze, or any of the Chinese philosophers. For the Chinese thinkers

have not been in the habit of regarding the world of phenomena, including the affairs of men, as either nonexistent or far apart from the world of higher reality. They are manifestations of the identical *tao*. Further, every quality in the wide expanse of the universe contains or implies the imminence of its opposite, which is not in conflict with it but is complementary to it. Their attempt for mutual accommodation reaching ultimately a state of harmony or equilibrium is the attainment of what Plato would call justice.

This brief survey of the radical philosophical and psychological differences between the Indian and Chinese people is, I hope, useful in helping us to understand better some of the international problems with which they are presently engaged. When the border question arose and China was charged with the invasion of Indian territory and therefore with having committed an act of aggression, I believed, as the rest of the world was made to believe, that it must be so. But in the back of my mind I was doubtful. Is it possible, I kept on asking myself, that Communism in so short a time has changed the structure of the Chinese mind? Have the Chinese leaders deserted the heritage in which they were born and nurtured? Have they become rash and imprudent? I began then a careful study of the events. And I must confess that the more I study, the more I feel convinced that the facts, which cannot be entirely suppressed and distorted no matter how one tries, tell a story that is diametrically the opposite of what I have been made to believe. Of course, being of Chinese birth I am inclined to be prejudiced in China's favor, but it is not difficult to submit myself to the discipline of being as impartial as possible, since the facts seem to be so well established. The record, in so far as it is not twisted by the press of the free world, leads inexorably, I think, to the following conclusions:

1. That it is India, not China as it is generally believed, that is the aggressor nation.

2. That it is India that violated Chinese territorial integrity and not the other way around.

3. That it is India that made preparations for war on the border, and not China; that only a nation that was prepared for open

hostilities could say, as Prime Minister Nehru did on October 12, 1962, that he had instructed the Indian army to "throw the Chinese" out of the disputed territory, or, as Mr. Krishna Menon, then still Defense Minister, two days later said, "We will fight to the last man, to the last gun."

4. That it was China that consistently and patiently pleaded with the Indians to sit down for negotiations and not to resort to force. As late as October 13, one day after Nehru had sent what the *Manchester Guardian* called an "ultimatum" and the New York *Herald Tribune* described as being "tantamount to a formal declaration of war," China still called on Mr. Nehru to "pull back from the brink of the precipice," as she was "absolutely unwilling to cross swords with India."

5. That India was not accomplishing what she wanted from her five-year plans and that the results were meager as compared with what China could show with her plans. When Mr. Nehru's sister, Mrs. Vijaya Lakshmi Pandit, for whom I have much personal respect, in her broadcasts on the radio and on television, was telling the American audiences that China was envious of India's record of accomplishment, exactly the reverse was true.

6. That India was in fact in great financial difficulties, especially from 1960 on, and needed very badly massive financial aid from abroad to tide over these difficulties, and that the only way to obtain such aid was to precipitate a crisis with China at a time when China was in the grip of one of the worst famines in modern history. All that India needed to do was to make demands on China which she knew China could not accept and to say that China had encroached on her territory so that war on China would appear to be justified.

7. That the only country that was in a position to furnish financial and military aid is the same country that is interested also in having India leave the neutral or non-aligned bloc and come out openly on the side fighting against Communism.

8. That it was the intention of the United States to complete the forging of the iron ring around China, stretching all the way from Korea to the Pamirs.

9. That it was the intention of the United States to encourage Asians to fight against Asians.

10. That finally the whole episode is an example of *Realpolitik* in its most naked form.

Every one of these points can be substantiated by incontrovertible facts.

It will need much more space than this book will allow to give all the facts, but many of them will have to be given, however brief the account. The whole border incident confirms that the Indians may be the world's most capable metaphysicians in their quest for the realization of the infinite or of the ultimate reality, throwing out their great web of mysticism with its tat tvam asi, satyagraha, ahimsa, jnana, moksha, sunyata, and all the rest of these abstruse terms; but when it comes to the realm of maya, to which political behavior unfortunately belongs, the Indians can be as hard as nails. They then depend not on philosophy to guide them, but on the *Arthasastra* of the chief adviser of Chandragupta, which is, in a word, a compendium of cold cynicism. There have been Indians who sometimes feel that this cynicism will lead India nowhere. Sri Aurobindo (1872–1950) used to say in the columns of his *Bande Mataram*, "Our actual enemy is not any force exterior to ourselves, but our crying weaknesses—our cowardice, our selfishness, our hypocrisy, our purblind sentimentalism." * But this view is not shared by the majority of the Indians. They have lost the sense of humility, which was still a virtue in the Buddhist scheme of things; it never developed in Hinduism. They have not learned to look at themselves as others see them. They have become chauvinistic, not only in a political, but also in a spiritual sense, as when Dr. Sarvepalli Radhakrishnan could say that all roads in Asia led to India. One would think that a scholar would show more modesty and restraint. Long ago the Islamic scholar al-Biruni (973–1048) in his *Story of Indian Civilization* made the observation that the Indians were too self-centered to recognize the existence of outside nations, because they had too strong a sense of pride, of what the

---

* *Haridas Mukherjee and Uma Mukherjee,* Sri Aurobindo's Political Thought, *p. x.*

ancient Greeks would call *hubris*. Other nations have their pride, but at least they have the saving quality of self-examination. The Chinese, for all they have been able to accomplish on the mainland, are very humble. Time and again they admit that they are very backward and that it will take them decades before they can become a modern nation. Not so the Indians. The absence of the sense of proportion prevents them from seeing themselves as anything but the "most spiritual" of nations. Is it any wonder that the border incident flared into open conflict? The Indians decided to "throw the Chinese" out of the disputed area and to teach them a lesson, without inquiring in the first place whether they were in a position to do so.

And now a résumé of a few facts relating to that conflict. We must first begin with the status of Tibet.* Its early contact with China has been discussed previously (p. 56). As in the case of many European courts, marriage played an important part in territorial distribution. By A.D. 641 the Tibetan king Srong-tsan Gampo had married the Chinese princess Wen-Cheng of the T'ang Dynasty. The relationship between Tibet and the Chinese court from then on, both politically and culturally, became increasingly more intimate. It was the Chinese queen who persuaded the king to have his people give up tattooing their bodies. Like any doting husband he agreed. She also had them discard the skins and furs with which they wrapped themselves, and in their place put on Chinese dress. To this day the Tibetans wear the clothes of the Chinese which prevailed in the Ch'ing Dynasty. Finally she gave instructions that the sons of the Tibetan aristocracy be properly educated in Changan, then the Chinese capital, in the Confucian classics. Those again were duly carried out. She must have been quite a strong-willed woman, but then there have been many women of this type in Chinese history.

Even as we come to relatively recent history, when the influence

---

* *The number of books on Tibet is increasing as a result of what has been happening there. Most of them are strongly biased. Perhaps the most scholarly and the best documented book is the one by Dr. Li Tieh-tseng. The notes and bibliography alone of* The Historical Status of Tibet, *written in 1955, run over 85 pages. It is an indispensable book for any impartial study of that part of China.*

of the Chinese court began to wane in the eyes of the Western powers, we find the following facts:

1. The British recognized Tibet as a dependency of the Chinese Empire in 1792. That legal commitment never came into question even at the height of British imperialism throughout the nineteenth century.

2. When the British in 1904, under the leadership of Sir Francis Younghusband, broke into Lhasa for no justifiable reason, the American ambassador in London, Joseph H. Choate, was instructed in June of that year by the State Department to remind the British Foreign Secretary, the Marquis of Lansdowne, that Britain had three times recognized Chinese sovereignty by negotiating with the Chinese government on questions relating to Tibet. He "assumed" that the British "still regarded Tibet as a part of the Chinese dominions." As late as 1933, when I happened to be on the same steamer bound from Shanghai to Europe, I recall that Sir Francis still resented the American protest.

3. It has been the practice of the Chinese government to allow as much local autonomy as possible to outlying areas that came within the empire and not ruthlessly to eliminate their differences. In the case of the Tibetans this autonomy was given to them during the 1270's by Kublai Khan and still found a place in the Treaty of May 23 of 1951. It is a seventeen point agreement known as the Agreement of the Central People's Government and the Local Government of Tibet on Measures for the Peaceful Liberation of Tibet. It is clear that the agreement is not one between two sovereign states, but between the Central government and one of its local governments for the enforcement of certain specific measures, one of which was the reorganization of the local army into the People's Liberation Army.

4. In November, 1950, when El Salvador requested that Tibet be included on the agenda in the United Nations Assembly for that year, not a single country was in support of the suggestion in the General Committee. The Committee was correct in its position. Tibet has been and remains an integral part of China, and what goes on there is purely China's domestic question. Both Communist China and Nationalist China are completely at one on this matter.

5. Four years later, in 1954, India signed the treaty with China which accepts the fact that Tibet is an inalienable part of China.* It was in that treaty incidentally that China made clear her views of peaceful coexistence, about which there still seems to be much doubt. The Five Principles of Peaceful Coexistence (*Panch Sheel*) include: (a) mutual respect for sovereignty; (b) mutual non-aggression; (c) non-interference in each other's internal affairs; (d) equality and mutual benefit; and (e) peaceful coexistence. The same principles were incorporated a year later in what came to be known as the Ten Principles of Peaceful Coexistence at the Bandung Conference. It was on the basis of these principles that a number of treaties of peace and friendship were signed by China with many countries of Asia and Africa.

6. Without going into any historical details, I think this brief résumé should be enough to show the position of Tibet and her relation with China. The doubts that some people, perhaps sincerely, entertain in regard to this status and the troubles that others deliberately and willfully create by making use of these doubts, probably could never have arisen if the Chinese government had adopted the policy of most modern governments, even in relatively recent times, in a total elimination of the "aboriginal" peoples. To have carried out such a policy of genocide against probably less than half a million people in an area of 580,000 square miles (or one person in a square mile), during any one of the powerful dynasties in Chinese history, would scarcely be a difficult thing to do, but China would not be China if she so much as entertained such an idea. China never had dreams of imperialism.

Living under the same government in China today there are some forty national minorities where divergences of language, speech, religion, social customs, and manners are not only tolerated but even encouraged. Tibet is one of these minorities. To argue, as many do, that she is therefore an independent country, with attributes of sovereignty, would completely miss the mark. On the

* *On this treaty Prime Minister Nehru, in his speech in Parliament, said, "We have done nothing better in the field of foreign affairs than signing this agreement over Tibet."*

basis of a similar argument Belgium should be divided into two countries of the Walloons and the Flemish, and Switzerland into three countries. In fact none of the countries of the world can escape from being divided up into as many countries as there are races, languages, or religions. Neither Britain nor France nor Germany nor Soviet Russia nor even the United States could become an exception. And where will India be if such a criterion were used? Six hundred independent states with six hundred sovereignties? India did the only correct and wise thing in recognizing that Tibet is an integral part of China, as she certainly is.

But while she did that, India was at the same time doing things that contradicted that position. Throughout the nineteenth century India was part of the British Empire. Britain also made inroads into Tibet which were *ultra vires*. When India declared her independence, what she should have done then and subsequently was to enjoy the full benefit of her independence within her own boundaries and to retreat from the areas beyond those boundaries into which the British Raj had intruded or trespassed. If India did that, there would have been no border issue with China. But she refused to do so on the ground that what Britain had acquired became as by right India's inheritance. It is this unwise and irrational stand that has brought trouble to China as well as to a number of India's neighbors. That is why one Pakistani writer, Mr. Yussuf Buch, maintained that until there is a Himalaya conference to settle those problems that have been left behind upon the dissolution of the British empire in the Indian subcontinent, there will be continuous friction between India and her neighbors.

By holding fast to what she considers the gift of the British empire to her, India does not remind us of the spiritual grandeur of her great teachers of the Vedas and the Upanishads, but of the pettiness, the "avarice, envy, pride," which Dante condemned in his *Inferno* (Canto V, line 74), or of the "cowardice, selfishness, and hypocrisy," which her own Sri Aurobindo considered India's enemy. What India has done on the border issue is an example of the ruthlessness and cynicism of Kautilya. This is to be expected. For, as I said previously, in the realm of practical politics the Indian has not had the guidance of ethical and moral scruples, which are needed to act as a brake on undesirable action. And political action without restraint becomes the pursuit of unbridled selfishness and therefore undesirable. Even the Bhagavad-Gita does no more than remind the pious Hindu of "my station and its duties"; it does not provide the necessary moral control which makes human relations as well as the relations between nations and peoples tolerable and indeed possible.

According to Kautilya's *Arthasastra,* which has served as the political bible of the Indian for many centuries, there are three types of conquests, all of which are permissible as long as the conqueror can get away with them. They are righteous conquest (righteous from the point of view of the conqueror, of course), conquest for greed, and demonic conquest. *Dharmavijaya, lobhavijaya,* and *asuravijaya.* The first is conquest in which a defeated king is made to render homage and tribute, the second is where an enormous booty is demanded and large portions of enemy territory are annexed, and the third involves political annihilation of a conquered kingdom and its incorporation in that of the conqueror.

In any dispassionate study of the border question between China and India it is difficult not to have the impression that India is practicing one of those three types of conquest or a combination of these to the full extent that circumstances will allow. I shall present the facts as they happened and leave the reader to draw his own conclusions.

First of all, the long and spacious area separating China and India is a kind of borderland. The boundary is nowhere well defined. It is an area of very high mountain ranges, most of which are not inhabited, as in fact they are practically uninhabitable. This geographical fact is true also in varying degrees of the areas separating China from Pakistan, Nepal, Sikkim, Bhutan, Burma, Thailand, Laos, and Vietnam. With none of these countries has this boundary question arisen. Demarcation work had been going on for many years before the new government took power in China. Differences were inevitable, as in all such cases. But with patience, good will, a spirit of give and take, and above all with sweet reasonableness and a desire to maintain friendly relations, it was not

impossible to overcome these difficulties, and they were all overcome. This was as it should be. India became the solitary exception. China showed the same spirit of conciliation. There is reason to believe that she was even more conciliatory to India. The
Chinese leaders were conscious of the long and truly unique record
of a historic relation that goes back two thousand years, always
based on the high level of cultural and spiritual exchange. It was
marred by two occasions of attacks on China and Tibet when India was under Islamic rule, which therefore exonerated her. In
1205, at a time when China was under severe strain, having lost all
her territory north of the Yangtze River to the Jurchens and
Khitans, Ikhtiyar-ud-din invaded Tibet and penetrated the Himalayas with an army of 10,000 men. When he failed to take a gar-
risoned city, he began retreating, only to find that his retreat had
been cut off by a scorched earth policy carried out by the local
population. It was much like Napoleon's retreat from Moscow.
The sad and bedraggled army was cut to pieces, and all but one
hundred horsemen were killed.* The second Indian expedition into
Tibet also caught China at a weak moment. The Yuan Dynasty
had begun to disintegrate, and so Mohammed Tughlak in 1337
thought the time had arrived to surprise Tibet. It was a formidable
army of 100,000 men that he assembled. On they went from the
scorching plains and steaming jungles of India, up the cool and
verdant slopes of the mighty Himalayas, and everyone thought that
it was going to be an exhilarating and pleasant excursion. Then
came the snow and ice. But on they pushed through the mountain
passes formed by the massive and towering precipices until a sudden storm blinded their eyes, which made both advance and retreat
difficult and hazardous. Men and animals began to perish by the
hundreds. It was then that the enemy came out to massacre the
invaders. They were killed almost to the last man. Only two horsemen survived to tell the story.

Now, after more than six hundred years the Indians are at it
again. This time it is no longer the Moslems who are in command. It is the Indians themselves who thought that they had mas-

* Cambridge History of India, *Vol. III, p. 49.*

tered the secrets of modern war and overcome the insuperable difficulties of nature. This was what happened.

The first armed clashes on the border took place between August and October of 1959. The territorial stake was large. The Northeast Frontier, which was previously carved out by the British, out of undemarcated territory, stretches for hundreds of miles to the east of Bhutan; it covers some 35,000 square miles. That had been under the occupation of the Indian troops by 1951. The whole area was regarded by the Indians as a legacy from the British. It was difficult, even impossible, for the Chinese then to prevent the Indians from doing much as they liked, for the Chinese had not yet emerged from the life-and-death struggle of the Korean War. In the west is an area of 13,000 square miles called Ladakh and commonly known as Little Tibet. It has always been Chinese territory. After the clashes in the fall of 1959 the situation promised to become serious. And so, on November 7, the Chinese proposed that further incidents should be stopped and negotiations should begin at once to settle the entire border question. They proposed further that the troops on both sides should withdraw twelve and one-half miles (twenty kilometers) from the line of actual control so that they would not face each other and precipitate further fighting.

This Chinese proposal was promptly rejected by India. That was a pity, for India had everything to gain by accepting it. The Northeastern frontier area had the McMahon Line running along the watershed of the mountain range as its northern boundary. The line had no legal standing and was therefore never accepted by any Chinese government. It was arbitrarily drawn in 1914.* China, by

---

* On the legal status of the McMahon Line I wrote a letter of explanation to the New York Times on November 29, 1959, which it published a few days later. (See Appendix C.) Mr. Christian Herter was then Secretary of State, and one day during a press conference, on being asked what he thought of that boundary, he answered that from "an objective reading we have no basis to go on." In the same conference, which he gave on November 12, 1959, reported verbatim in the New York Times the next day, Mr. Herter also said, "The border . . . has been for many years pretty ill-defined. And I don't think that we have any first-hand knowledge, particularly from the point of view of the northwestern area [Ladakh] with respect to the definitive border that could be rightly claimed by either side." The only possible course of action would be to sit down and negotiate, which was what China persistently

making the proposal, almost implied that she was willing to consider the validity of the line. But India thought that the whole area up to the line was hers already. Next, she intended to put all of Ladakh under Indian control. In other words, she was not going to lose one inch of the entire 48,000 square miles which had been in dispute and never demarcated since time immemorial! Is it unreasonable to assert that this sounds like a page from the *Arthasastra* in a modern version? This is an example of naked aggression on the part of India, and yet for years the American public has been told that China is the invader, not India; China is the aggressor, not India!

Let us turn to the McMahon Line again. That it has no legal status is fully borne out by many maps, some official, and other public documents:

1. The Survey maps of the Government of India for 1938 and earlier (as for instance for 1917) on *Tibet and Adjacent Countries,* followed by the 1943 and even the 1950, 1951, and 1952 editions, made no mention of the McMahon Line. The whole area was marked in all of the maps "undelimited," showing the line of "customary usage," which is very much to the south of the so-called McMahon Line.

2. The map in the 1929 edition of the *Encyclopaedia Britannica* made no mention of the McMahon Line. The 1911 or eleventh edition shows unmistakably that the southern boundary of Tibet is the eastern extension of the southern boundary of Bhutan, which is very much more to the south of the imaginary McMahon Line to appear three years later.

---

wanted but what India as persistently refused. When asked, "Haven't we ever backed the McMahon Line in any way?" the answer was, "I don't think that we have ever backed it." When Mr. Herter was further pressed, with reference to the entire Sino-Indian border, as to whether he wished "to leave the impression . . . that the United States has no view whatever as to the rightness or wrongness of this issue between the two governments," he replied, "I think you are probably correct. I doubt whether any American has ever been on the border to see whether these particular boundaries have been properly delineated or not. We naturally presume [because the United States has backed India all the way] that the claims made by the Indians are entirely valid claims, but from the point of view of what you might call an objective reading, we have no basis to go on."

3. The sixth edition of the *Oxford Advanced Atlas,* compiled by John Bartholomew, cartographer to His Imperial Majesty, made no mention of the McMahon Line. In a letter published in the New York *Times* for November 18, 1962, after hostilities broke out between China and India, Mr. John O. Crane wrote, "This evening [November 14] we pulled out our 1940 *Oxford Advanced Atlas* by Bartholomew to show our 12- and 14-year-old sons the McMahon Line. Imagine our surprise to find, instead, the boundary line between India and Tibet to be virtually that now claimed by China."

4. Prime Minister Nehru's own book *The Discovery of India,* in its third edition of 1951, not only made no mention of the Mc-Mahon Line, but also "put the boundary between northeast India and Tibet somewhat closer to the line the Communist Chinese claim than to the border fixed by India" (New York *Times,* February 27, 1963). In other words, the boundary in Mr. Nehru's own book, published as late as 1951, agrees almost entirely with the boundary in 2 and 3! The book was subsequently withdrawn from sale in New Delhi. The first Indian edition of another book, *The Culture of Southeast Asia* by Reginald Le May, for which Mr. Nehru wrote the foreword, has a map that also shows the line of the Northeast Frontier area lying far to the south, whereupon the newspaper *Flame* "published a front page article this week headed 'This is Treason' and suggesting a Parliamentary inquiry" (New York *Times* of the same date).

5. Henry Twynam, who was Governor of Assam in 1939, had this to say about the McMahon Line in a letter to the London *Times* published on September 2, 1959: "The McMahon Line which sought to secure the main crest of the Himalayas as the frontier [between India and the Tibet area of China], does not exist and never has existed." These are very positive words, and then he went on to say and to explain: "The important point is that Tibetan settlement, and with it Tibetan religion and culture, extends *south of the crests of the Himalayas.* In 1939, acting as Governor of Assam, I was shown by the political officer of the Balipara frontier tract lantern slides which beyond all doubt show the Tibetan characters of Tawang [featured very prominently in

the October, 1962, fighting as an Indian town very much to the south of the McMahon Line; the very name suggests its Chinese origin], which he had recently visited with an escort of Assam Frontier Rifles. Since then, exploration has shown that there comes a point in many areas along this frontier where Assamese contacts give way to Tibetan. Tibetan villages . . . take advantage of the cool areas of grassland [south of the Himalaya crests] suitable for the grazing of yaks. It seems very unlikely that Tibetan villages will be found except in areas adjoining Tibet." This explanation by Henry Twynam is both precise and explicit.

The McMahon Line was part of a major attempt by Britain to detach Tibet from China during the Simla Conference of 1913–14. A "treaty" was signed by Sir Arthur McMahon and a Tibetan representative. There was no Chinese signature attached to the document. Even the Tibetans did not ratify it, and as late as 1947 six Tibetans officially declared nonrecognition of the lands taken by India from Tibet as a result of that line. As for China, she declared from the very beginning of the Simla Conference that "the Chinese would not recognize any treaty or similar documents which might then or thereafter be signed by Britain and Tibet." The Chinese Minister in London made a similar protest on July 3 and 7 of 1914. The Nationalist Government made five further protests in July, September, and November of 1946, January of 1947, and the last one on November 18 of 1949.

This then in a summary way is the record of the McMahon Line.* And yet the American public, through the years, has been

---

* Colonel Sir Arthur McMahon must have had a pair of strong legs and feet, which he used to good advantage. He covered long distances on the boundaries of many countries and became an expert in demarcation. In 1894–96 he drew the boundary between Baluchistan and Afghanistan; in 1903–5 he became arbitrator in the boundary dispute between Persia and Afghanistan. In 1911–14 he became Foreign Secretary to the Government of India. It was in 1913 as the British plenipotentiary at the Simla Conference that he pulled out the line that has since been named after him and became the bone of contention between China and India. He then went to Egypt after the First World War broke out. On his retirement it was both proper and fitting that he was made the Chairman of the London Foot Hospital. Later he was made Chairman of the Liverpool and Manchester Foot Hospitals. He died in December of 1949.

led to believe that the line does exist, and has legal validity and that by coming south of the line China violated India's territorial integrity. The truth is, as we now see, the very opposite. It is India that has consistently violated China's territorial integrity. Occasionally a voice calling for justice and fair play is heard, but only after considerable damage has been done. Here is one letter from the New York *Times* which I should like to quote at some length:

To show that we are a mature people capable of carrying responsibilities in a world where many grave issues are still far from being solved, I hope that we shall exercise the utmost restraint in all that we say and do. Our stature in the world will be immeasurably increased if it is made to understand that what we went in for is merely to see that *justice is done* [my italics] in the solution of its problems. *That is the only stand which is worthy of a great nation like the United States* [my italics]. That is the only way to win respect of the other peoples. We must be unequivocal in our search for fair play. We do not brook bias, prejudice, or offer aid in the cause of injustice.

Take for instance the dispute between India and China. The issue for years has been presented to the American public in lurid colors unfavorable to China, simply because China happens to be Communist. But for a just solution of the dispute, which is what we should insist upon, we must realize that it has nothing to do with Communism at all. The question is basically and essentially one of adjustment in the relationship between China and India. Any other Chinese government, including the Chiang Kai-shek government, will not do any less than what is being done by the Chinese Communist government, if it is in a position to have its wishes respected and enforced. What China is attempting to do is to plead with India not to insist upon enjoying the fruits of 19th-century British imperialism when India herself was a victim of that imperialism. Surely no reasonable man will quarrel with that view. That is the core of the issue, and we have deliberately ignored it, purposely distorted it. Why we must say, with the Indians, that the McMahon Line is the boundary between the two countries when it has absolutely no legal validity whatever is beyond me: it is an example of our continual infidelity to historical truth.

Now that we are, I hope, in a stronger position and therefore better qualified to help in the solution of the world's problems [referring to Soviet Russia's agreement to dismantle the missile bases in Cuba], let us insist that America stands for fair play in the settlement of the border dispute between China and India. That is the only criterion we recognize, for that is the only criterion which will create the image of an America as being above one-sidedness and as being the arbiter of justice. It is a priceless image worthy of our unremitting effort. The moment this is unmistakably clear to the leaders of India, they will change their policy and begin to assume an attitude of sweet reasonableness. As in all great decisions to change from a position that can stand improvement, this one also requires courage. Are we equal to the challenge?

Let us now turn to the western end of the boundary between China and India, Ladakh, which has been likewise causing trouble between the two countries. The following facts are, I think, relevant:

1. One of the early books on Ladakh was by Alexander Cunningham. It was simply called *Ladakh* and was published in 1854. Among other things it says, "The general aspect of Ladakh is extreme barrenness. Seen from above, the country would appear a mere succession of yellow plains and barren mountains capped with snow." "No trace of men nor of human habitations would meet the eye." "Ladakh is the most westerly country occupied by the Tibetan race who profess the Buddhist faith [as distinguished from Hinduism in India]." "Ladakh is derived from the Tibetan word *La-tags.*" "The relations with Tibetans are those of two peoples speaking the same language and holding the same faith." "The great mass of the people of Ladakh [then 150,000, now 200,000] are all of one race or caste. They intermarry and eat together."

These statements, though brief, are eloquent. They show the extreme aridity of the area of some 13,000 square miles, its high altitude, its absence of human habitation in most of its parts, its closeness with Tibet (hence commonly known as Little Tibet), its racial, linguistic, and religious identity with the people of Tibet, thus making them entirely different from the peoples of India.

2. Moorcroft, who lived in Ladakh in 1820–22, in his *Travels,*

which Cunningham quoted, made the statement: "The earlier history of Ladakh is that of Tibet in general as it originally formed one of the provinces of that kingdom, governed as to temporal matters by an independent prince and in spiritual affairs by the Guru Lama or chief pontiff of Lhasa."

3. Sir John Davis, who was the first British Minister to China, in his book *Chinese Miscellanies,* published in 1865, said, "China's frontier is between Ladakh and Kashmir."

4. *The Cambridge History of India* (Vol. I, p. 33) says, "Ladakh is a province of Tibet."

5. G. W. Hayward, in an article on Ladakh in the British Royal Geographical Society *Journal* of 1870 said that Ladakh stretches from the Karakorum Pass to Changchenmo, which is what the Chinese have always said.

6. The official *Survey of India* as late as in its 1943 edition gave no boundary at all. Even in its 1950 map it simply says, "Boundary Undefined."

7. There is, however, a customary boundary based on historical traditions and usage. That was shown by John Walker, who inserted it in his map on orders from the East India Company and included in Major Alexander Cunningham's book cited above.

8. Sir Arthur Lothian, India's representative, in an attempt to limit the boundary between Tibet and Ladakh (1923) said in a letter to the London *Times* (December 11, 1959) that no result was attained. The attempt followed the abortive conference of 1899, when Britain likewise asked China to delimit the boundary. China's position was that it was unnecessary since Ladakh is a part of Tibet and therefore is a part of China.

9. The road in Aksai Chin was originally an old trail used for centuries by China, especially during the Ch'ing Dynasty, to link Sinkiang with Tibet. The Chinese government has now simply widened it into a motor road which was constructed between March 1956 and October 1957 without India saying one word about it. In fact, India was not even aware that such a road was being built in all the twenty months. Is it possible that India was not aware of what went on in its "own" territory? The construction was a major piece of engineering work comparable to the construc-

tion of the Burma Road during the war. It was a "gigantic task." Tens of thousands of Chinese laborers were employed in the work. If the territory through which the road passed was indeed Indian territory, surely one would expect the Indian government to know something of what was going on. If the road took nearly two years to complete, it took another two years before there was any protest from India. This protest came in 1959, and this was how Mr. Nehru explained it to his Parliament on February 23, 1961:

> It was not clear to us whether this proposed motor road crossed our territory. The first suspicion that this might be so came to us in 1957 from a map published in Peking. We did not even then know definitely whether this transgressed our territory . . . As we did not have proof we did not protest then.

Imagine Soviet Russia building a long road through Alaska, and the American government having no knowledge of it till two years after its completion! The fact of the matter is that India never exercised any jurisdiction over the territory it is now claiming.

10. Prime Minister Nehru had previously made three statements before his Parliament on Ladakh, which it would be interesting to compare with the statement quoted in 9:

> a. This is the boundary of the old Kashmir state with Tibet and Chinese Turkestan [Sinkiang]. Nobody has marked it. [August 28, 1959]
>
> b. This area has not been under any kind of administration. [September 10, 1959]
>
> c. During British rule, as far as I know, this area was neither inhabited by any people nor were there any outposts. [November 23, 1959]

These were all statements made after the clashes between China and India had taken place. And now all of a sudden India claims all of Ladakh with its 13,000 square miles as a part of Indian territory! Isn't this a glaring example of the kind of conquest of foreign land that was taught by the *Arthasastra* as early as twenty-three hundred years ago? I think that any fair-minded and reasonable person, reading the list of the ten arguments, can come only to one conclusion: that India has no claim whatever over one inch of the territory of Ladakh, or at least she should sit down and negotiate with China to see how much of the territory she is entitled to. But then, for all the spiritual qualities that India may have taught and developed in its long and distinguished history, I hardly believe that fair-mindedness and being reasonable are among them.

For consider what happened between the clashes in August of 1959 and the open hostilities beginning in earnest on October 20, 1962:

1. On November 7, 1959, when China proposed that negotiations should begin at once to settle the entire border question, and that both parties should withdraw twelve and one-half miles from the line of actual control, India's reply was that no such negotiations could take place until the Chinese had accepted not only the McMahon Line but also the boundary in Ladakh, which India had by then unilaterally defined.

2. Having called the Chinese presence in Aksai Chin (these are Uighur words, not Indian, meaning "the desert of white stones") an "aggression," the Indians now began applying military pressure to oust the Chinese. All through 1961 and 1962 the Indians had some measure of success. They had a series of clashes with the Chinese, who were not prepared for war and offered little resistance. Mr. Nehru became jubilant, and reporting to his Parliament on June 29, 1962, said:

> India had opened some new patrol posts endangering the Chinese posts, and it was largely due to movements on our side that the Chinese had also to make movements. It is well known in knowledgeable circles in the world that the position in this area [Ladakh] had been changing to our advantage, and the Chinese are concerned about it.

3. On August 13 and 14, Mr. Nehru felt confident that India's military measures were yielding results. Perhaps it would not be long before all the territory south of the McMahon Line and all of Ladakh would be in Indian hands. Addressing Parliament again he said:

We have concentrated on increasing our strength, military strength, strength in communications, roads, etc. We have a special border-roads committee which has done very well—I do not know how exactly—thousands of miles in very difficult terrain. We built up our air supply position by getting aircraft—big aircraft—from various countries; we have got some helicopters too, but in the main it consisted of big transport aircraft. There were some from the United States and some from the Soviet Union . . . We improved our military situation, our supply situation, and we have got our troops in various areas there with forward posts. If they [the Chinese] have got nine posts, we have got twenty-two or twenty-three or twenty-four.

4. The Indians, of course, are known to be peace-loving people; they are known also to have made no military preparation so that when open hostilities broke out more than two months later, they were completely taken by surprise! The facts unfortunately show a different picture. While the Indians were building up their military superiority, it would have been too much to expect that the Chinese were sitting idle. Still the Indians had supreme confidence, and it is not therefore difficult to see why they repudiated every proposal for restraint, compromise, or negotiation. What happened on the following dates is revealing. The Indians then were at times even arrogant:

a. On August 22, an Indian said that before any discussions could be held, the border in Ladakh must be restored to the "status quo," that is, the Chinese troops must be withdrawn behind the line as defined by India.

b. On September 13, the Chinese replied that there could be no preconditions. Again they proposed that each side withdraw twenty kilometers (twelve and one-half miles) and that the representatives of the two countries meet on October 15 in Peking and then in New Delhi alternately.

c. On September 19, the Indian note agreed to the proposed date and place but reiterated India's stand that the discussions should have the prescribed object of "defining measures to restore the status quo in the western sector [Ladakh]."

d. On October 3, the Chinese note repeated that both sides should speedily start the negotiations without raising any

objection to the discussion of any question that either side
might see fit to bring up.

e. On October 7, the Indian government rejected the proposal
and summarily called off the meetings, which were scheduled
to begin on October 15 at Peking.

f. Five days later, on October 12, Mr. Nehru announced that he
had instructed the Indian army to "throw the Chinese" out of
the disputed territory. The news media of the world were this
time taken by surprise and regarded Mr. Nehru's words as
being in the nature of an "ultimatum" (*Manchester Guardian*), or "a formal declaration of war" (New York *Herald
Tribune*). The *National Observer* also said, "Last week
Nehru turned to a new and more dangerous task: he ordered
his army to drive the Chinese out of the Northeast Frontier
region."

g. The next day, on October 13, China still called on Mr. Nehru
to "pull back from the brink of the precipice" as she was
"absolutely unwilling to cross swords with India."

h. Mr. Krishna Menon, on October 14, then still India's Minister of Defense, now came into the picture and declared, "We
will fight to the last man, to the last gun."

i. On October 15, Mr. Nehru called on his people for discipline
and sacrifice.

j. On October 16, the Indian Defense Ministry instructed ord-
nance factories to start maximum production even if it meant
three shifts on a round-the-clock schedule.

k. On October 17, China began charging India with repeated
violations of China's air space and invited India to shoot
down any Chinese planes if they flew over Indian territory.

l. India began large scale hostilities along the entire line on
October 20, 1962.*

We can see from this compact summary of dates that it was
India who all along was firm, aggressive, adamant, and unyielding.
There was to be no compromise for her. Her attitude was com-
pletely military. She would not agree to any negotiation that did

---

* *I am indebted to Mr. Felix Greene, to the* Far East Reporter, *and to the*
Monthly Review *of January 1963 for making these facts available to me.*

not in the first place establish the condition that both of the disputed areas of Ladakh and the Northeast Frontier area south of the McMahon Line, every inch of the 48,000 square miles, were Indian territory.

Little did Mr. Nehru or any Indian leader realize that four days after the hostilities began, the Indian lines would crack on all fronts. From that moment on, China spoke. But it was still the voice of conciliation. For on October 24, even as the Chinese troops were advancing, Mr. Chou En-lai still made the attempt to stop the hostilities and to bring the two parties to the conference table. He dispatched a message to Mr. Nehru with a three-point proposal:

1. Both parties affirm that the Sino-Indian boundary question must be settled peacefully through negotiation. Pending a peaceful settlement, the Chinese government hopes that the Indian government will agree that both parties respect the line of actual control along the entire Sino-Indian border, and the armed forces of each side withdraw twenty kilometers [twelve and one-half miles] from this line and disengage.

2. Provided that the Indian government agrees to the above proposal, the Chinese government is willing, through consultation between the two parties, to withdraw its frontier guards in the eastern sector of the border north of the line of actual control . . .

3. The Chinese government considers that, in order to seek a friendly settlement of the Sino-Indian boundary question, talks should be held once again by the Prime Ministers of China and India. At a time deemed appropriate by both parties, the Chinese government would welcome the Indian Prime Minister to Peking; if this should be inconvenient to the Indian government, the Chinese Premier would be ready to go to Delhi for talks.

These considerate proposals for peaceful settlement, couched in language that was courteous and conciliatory from beginning to end, were given to India by China at a time when the Indian forces were reeling back in a war that India herself precipitated. But India's arrogance was unabated. The Indian reply was prompt. It was full of her characteristic pride. It rejected the proposals on the same day they were delivered. Three days later came a supercilious note from Mr. Nehru: "My colleagues and I are not able to understand the niceties of the Chinese three-point proposal, which talks about 'lines of actual control' . . ."

All hope for negotiation and conciliation now vanished. There was no alternative but to continue fighting. Some three weeks later, by November 16, the Chinese troops had scaled the Himalayas and were looking down on the vast plains of Assam, threatening India's rich oil fields and the tea plantations from which she derives her foreign exchange. The main position, south of Tawang, was outflanked, and the still more important city of Tezpur on the Brahmaputra was in panic. Civilians and military personnel alike rushed to seize every available means of transportation to proceed down the river. It was at this point that the entire press of the world was in a state of hysteria. The *New Statesman* in London pronounced the Chinese military operation as being "the most brilliant in history." There was nothing to prevent the Chinese forces from taking Assam—or even Calcutta—if they wanted to. For a bare thirty miles or so Assam could have been cut from the rest of India. Then came one of the most extraordinary events in military history: on November 21, the Chinese government made the announcement that they would unilaterally cease operations on the entire line to begin on the following day, and that from December 1, the Chinese forces would withdraw, on the eastern sector, to a line twenty kilometers *behind the much hated McMahon Line* and, on the western sector, to a line also twenty kilometers *behind* the line of actual control as it existed on November 7 of 1959. The whole world was stunned. Nothing like this had ever happened in any military campaign, ancient or modern. The Chinese government was true to its word. On November 22, all fighting stopped. On December 1, the Chinese forces were back to where they said they would go. It was reported that many Indian people shed tears when the Chinese soldiers left, so well had they been treated. And all the prisoners of war, after their wounds had been attended to, along with all the captured munitions, after they had been properly assembled (and some even polished!) were returned to India.

Fantastic as some of these reports were, I feel that many of them are quite believable, as there was nothing that the Chinese would not do to produce the best impression on the Indian masses and to show them how unreasonable the Indian leaders were. The Chinese never gloated over their military victory. In fact they felt sad that they had to come into armed conflict, and that India's defeat might have even compromised her self-respect. So on December 1, after the Chinese forces were back to where they started from, Premier Chou En-lai at once sent a letter to Prime Minister Nehru in which he reiterated that the task was "to terminate the border conflict, separate the armed forces of the two parties, and create a proper atmosphere so as to settle our boundary differences through negotiations" (London *Times,* December 2, 1962). Moreover, the Chinese government "in taking its decision [on the cease-fire and the present withdrawal] had given full consideration to the decency, dignity, and self-respect of *both* sides" (italics mine).

But India still refused to negotiate. Why does India find it so difficult to accept negotiation? The answer must be sought not in the border dispute itself, but in the general conditions in India. India was then, as she is now, in the most difficult financial, economic, and social circumstances.

It is a matter of common knowledge that India, in carrying out her five-year plans, must depend for their success on the considerable amount of foreign aid from the capitalist countries and especially from the United States.

In 1948, when India had just become independent, the foreign investment was over 2,560,000,000 rupees (a rupee is one-fifth of a dollar). By 1960 it had increased to 6,550,000,000 rupees—150 per cent in thirteen years. British investment during the period doubled, while U.S. investment increased sevenfold. In a document presented by his cabinet to Mr. Nehru in 1951, foreign capital was said to control 97 per cent of India's petroleum industry, 93 per cent of her rubber industry, 90 per cent of her match industry, 62 per cent of her coal mining industry, and 21 per cent of her cotton industry.* Since this amount of foreign investment was still insuffi-

---

* *The* Far East Reporter, *"The China-India Conflict," p. 7.*

cient, the Indian government offered all kinds of inducements to
foreign capital, so that by mid-August of 1962, according to a report by ECAFE, foreign private investment in India rose from
$537,000,000 in 1948 to $1,073,000,000. During the same period, according to a report on the International Cooperation Administration, the United States granted or promised some $4,754,-
000,000. The U.S.-controlled International Monetary agencies
gave an additional $1,844,000,000, or a grand total of $6,598,000,-
000. One single grant of $240,000,000 was given to India, which
was the largest to any single country since the end of the war.

For all these astronomical figures, the Indian Finance Minister in
1960 was already saying, "Our resources are almost at rock bot-
tom; there is no scope for running them further down; we have
thus to depend wholly on foreign aid for the financing of our developing plans."

But here are some comments by the leading journals. The New
York *Herald Tribune* (July 9, 1962) said, "India's third Five-
Year Plan is showing signs of running out of gas." On July 12, it
described Finance Minister Desai's efforts as "touring Europe with
the hope of drumming up more financial aid from the Common
Market countries." In its editorial of August 16 it said, "The
World Bank provided another billion dollars toward India's economic development; without this sizable sum of money India
would be unable to achieve the goals set for the second year of its
third Five-Year Plan." *Barron's* magazine was saying almost the
same thing. "India's Finance Minister," it said on July 16, "is
chasing through the capitals of Europe in pursuit of $220,000,000
to finance the second year of the third Five-Year Plan; meanwhile,
India's liquid assets have been dropping inexorably to new all-time
lows." The *Christian Science Monitor* on November 15 said, "Today India's foreign exchange reserves practically have disappeared
and there is no money to pay for maintenance imports . . . India
is increasing, not decreasing, its reliance on foreign capital."

These figures hardly seem to show that India is making rapid
advances in her work of economic and social reconstruction. The
situation is more like that of China on the eve of the Communist
takeover. The leaders in India were desperate; their only salvation

was a continued dependence on U.S. capital. To acquire this support it was necessary to precipitate a foreign crisis, which would persuade the United States government to multiply its assistance. It was thus *essential* that India should have the border dispute with China. All that she needed to do was to start the conflict by refusing any compromise (hence the persistent rejection of all negotiations, however favorable) and by making demands on China that she knew China could not accept. As for the United States, she had nothing to lose and everything to gain by opening up another cold war front, taking India within her fold, keeping Asia divided, and forging another link in her war against Communism to the north of the subcontinent. This conclusion is borne out by many observers:

1. Mr. Edmund O. Clubb, the last U.S. Consul General in Peking, writing in the *National Observer* for November 12, 1962, made the following remarks: "For the United States, in one sense, the Sino-Indian conflict has been a windfall. Soviet influence in India has been weakened; leftist Indian Defense Minister Krishna Menon, until recently a possible successor to Mr. Nehru, has been toppled from power; and America's ties with India have been strengthened as a result of prompt American military assistance . . . Neutralist India, not pro-Western Pakistan or Thailand, clearly has become the strategic key to southern Asia and principal balance to Communist China." The fear, in other words, of a neutralist India, with her immense population and massive resources, falling within the Communist bloc, could now be laid aside.

2. The *Wall Street Journal* on July 9, 1962, wrote, at the time when the question of aid to India came up for debate in the Congress, "The administration is defending its request for a boost in economic assistance to India on grounds that India is a bulwark against Red Chinese encroachments in the Far East."

3. The New York *Herald Tribune,* in its editorial for August 16, 1962, commented, "The United States and its allies have had to evaluate continued . . . aid to India in relation to a likely development of closer ties between India and the Soviet Union."

4. Senator John J. Sparkman, Acting Chairman of the Senate Foreign Relations Committee, speaking on television on June 9,

1962, said, "We know right now that India is pressing very hard against Communist China on her northern boundary line and her Northeast Frontier . . . I feel we ought not to be discouraging India at the very time she is moving in the direction we have been wanting her to move for a long time."

5. And, finally, during the fall of 1961, when the elections were in full swing, Krishna Menon came out with the ingenuous statement: "The United States has been pushing us to go to war with China."

By rejecting all offers of negotiation or a peaceful settlement of the border dispute with China, it is clear that India has moved decisively to the right politically and into the Western camp internationally. All that these pages attempt to show is that the boundary conflict between China and India is not what is has been made out to be. The ways of international politics are tortuous, but they are also obvious. The United States has in a sense scored a victory in forging another link in the chain of containment around China and in persuading India not only to join in the cold war on her side, but also to do the actual fighting. That is what she wanted, and that is what she has succeeded in accomplishing.

In doing so, the United States has lost the friendship of Pakistan, and reduced the strength of such alliances as CENTO and SEATO, of which Pakistan forms a vital part. Even granting that this is a minor loss—which it is not—are we so sure that in supporting India against China, the United States has gained the long-range objectives of laying the foundations of a peaceful world? Can the ends of peace, in this nuclear age, be attained through antagonism, division, through the pitting of one nation against another, and through policies of containment? I hardly think so. I am still old-fashioned enough to believe with Karl Jaspers * that it is not enough even to find new institutions to solve our basic problems. "We must change ourselves," Jaspers said, "our characters, our moral-political wills." "Man must change if he wants to go on living." "The change can come only in every man's manner of liv-

* Karl Jaspers, The Future of Mankind (Phoenix Books, 1963), pp. 24–26.

ing. Every little act, every word, every attitude in millions and millions of people matter. What happens on a large scale is but a symptom of what is done in the privacy of our lives . . ." "What we need now, in the face of extremity, is more than a better insight: it is a change of heart."

The United States has the prestige, the strength, not only physical strength, but moral strength as well, at least to initiate this change; but she is not doing so. She is not attempting to work for the Great Commonwealth of mankind for which Confucius labored so strenuously twenty-five hundred years ago. That is the pity of it. The Sino-Indian conflict is one out of many opportunities that the United States could have used to bring nations and peoples together. That would have immeasurably increased the prestige of the United States and her stature as a truly great power. Instead of that she has split the nations more widely asunder, hoping thereby to promote her national interests. But it is a shortsighted policy. The United States, as a great power, can and must do something worthier for the cause of world peace.

VII THE UNITED STATES AND JAPAN

UNITED STATES POLICY toward Japan, like her policy toward India, is quite transparent. She is doing everything to build up Japan as a counterbalance to China, just as she is building up Germany as a counterbalance to Soviet Russia. It is again a short-range view. To a limited extent the policy may succeed; but the question is: Will it bring peace, the kind of peace so indispensable in a changed world? That, as it seems to me, should be the only criterion in assessing the value of any major U.S. policy.

But even as a short-range view, I feel the United States will eventually find Japan much more difficult to handle than India. India is relatively easy to deal with because—for all the immensity of her population and of her territory—the facts of her life are exposed and in full view.

When we turn to Japan, we find the issues there are more complicated. This is a defeated nation, not defeated as a small power, but as a big power that had gone far in the creation of a mighty empire. Throughout history, but certainly from the beginning of the Meiji era, every act, every thought of the Japanese, as a nation or as individuals, was directed toward the consummation of this supreme objective. First the success of the war against China in 1894, which led to the cession of Taiwan to Japan. Then the defeat of Russia in 1905, which showed that Western nations were just as vulnerable as any nation. Then came the unexpected bonanza from the First World War of 1914, in which the Western nations were engaged in annihilating one another, so that all of Asia was left to Japan to do with as she pleased. In these gigantic leaps, at intervals of ten years each, the Japanese came to the point of believing that their Emperor was indeed descended from the sun goddess Amaterasu and that the whole Japanese race was of divine origin and meant to dominate the world. The belief grew into a faith, and those of us who were in China through the 1920's and 1930's knew that Japan's plunge to consolidate her holdings into an extensive empire was inevitable. Any nation that tried to obstruct her would have to be crushed. The only nation that was in a position to thwart this grandiose plan was the United States. The climax came with Pearl Harbor, and then the shattering of the dream. Thus, in the image of the Japanese, no matter what and how much America may do for them, it was she who has reduced them to what they are today—a defeated and humiliated nation. The huge population, which was deliberately increased with the intention of filling the spaces of that unrealized empire, must now learn to live and survive on four small islands which make up the original Japan. The feeling of being frustrated and the psychological changes that have already taken place and will continue to exercise great influence on every phase of Japanese life are something that we as outsiders cannot fathom or understand. But to think, as many do, that because the United States is helping to build Japan's economy from the scrap heap to the conditions of an almost affluent society, the Japanese must therefore nurture friendly feelings is, I feel, naïve and premature.

The Japanese are under no illusions as to where they stand. Today there is not much they can do, but tomorrow is not going to be merely an extension of today. Premier Eisaku Sato has already suggested that Japan should play a more active part in Eastern Asia. These are ominous words. The present constitution was drafted by American hands and imposed on the Japanese by the occupation forces. As yet they will not build up their military strength, even if they are permitted to do so. But when the time comes, which will not be far off, they will have that strength whether the permission is given or not. There are already portentous indications. We have been told, for instance, that the ashes of Hideki Tojo, along with those of six others, have been enshrined somewhere up in the mountains facing the Grand Shrines at Ise, and that Tojo is being worshiped as the last of the samurai. This may be only a rumor,* but what is not a rumor is that the whole

* George A. Packard III in his article "Japan's New Nationalism," Atlantic

of the Japanese nation is being galvanized into the belief that it is passing through an unprecedented crisis more serious than the Mongol invasion of the thirteenth century. It was then that Nichiren (1222–1282) came forward to preach a new and vigorous version of Buddhism. Religion it still remained, but it was religion with wide political implications. The appeal, so said Professor Masaharu Anesaki in his scholarly *History of Japanese Religion* (1928),* "found an easy acceptance among the virile warrior classes and the earnest peasants [from whom the soldiers were recruited] of the eastern provinces. Thus we find among the adherents many warriors, and among the monk disciples the sons of warriors." The Nichiren version of Buddhism provided the religious basis for the spread of patriotism among the masses.

What happened in Japan some seven centuries ago has begun to happen today on a much wider scale. The spirit of Nichiren is again being invoked to inspire and guide the phenomenal growth of one of the truly fabulous religious movements in postwar Japan. Its sheer numerical following comprising, as it does, nearly one-sixth of the entire population, or a total of some fifteen million people, shows the immense popularity of this new faith called Soka Gakkai. It is inscribed in four Chinese characters (the Japanese characters are the same) meaning "The Value-Creating Society." †
At the center of this new religious faith is the "Theory of Values" written by the first president of the society, Tsunesaburo Makiguchi, according to whom "the goal of man's life is to find happiness, and happiness results from the accumulation of the values of Beauty, Gain, and Goodness. Ugliness, Loss and Evil are anti-values, which

Monthly, *April, 1963,* said that *"the very existence of the memorial raises questions for the future of Japan."*
* *First Tuttle edition, 1963, p. 204.*
† *The literature on this religious movement is rapidly growing. Reverend Wilhelm Schiffer, S.J., in a meeting of the Asiatic Society in Tokyo on December 10, 1962, gave, I believe, the first systematic and scholarly presentation of the subject. The paper was printed in three issues of the* Asahi Evening News *(in English) from December 11 to 13. Some popular articles include "Japan's New Religion" by Niels C. Nielsen, Jr., Christian Century, October 9, 1957;* Newsweek *magazine, July 16, 1962;* Look *magazine, September 10, 1963; and the New York* Times, *November 10, 1963, May 13, 1964, and November 18, 1964.*

THE UNITED STATES AND JAPAN

lead men away from happiness." Truth finds no place in this scheme of values, for as Makiguchi says, "Truth shows a thing as it is; it is therefore an object of our perceptive faculty of reason, and not of our evaluating faculty. Therefore it is impossible that Truth ever becomes a value."

While ostensibly a religious group, Soka Gakkai is openly bidding for political power, for that is its original purpose. It is already the third-ranking political force in Japan, next only to the ruling Liberal Democratic Party and the opposition Socialist Party. It has fifteen representatives in the Upper House of the Diet and nominated forty-six candidates for the 1964 Diet elections, in addition to over a thousand members in the perfectural and municipal assemblies all over Japan. On November 17 of 1964 the Society published its party platform, which for the moment still stands for peace and disarmament, abolition of nuclear weapons, retention of the no-war clause in the Japanese constitution, but also, significantly enough, a more independent attitude toward the United States, and the establishment of diplomatic relations with Communist China.

No one is in a position to say what the strength of the Soka Gakkai will be five years from now. But the Japanese people are known to thrive on regimentation since time immemorial, and to have a party prospering on intense discipline within the framework of a psychology in which obedience and taking orders has been an entrenched national instinct, it is not difficult to predict that its political beliefs may, in a relatively short period, become a dominating factor in Japanese life. While sight-seeing recently in the many temples in Kyoto and Nara, which are visited every day by hundreds of school children, I was amusingly struck by their extreme orderliness without apparently being told to be so. The children carried identical satchels, almost of the same color, which they arranged in perfectly straight rows before they took off their shoes, which they again arranged in straight rows, to enter the temples. It looked as if they had gone through some paramilitary training; but I was told the orderliness was entirely instinctive.

The Japanese mind is at the opposite end of the Indian. It is without humor and it is in dead earnest to see that a thing is prop-

erly done. Individualism, such as the Americans understand it, or
as it existed in China in her long history until Communism took
over, is practically nonexistent in Japan. The many changes, which
now are a feature of the Japanese scene, and which seem to many the
harbingers of a new mode of living approximating that of the
United States, are, I believe, entirely superficial and have not made
any dent on the Japanese character. Militarism will remain as its
dominant trait; honoring the war dead, as it was done for the first
time since the end of the war at the Yasukuni Shrine in Tokyo,
which is the focus of Japanese nationalism and militarism, will become more frequent from now on; the spread of political parties
like the Soka Gakkai will become increasingly more popular; and
before we know it, all of Japan may be bristling with bayonets again,
for, as Dr. Inazo Nitobe said long ago in his *Bushido: The Soul of
Japan,* the strongest of motives among his people is "the sense of
honor, which cannot bear being looked down upon as an inferior
Power" (p. 117), and Japan today, as international politics go, is
not counted as a superior power. The question is: Is it possible for
Japan to feel that she is not an inferior power without being milita-
ristic? I believe that this is not impossible, but clearly not until conditions are created for her to feel completely secure and to be on
friendly relations with her neighbors.

Japan is not unaware that she is being built up today more as an
instrument of security for others than for herself. She has become
a vital part in the chain of containment against mainland China,
stretching all the way from South Korea to India and beyond. She
is not entirely free to be mistress of her own destiny. But there are
indications that her people are not happy with the situation. Some
of the articles in the political program of the Soka Gakkai are
among those indications. In the meantime, Japanese society continues to go through some significant upheavals, which are inevitable if we recall what went on in Germany after the First World
War. The feeling of frustration has been responsible for the disintegration of some well-established and complex social patterns.
As one Tokyo psychologist said, all Japan has become one
"broken family." The emperor image, since the emperor system
officially renounced its divinity on January 1, 1946, has disap-

peared, perhaps never to return. There is a high incidence of divorce, of juvenile crime, and of suicide. The sense of feudal loyalty is also gone, and with it the cult of bushido, which, for Dr. Nitobe and the people of the older generaton, was the motivating force of Japanese society. The younger generation is now being caught between two worlds, the one dead, and the other powerless to be born. As it is well said by one Japanese youth: "The truth with us Japanese youth today is that there is nothing specific to which we can attach our national enthusiasm. Before the war there was the Emperor and nationalism." But these manifestations of uncertainty cannot survive for long. The efforts of Soka Gakkai and related organizations are seeing to it that nationalism is revived, or at least a national purpose is created to canalize the vitality of the younger generation in a specific direction. When that day comes, will Japanese society be willing to serve merely as an instrument for the satisfaction of the feeling of security for the United States? I hardly believe so. The Japanese will then not only see, but even tell the United States in the face, that it has, as Mr. Walter Lippmann said, "become grossly overextended in regions where it has no primary vital interest," that "United States security and well-being are not involved in Southeast Asia or in Korea and never have been," and that "since the end of the Second World War the United States has been committed far beyond its primary vital interests and far beyond its military and political reach."

Furthermore, with China again a power to be reckoned with, Japan will have to resume the responsibility of following her own interests—and there is every possibility that she will re-establish relations with her neighbor. The China of the future will not be the China that Japan has known, or better still, misunderstood, since the inception of the Meiji era. Her leaders are beginning to realize, I feel sure, that the entire earlier period constituted a colossal misreading of the Chinese character. From now on they will delve much more profoundly into the nature of their historical relationship with China. After all, the ties are so many, and the relationship was so close and intimate from the end of the sixth century. One thing they will discover again, if they have not done so already, and that is that everything of value in Japanese life is somehow inspired by Chinese influences, directly or indirectly. If these values have provided and stimulated the vitality of the Japanese, there should be no reason to doubt that they are not a source of at least equal vitality for those who created them. The evolution of a new pattern of conduct and of a policy drastically different from what was pursued from 1870 to 1945 would seem therefore to be inevitable.

The growth of national power in Japan since the Meiji era has necessitated the cultivation of the legend that everything Japanese is the product of her own creative genius. This concept of a national group, or collectivist soul, was started by Herder in Germany and magnified by Fichte. It proved to be an effective weapon in the war of liberation against Napoleon. It solidified and unified the Germanic peoples as nothing else did so effectively. When Japan decided to launch a policy of modernization, it was the most natural thing that she should take Germany as the model. Study missions were dispatched to all parts of the Western world, but neither the English parliamentary system nor the American constitutional system could satisfy the instinct for centralization or authoritarianism which is a peculiarly Japanese trait. Ever since the early days of the sixth and seventh centuries (during the Sui and T'ang Dynasties), when Japan came into intimate contact with China, all the important measures were initiated and introduced by those in power. The people were made to remain passive; they played no important part. The government welcomed the Confucian ideas of order and duty, but it was cool and unsympathetic to a basic Confucian idea, which was so eloquently developed and espoused by Mencius. All this is being substantiated by the recent studies of Japanese thought and institutions during the Tokugawa period, which immediately preceded the Meiji period. Mencius was all for the people, whom he regarded as being even above the Emperor in the hierarchy of values. He it was who asserted the right of the people to rebel against their ruler when he failed to promote their welfare. This is the famous theory of the mandate of heaven. There is one other Chinese thinker who made little impression on the Japanese, and that is Lao-tze, whose views of living in harmony with the cosmos were considered too anarchistic by the Japanese. The Japanese mind cannot conceive that by doing nothing everything is done. The concept of a First Cause much like Spinoza's *natura naturans* is alien to the completely practical and matter-of-fact mentality of the Japanese. The Indians and the Japanese are thus at opposite poles to one another. The Indians have been in the habit of losing themselves in the rarefied atmosphere of the suprasensuous world, while the Japanese have planted their feet so firmly in their immediate environment that they do not even see the stars above their heads. There are, of course, both advantages and disadvantages in the Japanese mental outlook. One advantage is that the Japanese have a tenacious hold on the realities of life. One disadvantage is that the Japanese in their nearly two thousand years of history have not produced a thinker of first rank, which is a unique phenomenon and one which has a vital bearing on Japan's international life.

Other nations borrow. In fact all nations borrow from one another to enrich themselves. But what they borrow acts as a kind of catalytic agent to stimulate their own thinking. Not so the Japanese. I don't know that scholars have made any specific effort to find out the reason. The Japanese are among the most intelligent people in the world, and yet we find it difficult to name any Japanese who, as thinker and searcher for truth, attains a position of real distinction or honor. There must be a reason. What then is the reason? My own explanation is that in the development of human thought philosophical speculation has usually followed in the footsteps of the earlier mythological beliefs, whose validity it began to doubt and then to repudiate. This act of repudiation crystallized itself in the exposition of its own position by a systematic presentation of its own ideas, and it was these ideas that formed the beginnings of philosophic inquiry. Thus the Milesian and Eleatic schools of thought in ancient Greece followed in the wake of the Homeric mythology. The Upanishads in India were a logical and speculative development from the somewhat vague and inchoate thought of the vedas. The flowering of philosophic thought in China in the sixth and subsequent centuries B.C. followed the mythological presumptions of an earlier age. In the case of the Japanese, who had their Amaterasu, and their gods and goddesses, philosophical speculation might conceivably have developed in the natural course of events. Before they had this chance, however, they received the sudden and overwhelming impact of a mature civilization from the Chinese mainland, one which had already had two thousand years of history behind it, and which apparently provided all the answers that the Japanese wanted to know, thus making the development of their own independent thinking superfluous. They therefore never had a philosophy of their own, nor did they develop the capacity for creative and original thinking. At the time of the T'ang Dynasty (618–906) Japanese culture was still in its very early and, I may add, crude stage of development, while that of China was already cosmopolitan, profusely influential, and in a state of unrivaled excellence. The Japanese at the time did not even have a written language, and they were willing to go so far as to adopt and take over bodily a monosyllabic written language, which hardly seemed to fit their own Ural-Altaic, polysyllabic spoken language. That shows that the Japanese were prepared to appropriate anything from the mainland so long as they could thereby absorb the refinements of a civilization which had become embodied in the Chinese language. From that moment on, hardly anything was done in Japan without prior reference or consultation with what had already been done in China.

I say all this neither to glorify China nor to belittle Japan. Similar historical parallels have appeared elsewhere, though perhaps not on so massive a scale. When Virgil wanted to trace the lineage of his people back to the Greeks, and when Marcus Aurelius wrote in Greek rather than in his own Latin tongue, we do not thereby say that the Romans were appropriators. In the case of the Japanese, as we know all too well, they did draw freely and copiously upon the Chinese. Surely there was nothing wrong in this, but for some reason they developed an inferiority complex, which they have tried unconsciously to overcome or eliminate ever since. It has become a profound psychological problem. It is because of this that Dr. Nitobe said that his people "cannot bear being looked down upon as an inferior Power." It is also because of this that they always wanted to show that they could be better than China. How? By military force. This wholly irrational feeling explains to a very large extent the behavior of the Japanese toward the Chinese in modern times.

Japan's first attempt to evolve a civilized society was when Prince Shotoku Taishi introduced what is commonly known as the seventeen-article constitution, toward the end of the sixth century. It was not so much a constitution in the ordinary sense of the term as the application of the Confucian system of morals applied to government. Overnight Japan was converted, as Sir George Sansom said, from a tribal organization to a centralized country. Then came in rapid succession a whole series of innovations, always based upon some existing Chinese model, which brought Japan under the influence, power, and beauty of the older civilization. The first mission from Japan to China arrived in 630. In less than two hundred years there must have been some twenty official missions in addition to many private ones. The Taikwa or Great Reform (645–650), introducing a new system of land tenure, of provincial and local government, of taxation, and of the registry of population, was based on the system that then prevailed in the T'ang Dynasty. The Chinese language had been adopted earlier, and the first Japanese book, written entirely in Chinese, was the *Kojiki* (682). The first capital of Japan at Nara, modeled on Changan, was built in 710. Not only was the architecture of the government buildings and temples and the laying out of the streets entirely in the Chinese style, but all the laws, ordinances, public documents, and even the costumes of the courtiers, their etiquette, ranks, appellations, and political doctrines were of Chinese inspiration.

When shortly afterward the Japanese government was moved and established in Kyoto in the Heian period, there was an upsurge of interest in Buddhism, but the different sects followed on the lines of those already in existence in China. The Tendai sect was the Chinese Tien-tai; the Shingon was the Chinese Cheng-yen; the Jodo was the Chinese Chin-tu or Pure Land; and the Zen was the Chinese Ch'an. Of course every time a new sect was established in Japan, even though it had a Chinese prototype, something new and distinctively Japanese emerged. Men like Honen Shonin (1133–1212) or Shinran (1173–1262) or Nichiren (1222–1282)

or Eisai (1141–1215) or Dogen (1200–1253) or Soseki (1275–
1351) were all profoundly Japanese, and their teachings were conditioned by the special circumstances with which they were surrounded. But the most powerful impact of Chinese thought on
Japan was yet to come. During the Tokugawa regime, which enjoyed a long period of some 260 years of internal peace, just before the beginning of the modern Meiji era, Japan was absorbed in
the study of two schools of Confucian thought led respectively by
Chu Hsi (or Japanese Shushi 1130–1200) and Wang Yang-ming
(or Japanese Oyomei 1473–1529). During this period there is a
long and distinguished list of Japanese scholars and thinkers whose
teachings still exert a powerful influence on the older generation of
Japanese today.*

The relationship between China and Japan in this period formed
one of the happiest chapters in their history, and I feel sure that
there are still many in Japan who wish that this relationship could
be restored. There was, for instance, one scholar from China whose
relationship with Japan transcended all national differences. He
was a loyalist of the Ming Dynasty who left China under Manchu
rule to live in Japan. Those were the days when Japan closed her
doors against all foreigners, but Chu Shun-shui was not considered
a foreigner. He had a Japanese student Ando Seian (1622–1701)
who negotiated successfully with the governor on Chu's behalf for
a permit to stay. The story is so beautiful that it is best to quote
Chu's own words in a letter to his son. "Ando shared with me his
rice allowance of 80 piculs, sending me 40 and visiting me twice a
year. He lived frugally, wearing plain clothes and feeding on
coarse rice and vegetables. His best meal would consist of a dish of
small fish. He had a Chinese pan to cook his food in, but it often
looked dusty and rusty because nothing was ever in it. His friends
would reprimand him, but he cared little for what they said, because he was happy with his poverty and pleased with his *tao.*" So

---

* These thinkers include Fujiwara Seika (1561–1619), Hayashi Razan
(1583–1657), Yamazaki Ansai (1618–1682), Kaibara Ekken (1630–1714),
all of the neo-Confucian school; Nakae Toju (1608–1648) and Kumazawa
Banzan (1619–1691) of the Oyomei or idealist school; and Yamaga Soko
(1622–1685), Ito Jinsai (1627–1705), Ogyu Sorai (1666–1728) and Muro
Kyuso (1658–1734).

strong was the influence of Confucius on the life of Ando. Ando himself also gave an account of what happened. "When I learned," he said, "that the governor has given you [Chu] permission to stay, I was so glad that I could not sleep. I returned to my house and decided to give half my rice allowance to you . . . You said it was too much. As my teacher I regard you as holding a position equal to that of father and sovereign [how Confucian!]. Since a man can die for either of them, that matter of rice is not worth mentioning. I should have kept only a third for myself, but knowing that you would not accept it, I took the middle road and divided my rice allowance in two halves. Because you are honorable and righteous, you will refuse anything which comes from unclean hands. I hope you will not consider my offer as coming from unclean hands." *

Chu Shun-shui lived on in Japan, took a Japanese wife, and died at the ripe old age of eighty-two (1600–1682). But before he died, he performed one valuable service for his host country. Among his students was Tokugawa Mitsukuni (1628–1700), in whom Chu stimulated a deep interest in Chinese history. Since Chu's steadfast adherence to the Ming cause was a symbol of his unswerving loyalty and patriotism, Mitsukuni had him as his chief adviser in the rewriting of Japanese history, and that has had a profound influence in the subsequent development of the Japanese nation.

This sketch of the relationship between the Chinese and the Japanese is based on historical facts that go back to the very early days of Japanese civilization. I see no way in which these facts can be concealed or twisted, and yet this is what is often attempted. Scholars, both native and foreign, have tried to show that the gagaku or kabuki is Japanese, haiku is Japanese, Sesshu and Japanese painting are Japanese, the frescoes of Horyuji were Japanese, Todaiji and all the temples are Japanese, the women's dress is Japanese, sitting on tatami is Japanese, sake is Japanese, go-chess is Japanese, the written language is Japanese, Zen Buddhism is Japanese, and so on down the list. Of course they are Japanese or

* *Tokutomi Iichiro:* Tokugawa Bakufu, *Part II, Vol. 16.*

have a Japanese flavor, but does it make them less Japanese because their roots happen to have sprung from the Chinese soil?
They have been with the Japanese for so long that they have become
an essential part of the Japanese soul. But their Chinese origins
cannot be repudiated any more than the Western nations can repudiate the spirit of inquiry of the ancient Greeks or the Roman feeling for law and political organization. The younger generations of
postwar Japan are now tampering with these established values by
substituting for them those of the West. All they have done is to
increase their frustration, to create a deeper want of direction and
purpose, a greater spiritual vacuum, more chaos, confusion, and
uncertainty.

There are, as it seems to me, three ways in which the problem of
Japan can be solved. First, the Japanese can choose to turn their
backs on the past, as many of them are doing, and follow the
West. A visit to the larger cities in Japan, especially Tokyo, would
seem to confirm that this is the road that the Japanese have
chosen. It is also the road that the West would like the Japanese to
choose. In many respects, this policy has succeeded. The emperor
system, for instance, with its concept of divinity, was obviously
out of keeping with the modern world, and has now been di-
vested of its pretensions. The raising of the status of women was
a desirable act. But care should always be taken to exercise judgment and good sense: changes should not be made simply because
they happen to be of Western origin. In this regard, the Japanese,
thanks to centralized control, have a much better record to show
than the Chinese, many of whom, especially during the last half-
century of missionary penetration, became pale shadows of themselves or of their forebears—no longer Chinese, they had lost their
identity. The Japanese government, on the other hand, has always
taken matters into its own firm hands. While encouraging and promoting science and technology on an extensive scale, it has allowed
only such Western ideas and institutions to come into contact with
Japanese life as it deems to be useful. But the bars have been taken
down in the postwar period, and anything may happen. Even so,
the dangers are likely to be superficial, and the present social
disturbances in many cases are likely to decrease rather than in-

crease in severity, particularly when there are such organizations as the Soka Gakkai to act as watchdogs.

However, if these reactionary movements succeed too easily and too soon, there is danger of another kind. They may lead to a recrudescence of the military spirit, which is the second way of solving the Japanese problem. The re-emergence of militarism in Japan has always been a great possibility. Its roots lie deep in the past, and old habits die hard. Many Japanese think that their country must go through another war to regain her honor. Instead of an effort to curb the spread of militarism, there now seems to be every encouragement of it. One recent event, for instance, has come as quite a surprise to many who are studying the Japanese scene. On December 7, 1964, the Japanese government saw fit to confer the highest decoration for a foreigner, the First Class Order of Merit of the Grand Cordon of the Rising Sun, on General Curtis LeMay, Chief of Staff of the United States Air Force. In March, 1945, U.S. planes, under orders from the General, ravaged ten square miles in the industrial center of Tokyo; later, as Chief of Staff of the U.S. Strategic Air Force, he played a part in the atomic bombing of Hiroshima and Nagasaki. The award is something that only the Japanese can understand. What went on in their minds before they arrived at the decision? What kind of logic did they follow? The Japanese are not unaware of the power and influence of General LeMay in the United States. Is the award an indication of the exaggerated respect that Japan still has for military might? Or is it an earnest of what Japan proposes to do in the military sphere?

For a full century China was weak, offering a constant invitation for Japan to take advantage of the situation. The Japanese should have been the first people to understand the vital forces that have created Chinese history, for no two peoples have been so close. If only they had asked themselves why a civilization has lasted as long as that of China, they probably would not have been so reckless. If China did not have within her the strength to resist the pressure that was brought against her through the ages, she would have perished many times over. The Japanese certainly realize now that the China of today is no longer the China of the nineteenth century. Whether she is Communist or not is immaterial, though it is the Communist regime that has put her where she is: the important thing is that China has suffered a dramatic turn in her fortunes, so characteristic of her long history. The last ebb in Chinese history began shortly after the death of Chien Lung, and now we can confidently say that it is at the beginning of another tide. I believe it will be the better part of wisdom for Japan, as a very close neighbor and disciple, to be cognizant of this fact and shape her conduct accordingly. I have previously referred to Dr. Nitobe's remark, because in a sense it is quite representative of Japanese thinking. Japanese scholars who are well versed in Chinese political thinking should be aware that the concept of *wang tao,* to which all political action should be directed, means the attainment of justice among nations and the diffusion of moral ideas in the international order. It is this *wang tao,* as against *pa tao,** which elevates the stature of a people, not its military might. China has not forsaken that point of view at any period of her history, though her own weakness and inability to enforce it have at times made it inoperative. But it will prevail just as soon as the opportunity arrives.

When Chinese history is read and understood in the proper light by the Japanese, as it will be, there is no doubt that Japan will proceed on the third way to the solution of her present problems. Any repudiation of her past, which the first solution envisages, will destroy her best instincts: it will mean spiritual suicide for the Japanese people. To become a military power again, as suggested by the second solution, would mean physical suicide. The most rational, the wisest and the most sensible course of action open to Japan is to explore all the possibilities of her racial and national heritage, to preserve and keep untarnished her historical personality, and to proceed with her plans for modernization in keeping with that heritage and personality. The Japanese should have as little reason to nurse an inferiority complex as the English have because their roots go back to ancient Greece and Judea, or the Americans because many of their ideas and institutions are of British and Continental origin. The original Chinese elements in Japanese culture

---

* *Domination over other nations through military power or force.*

have been there for so long and are so well blended that they have become for all practical purposes Japanese. It is essential that the Japanese get rid of this inferiority complex. One does not get rid of it by concealment or suppression, but by exposure and by frank and open acknowledgment. After all, an American does not have to bolster his pride and sense of honor by saying that the language he uses is not of English origin, but is America's own. This is precisely what the Japanese have been taught to do, in their national educational policy, in regard to the Chinese language, which they use. When I told my Japanese friends that I did not understand Japanese (I admit that with shame) and began to communicate with them through the Chinese written characters, they were surprised. "But you said you do not understand Japanese," they said. They were unaware that Japanese characters are Chinese!

Peace, tranquillity, serenity, economic prosperity, refinement of manners, beauty of conduct—there are few countries in the world that are blessed with these qualities all at the same time as in Japan. Indeed, rather than having an inferiority complex, the Japanese have every reason to feel superior. Japan must stay neutral, discard militarism, cultivate friendly relations with all the nations of the world—and show them how a peaceful country, free from bayonets but secure within its boundaries, however limited they may be, can achieve the happiness and advancement of its people.

There are cycles in the affairs of men that are beyond human control. The dominance of the Western world by the descendants of the Greco-Roman tradition has lasted some five hundred years. It has brought glory, but also misery and exploitation, which have come from its emphasis on power and physical strength. With the next century, the Eastern world will have the unique opportunity of putting into practice again what it has always taught in the past. It will have completely mastered science and technology, which are the supreme accomplishments of the West, but while making use of them, they will no longer be tools of torture or weapons of oppression. Mencius said long ago that physical force has never subdued anyone: it is the conquest of the heart that makes conquest complete and final. It is the only kind of conquest suited to the atomic age. There is no reason why Japan should not be a leader in this new era. She has inherited a rich and bountiful past, which she shares with the older neighbor; she has all the conditions for happiness and prosperity.

Where then does the United States come in? As in the case of India, the United States can make it possible for Japan to play this role—as a reconciler of the East and the West, of the old and new. This is what China has always sought to do. With a complete understanding thus established between these two peoples, they can bravely go forward to help create a world rich in its diversity, with each human segment proud and free to develop its own unique qualities while respecting and admiring the accomplishments of the other segments. Why must there be domination and conquest, to be followed by certain destruction, when unhampered development, each according to its genius and mutual consideration, is the road to the fulfillment of life?

EPILOGUE

T HE HISTORIC ROLE of the United States is to bring all nations together within the framework of genuine co-operation.

The image of the United States continues to be embodied in the ideals of the Declaration of Independence. If these ideals collapse, we collapse with them. The image cannot be long sustained if all we aim at is promotion of national self-interest.

I do not think and believe, therefore, that the interests of the United States are served by the acceptance of the advice of a distinguished former Secretary of State, who only recently, in a speech given at Amherst College in the early part of December 1964, said, "The discussion of ethics and morality in our relations with other states is a prolific cause of confusion." Exactly the reverse is true. It is the absence of ethical or moral values that is responsible for all the confusion in our international relations. Mr. Dean Acheson went on to say, "The righteous who seek to deduce foreign policy from ethical or moral principles are as misleading and misled as the modern Machiavellis who would conduct our foreign relations without regard to them." There is no compromise for the moral law. Either one is moral or one is immoral. Mr. Acheson's advice is a reversion to Machiavellianism and to the principles of Kautilya. The righteous cannot be misleading, nor are they misled; they become so only when they are not righteous enough.*

---

* The influence of Mr. Dean Acheson on the present Administration is still being felt, but I do not think it wholesome. He is all for the American "image" being able to take care of itself. And he has no use for moral or ethical "interference" with the course of international affairs. In a New York Times Magazine article (July 4, 1965) Mr. Henry F. Graff made the remark: "Bundy [McGeorge] said he had come to accept also what he learned from Dean Acheson—that, in the final analysis, the United States is the engine of mankind,

215

John Donne said long ago that "no man is an island, entire of itself; every man is a piece of the continent . . ." It is only in that sense that our new international order can be conceived. It does not mean the imposition of the will of one nation on the rest of the world. It must be a plurality of wills. Such a society was attempted in the China of twenty-five centuries ago. China was then divided into as many states as there are in modern Europe. The same confusion and conflict of national interests prevailed. Fighting among these states was continuous until Confucius made his appeal to those great moral values of benevolence, humanity, justice, equality, and humility. He succeeded beyond all measure. It is true that he did not see the result of his teachings during his own lifetime. But he set a norm of conduct to which the states at first grudgingly, then willingly conformed. When the Han Dynasty (221 B.C.–A.D. 220) appeared, that unity became an accomplished fact. It has remained ever since. There were, of course, moments

---

and the rest of the world is the train." The Times *editorial on the same day rightly took exception to this view. "Taken literally," it said, "this notion can be interpreted by Communist propagandists and by many non-Communists as supporting the charge that the United States seeks world domination. There is an implicit arrogance in this idea. . . ." Whereupon Mr. McGeorge Bundy, sensing the mischievousness of his unhappy statement, immediately followed up with a letter next day that Professor Graff "honestly misunderstood me." "We believe," he continued, "as nearly all Americans believe, that the United States must act with full respect that other nations have their own purposes and energies." Did Prof. Graff really misunderstand Mr. Bundy? For following the engine-train idea he took the trouble to explain that Mr. Bundy wanted him to know that "he was not expressing chauvinism, but simply passing judgment on the usefulness to the world of American energies." This is as if Prof. Graff wanted to make it quite clear that Mr. Bundy was not being misquoted. It is because later, Bundy thought, it might be taken to mean what the editorial interpreted, that he felt uneasy, turned away from the Achesonian concept, and issued a new statement. However that may be, I think that the engine-train idea does dominate a good deal of White House thinking. In the otherwise marvelous civil rights speech of March 16, 1965, heard throughout the world, Mr. Johnson made this remark: "This is the richest, most powerful country which ever occupied this globe. The might of past empires is little compared to ours." I wonder how non-Americans reacted to such a sentiment. Why talk of "occupying this globe" as if it were America's private property? Besides, the Roman Empire, in its days, was perhaps, in relation to the rest of the then known Western world, even richer and more powerful, but that did not prevent it from precipitate decline not long afterward. As the poet said:* Mais où sont les neiges d'antan?

of weakness when political unity was rent asunder, but the basic cultural and spiritual unity that was born of the Confucian ideals always prevailed. That was what Professor Tawney observed. As one minister in the Han Dynasty said to the Emperor: "Sire, you can *conquer* the empire on horseback, but you can never *rule* the empire on horseback."

I believe human beings are basically reasonable. I do not think that *Ta Tung* (the Great Commonwealth), as conceived by Confucius, is beyond our reach. There is in our atomic age no alternative—either that or the total destruction of mankind. When the Great Way prevails, said Confucius, there is justice for the entire world.

In Isaiah it is also said, "Come now and let us reason together." Many find this as a key to the understanding of President Johnson's personality. If this is the case, we have reason to hope that great things will come out of the present Administration. It is in this hope that I propose the following Five-Point Program, to reduce the existing tension between the United States and China:

First, let us look at China. It is no secret that the United States is the one country to which she is now most hostile. Every once in a while, in those massive rallies and demonstrations in the huge square in front of the T'ien An Men, the United States is singled out as the citadel of imperialism; and every man, woman, and even child is made to believe that there can be nothing more wicked than American imperialism. The Chinese have always had a sense of moderation, and they have reason to be proud of it. Not so long ago there was a bond between the two countries, even to the point of being sentimental; today there is intense animosity. What has happened to bring about so dramatic a change? Is it the nature of Communism to hate? It may be so. But in the case of China this hate and anger against the United States is not something vague and general: it is selective, it is directed and concentrated on the *policy* of the U.S. government and not against the people. The difference is an important one, and is illustrated tellingly by what happened to Mr. Felix Greene, who has now made three trips to the Chinese mainland. On one occasion when he found himself in one of those massive rallies in Peking, the crowd broke out in the usual anti-

American manifestation. He became uneasy, as anyone from
America would. After the demonstration was over, the crowd directed their attention to this tall and lanky figure, whom everyone
suspected to be an American. One person asked him if he was
from the United States; Mr. Greene did not deny it. And then
something most unusual happened. Instead of attacking him, the
crowd started to laugh. They were overcome by the humor of the
situation and left Mr. Greene in a state of bewilderment and em-
barrassment, but completely unharmed. In other words, even
though the people were in a state of excitement, they had enough
presence of mind to know that an individual American has nothing to do with the policy of his government.

Now, with regard to the reason for the widespread hostility toward
American policy, everyone in China understands that from the
day of the success of the revolution and the establishment of the
new government at Peking, not one moment has passed in which
America has not done something to hurt or even to destroy it. Nonrecognition and American effort to prevent China from being represented at the United Nations are relatively minor issues. But the
fact that the United States, through superior military force, violates China's territorial sovereignty by refusing to allow Taiwan to
come back to the mainland, that the United States has frequently
violated China's national sovereignty by flying over China's air
space or going into China's territorial waters to perform acts of
espionage, that the United States has consistently forged a ring of
iron around China through her policy of containment, that the
United States has egged on China's neighboring countries to
assume a positively aggressive and antagonistic attitude toward
China as in the case of India or at least an unfriendly one as in the
case of Japan, that the United States has used every effort to isolate China by cutting off trade with the rest of the world, that the
United States conducts a continual and sustained progaganda
against China, that the United States stations the powerful Seventh
Fleet in the western Pacific close to the Chinese coast, that the
United States piles up all its lethal weapons in Okinawa and Guam
for possible use against China—it is these and many other things
that America has done and is still doing that have stimulated and

brought about this anti-American feeling. It would be unreasonable
and inhuman, as anyone would think, for China to remain indifferent or be friendly to America if America in the first place and
from the very beginning has conducted a policy of unremitting hatred and provocation toward China. And then to add insult to injury
America blandly tells the world that she will not consider changing
her policy if China does not do so as a prior condition. Is not this
putting the cart before the horse? What else is there for China to do
but to respond with similar hostility if America is so relentless, so
persistent, so stubborn and so unyielding in her policy of hatred
toward China? Of course one can always say that when one's right
cheek is struck, one can turn the left cheek. But the Chinese will
reply that they have not become that hypocritical, that unfortunately
they are not Christian, and that it is for the United States as a Christian country to do so. Whatever the circumstances may be, we have
here a classic example of a vicious circle, which must be broken before there can be any reduced tension between the two countries or
any prospect of peace between them. And to show that the United
States *is* a Christian nation, it is right and proper that she should
take the first positive step and undo what she should not have done
in the first place. This leads to the second thought in our Five-
Point program.

2. The United States must assume the initiative in bringing
China and India together on the border issue, and not use it as a
weapon. More than that, the United States should realize that the
path of salvation for India is not in foreign wars or expansion, but
in building up a sound economy and a viable political system, in
training a proficient bureaucracy unhampered by corruption and
nepotism. India's salvation is internal: it cannot be achieved by
taking on hazardous external adventures, for these lead directly to
ruin and destruction.*

* *The now 30-year-old Rajmohan Gandhi, grandson of the Mahatma, on
returning to India to place his services at the disposal of his country, made
some significant remarks during an Indian Independence Day address in London on August 15, 1964, which were reported by the New York* Times *the following day. He said he intended to enter Indian politics "if they [the people
of India] will have me" as their leader. "I am determined now to mobilize the
Indian masses." Earlier in the year he had organized anticorruption protest*

The world has profound sympathy for what India has gone through in history. "Everything of any value" [in India], said one historian, "was taken long ago by the conquerors who have been coming here for a thousand years. They took the strength from the soil, the virtue from the women, and the willpower from the men. They left nothing behind but vices and weaknesses—the winning pliancy of slaves, the intrigues of degenerates, the superstitions of peasants. India is like an empty tomb: the gold gone, the jewels gone, nothing left but bones and a bad smell." The United States would do well to persuade the Indian leaders to avoid any foreign entanglements—for the border question with China is a relatively minor question, which can easily be solved through negotiation— and to concentrate instead on the much needed domestic reforms. I am convinced that such a step, the very opposite of what is being done today, will immeasurably enhance the stature and moral prestige of the United States.

In Japan's case, the United States has more to gain in the long run by giving Japan the freedom to pursue her own policy even to the extent of establishing a *modus vivendi* or normal relations with China. In this connection, Mr. George F. Kennan, for all his stand on containment, has made some remarks that are worth considering: *

> There is first [says Mr. Kennan] the fact that the establishment of better relations between Japan and the countries of the Asian mainland is, in the long run, an essential requirement, politically and psychologically, of Japanese policy. The instincts, outlooks and needs of the Japanese people simply will not tolerate for long

---

marches in six Indian states. He felt that the one, single corrosive force in Indian public life was corruption among its officials which would take nothing less than a revolution to root out. But he said he sought "a peaceful revolution where the energies, the feelings and desires of the masses are waiting to be tapped." He concluded: "There is no need for corruptible leadership in India. Corruption destroyed 40 to 60 percent of the nation's revenue!" Indian official circles in London promptly denied the charges. Mr. Gandhi has not been heard of since his return. To a Chinese ear the words and their denial sound familiar and ominous. The situation in China was similar before the Communist takeover.

* George F. Kennan, "Japanese Security and American Policy," Foreign Affairs Quarterly, October, 1964, pages 25–26.

anything that appears to be an effort to enlist Japan as a passive instrument in an all-out cold war to which no one in Japan can see a favorable issue generally and which seems to imply the indefinite renunciation by Japan of all hopes for a better relationship with the mainland. Anything of this sort can only exacerbate the divisions already existing in Japanese society, increase the difficulties of the Japanese Government, and be destructive of the foundations of the United States–Japanese relationship . . . [The United States] will have to shape the mutual security relationship between the two countries in such a way that it conduces to overcoming rather than prolonging the division now so unnaturally prevailing between Japan and her mainland neighbors.

Many of us may have our doubts—some Japanese have them, too—as to how much Japan would stand to gain, in the present circumstances, from the cultivation of closer relations with Communist China, in particular. But if these doubts have merit, this is something the Japanese will have to discover for themselves, as a lesson of experience. It will not do just for us to assure them of it. It need not be considered that American policy has failed if the effort to create a better relationship between Japan and the mainland proves abortive. What is important is that American policy should not be permitted to appear as an obstacle to the effort itself, but should rather reflect a generous tolerance for special Japanese needs and feelings, and should let it be demonstrated, at every point, that if there are limits to the possibilities for improvement of Japan's relations with the mainland, these lie in the outlooks and policies of the mainland powers themselves and not in the preoccupations of American policy-makers.

I believe this represents a fresh point of view, which will do much to enhance the effectiveness of U.S. policy and the prestige of the American government. At present we have been told there are something like two hundred U.S. military bases in Japan. What are they there for except to arouse the animosity of the Japanese? Japan's two most important naval bases are visited periodically by Polaris submarines. What purpose does this serve except to stir up demonstrations and to accentuate the Japanese feeling of inferiority? *

---

* *"Only a few days ago . . . the* Seadragon *docked again at Sasebo. Im-*

222

EPILOGUE

Japan has no reason to worry about her security for a long time to come, unless she herself begins to pursue policies that are provocative and inimical. Her defeat in the last war has actually become an advantage to her. U.S.–Japanese relations have never been better. For a long time before Pearl Harbor, these relations were Japan's major concern, a problem of her own making. That problem has now been solved. Her relations with Soviet Russia present no difficulties. The past conduct of Japan toward China has nothing to justify it except that China was powerless to resist. But China shows no vindictiveness.* She looks for understanding and friendship in the future with the Japanese. It is up to Japan herself to decide what the days ahead will bring. If she keeps her ambitions under control and forsakes her military posture, as we hope she will, she will really become one of the most enviable countries in the world. But unfortunately, nations like individuals are not consistently wise. One problem is already on the horizon. In the debate about the future of Taiwan, Prime Minister Eisaku Sato has given the impression—some say more than the impression—that Japan looks forward to a day when she may repossess the island. If the Prime Minister does actually stake such a claim, he will be performing the greatest possible disservice to his own people and to the cause of world peace. The question of Taiwan today is the most touchy, the most sensitive single problem in international affairs so far as China is concerned. Japan is not steering away from it and even tries to take advantage of it. The of-

---

mediately, 10,000 people gathered there in militant protest, thousands more demonstrated throughout the country, and countless others were silently indignant. Can we blame them? . . . Even today, more than 20 years after Hiroshima and Nagasaki, many citizens suffer from radiation poisoning and malformations . . . the submarines are dreadful reminders of past horrors and warnings of an even more horrible future. It is inconceivable to me, as an American citizen, that those responsible for the Seadragon visit could be so arrogantly indifferent to the damage it has done to the prestige of the United States and to our friendship with other nations." Theodore Brameld, writing from Fukuoka, Japan, in a letter published in the New York Times of February 15, 1965.

* This has been carried to a ridiculous extreme. The government under Chiang Kai-shek has not asked one penny of reparation from Japan after nearly fifteen years of massive destruction and the killing, often in the most cruel form, of millions of Chinese!

ficial spokesman for the Japanese Foreign Office was reported to
have said (New York *Times,* December 24, 1964) that he was
"firmly convinced" that the United States would protect Japan from
Communist Chinese nuclear threats." How he could have made such
a statement when the Chinese authorities have repeatedly said that
they are for the total destruction of all nuclear power as a military
weapon, is really beyond understanding. The Chinese government
only wants the world to realize that it is not beyond its power to
make the weapon, but that having done this she is interested in
total destruction by all the powers which now possess it. In this connection some of the remarks made on October 16, 1964, when China
exploded her first nuclear bomb, should be reassuring:

> The Chinese government has consistently advocated the com-
> plete prohibition and thorough destruction of nuclear weapons.
> Should this have been realized, China need not develop the nuclear
> weapon . . .
> The atom bomb is a paper tiger . . . This was our view in the
> past and this is still our view at present. China is developing nu-
> clear weapons, not because we believe in the omnipotence of
> nuclear weapons and that China plans to use nuclear weapons.
> The truth is exactly the opposite. *In developing nuclear weapons,
> China's aim is to break the nuclear monopoly of the nuclear powers
> and to eliminate nuclear weapons* . . .
> The Chinese government hereby solemnly declares that China
> will never at any time and under any circumstances be the first to
> use nuclear weapons.

The possession of the bomb by the Chinese government merely
reinforces its stand and gives it substance. Besides, no Chinese in
his proper senses would ever think of using the weapon on Japan if
Japan refrains from pursuing any policy of aggrandizement or military conquest as she did in the 1930's. Does the statement by the
Japanese Foreign Office official mean that Japan is already thinking of reviving her former policies toward China? It is this lack of
understanding on the part of the Japanese that sometimes makes
the Chinese wonder whether the Japanese understand their own interests. That China is not vengeful, that she is not vindictive, is for

every Japanese to see and feel. The tablet celebrating the cession of Taiwan to Japan in 1895 still stands in the Meiji Shrine in Tokyo: the Chinese government has not even asked for its removal! Do the Japanese believe that conciliation is a sign of weakness? The Japanese mind, I admit, is often not easy to understand and the latest information out of Japan is that the government has started the work of revising the school textbooks, eliminating all references to the mad military extravaganza, with all its atrocities, against the Chinese in the 1930's and the early 1940's!

Perhaps America understands the Japanese mind better, now that they have become so intimately associated for twenty years. We hope she does, for her role requires the understanding of the many ways in which the human mind works.

3. But the American mind is in a quandary itself. Words have often been used and actions taken that have produced the opposite of what was intended.

For instance, for the last fifteen years since the establishment of the Communist government in China, everyone knows that there has been a massive campaign of propaganda against that government. All the major organs of public information, both official and unofficial, join forces in painting it in the blackest possible colors. Nothing that that government ever did was any good. First, it was the mass murders and liquidations, of which horrible and exaggerated accounts were given. Then when the communes were established, there were lurid stories of utter ruthlessness and inhumanity. We were told that families have been mercilessly dissolved, men and women were separated and placed in slave camps, where they worked for no remuneration at all and they were all the time kept away from their children, who were taken care of by state nurseries. The Chinese have become a nation of blue ants! We were also told of the dangers of a population explosion which by the year 2000 would become so huge that the conquest of foreign lands by China would become all but unavoidable.* Finally,

---

* This, of course, is manifestly not true. All the efforts now being made by China, which Marshal Chen Yi and other leaders have taken the trouble to explain on more than one occasion, have never received any publicity in the Western press. Men are now being encouraged to marry at the age of

when famine came for three years between 1959 and 1961, it was freely predicted that the end of the "evil" regime was now in sight. Swarms of refugees came into Hong Kong at the risk of their lives to swell the dirge. Fantastic stories were extracted from them to let the world "know" that internal conditions had become so unbearable and the dissatisfaction among the people was so widespread that a massive revolt against the tyranny was expected momentarily. People were dying so rapidly and in such large numbers that if we believed the stories of Joseph Alsop, one observer computed, all of China's population would by now have perished many times over.

If we now make a sober estimate of all this trumped up publicity against China, what has been accomplished? Nothing, exactly nothing. Of course it was all meant to show that the days of the mainland regime, founded as it was on the lack of freedom, on tyranny, on a rigid police system, on mutual espionage, hunger, distress, mass starvation, and a total denial of all that makes life worth living, would soon collapse, and the Communist regime would then be over. But the inevitable has not come to pass. While the accusations are not entirely without foundation, we must admit that today China finds herself more confident than ever, conditions for the people have become infinitely better, in fact she is strong enough even to become a nuclear power, which requires both talent and resources. All of this makes the average person so confused that he does not know what to believe and follow. The explosion of nuclear power, in particular, coming as it did after Soviet Russia had withdrawn all aid to China, is a most perplexing and disquieting problem. How did China do it? The answer is very simple. We have a saying that faith can remove mountains. The Chinese have four little words. *Tse li keng sen,* which mean "re-

---

thirty and women at twenty-five, which is the ancient Chinese practice, and the men even run the risk of sterilization if they so much as make two women pregnant. I pity the members of my sex who from now on must rigidly put a brake on their romantic propensities. These strict measures of population control—there is no other word to describe them—are certainly news fit to be printed, yet even the New York Times, *the most respected of all papers, has made no mention of them. Along with all other papers, it continues to raise this population bogey of the Chinese.*

birth through self application." That is precisely what they have
done these years: they have applied themselves, and through self-
application they believe they can accomplish the impossible. These
four little words, I believe, will have a tremendous impact on the
future of all the underdeveloped countries in the world. Why look
for aid, especially when that aid is often given with strings attached, when energy directed by oneself with supreme confidence
can accomplish even more wonderful results?

Another example of how the results can be the very opposite of
what we say and wish is the so-called policy to isolate mainland
China. Mr. Adlai Stevenson even spoke openly of the "lone-wolf"
position of isolation of mainland China. Surely there is no indication of any loneliness when delegation after delegation from all
parts of the world visit Peking, year in and year out, either to take
part in celebrations and to negotiate for trade pacts of one kind or
another, or when officials from China herself travel to Africa and
Chinese workmen help to build roads even in distant Yemen.

Still another way being used to embarrass China or to hasten the
downfall of her government is to cut her trade with the rest of the
world. There is no indication that China is any the worse for it. In
fact, countries are vying with one another for trade with China.
Trade has been increasing steadily through the years. It expanded
by 25 per cent to 30 per cent in 1964. Trade relations have been
established with 125 countries and regions, of which 38 have concluded government trade agreements. The embargo imposed by the
United States on China from the time of the Korean War seems to
have stimulated rather than curtailed her foreign trade. One has
to stretch one's imagination considerably to believe with Mr. Stevenson that China is a big bad "lone wolf."

The policy of containment, the brain child of Mr. John Foster
Dulles, has likewise produced no result. The Indians were persuaded to take up arms against China with massive financial and
military aid from the U.S., only to show that India is completely hollow. The situation in South Vietnam has become a costly fiasco.
What is being lost does not consist only of things of a material
nature, but also the prestige of the United States as a great moral
leader of the world.

The most harmful myth as a propaganda stunt against China is, of course, the famous one that in the event of an atomic war 300,-000,000 Chinese, according to Chairman Mao Tse-tung, would still be left alive. This is an outrageous and unmitigated falsehood, which everybody has accepted as gospel truth. Felix Greene has now traced it to a speech made by Marshal Tito, who, as we all know, is opposed to Mao Tse-tung. The speech was given in Belgrade in 1958. It was reported correctly in the New York *Times* of June 16 of that year. Then in the editorial of the following day the *Times* described it as Tito's "revelation." From then on, Chairman Mao was given the full credit throughout the world as having fathered that absurd thought, even though the State Department's Office of Research and Analysis for the Far East (Asian Communist Division) stated in 1963: "As far as is known, the Chinese Communist regime has never officially expressed this viewpoint in print." * Indeed Mao never made any such statement in all of his published writings.

I have given a few of these samples only to show that notwithstanding Mr. Dean Acheson, mere strategic considerations, bereft of moral and ethical value, can be infinitely harmful. They work against the cause of peace. All this, in my view, should be carefully re-examined in the light of Mr. Johnson's new and eminently statesmanlike policy of "patience and generosity." To persist in the present policies, backed by however strong a force, can only mean that the United States will continue to be described as an imperialist power. Already, even in the United Nations, where American influence is so strongly felt, the United States is finding itself criticized as a colonial power. "Charges of colonialism, neo-colonialism and imperialism," according to the New York *Times* of December 22, 1964, "are being leveled at the United States in the 24-member UN Special Committee on Colonization." As long ago as 1921, Mr. Van Wyck Brooks made the statement: "Few Americans know, even today really know—I mean apprehend—that America is an empire, with all the paraphernalia of imperialism." It was then not so offensive, abusive, and flagrant, but now,

---

* *Letter by Jonathan Mirsky in the New York* Times, *written on December 4, 1964.*

these UN delegates must feel, as "leader and protector of the free world," she is getting to be increasingly so.

4. And now to end as I began, and as I have said throughout these pages, the first and the most pressing problem that awaits immediate solution to ease the existing tension in the world, or at least between the United States and China, or to dispel the impression of imperialism, is that of Taiwan. If President Johnson's new policy is to produce results, the solution will have to be found in the full, complete, and unconditional restitution of the island to the sovereignty of an undivided China. All the arguments about two Chinas, are specious. The idea of self-determination is a good one, but it must be used with discretion and not in any indiscriminate manner, or the world would be in utter confusion and chaos. President Woodrow Wilson first made use of it only to serve the immediate end of dismembering the Austro-Hungarian Empire, which was put together, as in the case of Malaysia now, in an unnatural manner. It never was meant to be an inviolable principle to be indiscriminately applied everywhere and under all circumstances. Certainly it is not applicable to Taiwan, when the so-called Taiwanese speak the Chinese language, write the Chinese language, even have their names in the Chinese language, and have Chinese blood running in their veins. They are Chinese in every respect. In 1963 when I was passing through Tokyo, I had a seminar with a group of students from the University of Tokyo. Among them was a student from Taiwan who believed in the creation of an independent Taiwan, a thesis that I considered untenable. But we got along well enough. Finally I asked for his personal card, which he handed to me. His name of course was written in Chinese. I then asked him to read his name. It was read as any Chinese would read it. I finally asked him how he could say that he was not a Chinese but a Taiwanese. Where did the Taiwan part come in? We both laughed and understood each other. The fact of the matter is that this alleged Taiwan-for-the-Taiwanese movement was created for definite political motives. The only true Taiwanese are a few headhunters up in the mountains, and even these have given up their practice because they came into contact with bad Chinese influences! My recommendation is that the sooner we forget all this

talk about Taiwan for the Taiwanese or self-determination for
Taiwan, which is all meaningless and inspired, the better it is for
peace in the world.

The Irish delegation to the United Nations, true to the creative
and imaginative resourcefulness of their race, has offered a new arrangement. It is a kind of variation of the same theme, but it is an
interesting variation. The suggestion is that both China and
Taiwan will be represented in the UN just as surely as Soviet
Russia and the Ukraine are both represented in that organization. I
said this is interesting and even perhaps worthy of consideration if
the administration of Taiwan, and its defense and foreign policy,
are directed from the central government at Peking, as those of the
Ukraine fall within the competence of the central government at
Moscow.

I feel that if the Taiwan question is properly and resolutely settled, now and with courage, all the remaining problems will be
solved in short order.* This is one of the cases where American
statesmanship of the highest quality is needed in an eminent degree. It requires courage, because it must be fearless in running
straight against the rampart of the China lobby and step on the
toes of those, including the China-born Henry Luce, who in one
way or another are implicated in that famous lobby. It requires
also knowledge and understanding of the China of the great traditions. Make no mistake about it: no Chinese government can
organize a society and leave out those traditions any more than
any Western government can create a new order and leave out the
Hellenic and Christian traditions.

The idea of dominating the world is entirely alien to Chinese
thinking, though Dr. Arnold Toynbee is right in his Denver interview of December 26, 1964, when he said, "The Chinese have a
world-state viewpoint in their tradition." Dr. Toynbee would have
done better if he went on to point out that the Great Common-

---

* *It cannot be overemphasized that the problem of Taiwan is basically the
one and only problem between America and China. If that problem is solved,
all, yes all, of the other problems are easy of solution. Conversely, if that
problem is not solved, that is, if the United States refuses to consider it as
China's domestic problem or to bring it back within the territorial sovereignty
of China, then there can be no normal relations between the two countries.*

wealth as envisaged by Confucius and by the other thinkers has no
relevance to the use of physical or military force even in a concealed form; it is based completely on the acceptance of moral
ideas by all human beings wherever and whatever they may be. Dr.
Toynbee, for all his copious knowledge and scholarship, seems to
lack the comprehension and perception of one of his countrymen,
Professor Joseph Needham, who in his letter to the *New Statesman*
on the first day of the year 1965 had this to say:

> A little reading about Confucianism [said Professor Needham]
> makes one realize that China is a civilization which for two and a
> half millennia has been deeply permeated by an ethical doctrine
> which admitted of no supernatural sanctions. If one takes the
> trouble to learn a little about Taoism one may understand that the
> ideal Chinese way was always to persuade, to lead from within and
> below, to let natural processes take their course, rather than to
> dominate, to enforce and to impose. Confucianism and Taoism
> were . . . each in their own different way . . . devoted to the
> coming of what some Christians would call the Kingdom of God
> on earth.
>
> Confucianism and Taoism are still today the indelible back-
> ground of the Chinese mind, and no one can understand China
> without them. The "renovation of the people" (*hsin min*) is a
> watchword 20 centuries old, a process that has many times been
> repeated, more often attempted, though never so deeply achieved
> as now . . . The fact is that Marxism in Cathay must be seen
> against an entirely different mental background from Marxism in
> Christendom.

President Johnson, in his State of the Union message, complained that "In Asia Communism wears a more aggressive face."
This may be true, but it is essential to bear in mind, as Mr. I. F.
Stone pointed out, "that the more aggressive face we see in the Far
East is in substantial degree the mirror image of the aggressive
face we steadily turn toward it" (*I. F. Stone Weekly*, January 11,
1965). We are always eloquent about the effect, but forgetful of
the cause.

So it is with this continual talk of war. China is in no position
for war, therefore she cannot desire it. She is so backward indus-

trially that it will take her easily three-quarters of a century to be
anywhere near where she wants to be. To talk of war under such
circumstances would be the height of folly. But if the world is fool-
ish enough to compel China to go to war, one thing is certain: both
the United States and China would be irretrievably hurt. Such a
war is bound to engender complications. The physical damage for
the United States would not be as serious as for China, but she
would be mortally shaken. A process of disintegration would
rapidly set in, leading, as in the case of ancient Rome, to ultimate
destruction and death. China would be destroyed physically, but
what remained of her in the country and in the villages would lie
dormant, perhaps for centuries, and would then blossom forth
with renewed vitality and energy into a new period of glory and
splendor. It has happened before. It can happen again. In the
meantime, the field would be open, as Senator Albert Gore warned
us, for Soviet Russia to take over. So let us not talk about war, but
keep in our mind, as it has been said many times before by perceptive people, that the destiny of the United States is in the Pacific
and that China is her natural ally. This seems to have been the
view that was shared by the missionary father of Mr. Henry Luce.

5. Finally, I come to the last of the Five-Point Program of the
immediate practical steps to be taken for easing the tension between the United States and China. I refer to China's representation at the United Nations. While from China's own point of view
the matter is not of such overriding importance, it is best for that
truly indispensable international organization, in its own interest,
to renew its consideration. It is essential that it not only survive,
but grow in strength and vitality. For the nations need it at this
period when they seek adjustment for a new pattern of relationship. And yet there are signs of weakening. It has "plunged,"
as General de Gaulle thinks, into "a crisis." Indonesia has severed
her relations with the organization: this is a danger signal. And
General de Gaulle himself said in no uncertain terms, during his
February 4, 1965, news conference, that "the United Nations
allowed itself to be led into going beyond the Charter, ignoring
the powers of the Security Council, and in 1950 the General Assembly took upon itself the right of deciding the use of force, and

this transformed it immediately into a battlefield for the two rivals."
Also, the United Nations allowed itself to indulge "in a series of
encroachments on its own legality," and has thereby "undergone
a deep change which . . . [has] cost the organization its unity,
prestige, and possibilities of functioning." Whether these observations by the General are just or not, there is no denying that the
organization has become an arena where the great powers continue
to jockey for position. They have contracted the habit, as the Chinese saying goes, of "grabbing the emperor in order more effectively to issue orders to the feudal lords." No organization, let
alone a vital international organization like the United Nations,
can survive on this basis. And the biggest joke remains that of imagining that the government in Taiwan represents 700 million
people or one-quarter of the world's population. While the "crisis"
is on, it gives the best opportunity for a reappraisal of the entire
situation. Indonesia must be persuaded to come back. China must
be properly represented. This is the time to revitalize the organization by following General de Gaulle's suggestion for a Five-Power
conference, including China, to bring the Charter up to date.

M. Edgar Faure, twice Prime Minister of France, speaking in
the Assembly Hall of the United Nations in the presence of its
leading personalities on February 1, 1965, made some memorable
remarks. They were the concluding words of his eloquent address
on "The Three Periods of Co-operation," and I quote them as a
fitting conclusion to these pages:

> There can be no genuine co-operation if great areas of mankind
> are cut off from its sphere. Although certain powers have not yet
> been admitted to these precincts by reason of historical circum-
> stances overshadowing your gatherings, and although, more spe-
> cifically, Germany must still await the settlement of a diplomatic
> prerequisite, it is hard to understand in this day the prolonged
> absence of China, which was not only a signer of the Charter but
> an inviting and founding member of your organization. Even
> though in this address we have given much attention to history,
> the status quo and a longing for the days of yore cannot indef-
> initely keep the upper hand over the logic of the real and the im-
> mediate. From the point of view of efficiency alone, how can . . .

disarmament, how can . . . human betterment, which have become for us an obsssession, be dealt with, how can we, shall I say, approach them in any comprehensive way if we completely disregard the greatest concentration of human beings who have ever been gathered within the organic framework of a nation?

I think this is truly the voice of reason, the kind of sentiment that President Johnson himself would wish to have uttered. But, unfortunately, there are obstacles, and all we have been hearing through the years is the raucous voice of passion, of emotion. The absence of the voice of reason does no good to the country; it undermines the respect of the world for a country which, by virtue of the most favorable combination of circumstances—its wealth, its strength, but above all its great moral prestige and the inheritance of a noble legacy of justice and freedom for all—should be its natural leader. And yet, as Mr. Emmet John Hughes complains,* "There is no Asian people, no African government, no European foreign office that *today* gravely respects American policy in the Far East."

It is true, as Mr. Hughes further complains, that we do not have an Asian policy. What we have been having is a series of moods, attitudes, and postures, compounded of pride, superciliousness, arrogance, over-confidence, stubbornness, lack of imagination, and a flat refusal to look at the world from another point of view. We have paid dearly for all of these in Korea, we are paying dearly in South Vietnam, and we shall continue to pay dearly elsewhere. "There can be no peace in Asia [nor for the United States for that matter] without a new American policy toward Red China—a policy looking toward both diplomatic recognition and negotiation."

Sir Winston Churchill, in the last volume of his memoirs, made this observation: "The United States stood on the scene of victory, master of the world fortunes, but without a true and coherent design." The United States cannot afford to continue to be without "a true and coherent design" toward Asia in this period of her history. In that design antagonism must yield place to co-operation and friendship, division to harmony and understanding.

* *"The Great Debate on Asia"* in Newsweek, *January 11, 1965.*

Furthermore, that design can never function and unfold itself properly without China's full and active participation. I am not only thinking of her massive population and unlimited resources; I am thinking particularly in terms of the enormous human values and of her contributions, through the ages, to make life richer, more refined, and more meaningful. She is the home of humanism par excellence, and this humanist tradition will help to make the world healthier and happier, and to develop an attitude of complete sanity toward everything which pertains to life.

APPENDIXES

APPENDIXES

MEMORANDUM ON THE
CHINESE QUESTION *

FOR ELEVEN YEARS since June 27, 1950, when President Truman despatched the Seventh Fleet to Taiwan, that island has become an important and complicated issue in international politics. It is not an issue which lends itself to any easy solution, because it is an issue involving all of China. A few suggestions for its solution have been made, but none so far has proved to be sufficiently acceptable. So the stalemate remains, and the situation drags on.

But it is a situation which, like others, is an integral part of the world picture; and unless it is placed soon under proper and effective control, its evil effects may spread, as they have already, for instance in Laos and other parts of southeast Asia, or it may itself become the cause of a major conflict between the United States and China. President Kennedy said during his recent birthday speech that in the forty-four years of his life, he had already known World War I, World War II, and the Korean War. That was too much for anyone's life, and he vowed that he would do everything to avoid another such catastrophe.

To do that it seems to me that one essential thing is stubbornly to make reason prevail in international relations, and not to allow emotion under any circumstances to gain the upper hand or get the better of rational considerations.

I am afraid the Chinese question has already drifted from a rational to an emotional sphere of response, and our first duty would seem to be to bring it back to where reason may again freely operate. The American people cannot forget the bitterness of the Ko-

---

* Given to the leaders of the U.S. government, January, 1961, by General Li Tsung-jen, former Acting President of the Republic of China. My thanks are due to him for giving me the permission to print it.

rean War. It continues to rankle, and that is quite understandable. The Chinese on the mainland, on the other hand, are exasperated beyond measure by America's constant interference with what they deem China's domestic affairs and by its imperialist or aggressive attitude towards matters which are specifically Chinese. The two standpoints are at opposite poles to one another. There is no common ground for even the rudiments of reconciliation. And yet in the interest of both nations and for the good of all mankind, there must be a determination to break the impasse before it brings incalculable disaster. There must be a resolution for peace. Is that possible?

I believe it is possible, provided both sides are willing to take a long view, to bear in mind that historically they have been on friendly relations, and that there is much in common in the basic instincts of their respective peoples which should provide the closest cooperation in building a peaceful world. There is no doubt that America works for peace. Equally there is no doubt that Communist China desires and must work for peace. Its vast program of modernization and industrialization cannot be carried out unless there is peace. It would thus be a real tragedy if, desiring peace, the two countries should drift into war and conflict. That can happen if passions on both sides are not placed under proper control.

Quite often human beings allow themselves to indulge in the luxury of wishful thinking. This is dangerous, because it blurs our vision and interferes with our judgment. There is no indication, famine or no famine, that the Communist regime in China is likely to disintegrate within the immediate or foreseeable future. Irresponsible journalism based upon inspired information coming out of Hongkong is trying to create this impression. Publicity coming out of Taiwan aims to do the same thing. Needless to say, it would be the height of folly if national policy should be predicated on such tendentious reportage. It is not only misleading; it could even give rise to another fiasco. The consequences then would be too great for the world to bear. Whether we like it or not, the China which the world has to deal with, in the sphere of practical politics and not in the world of make-believe, will be Communist China for some time to come.

This being so, let us ask what are some of the solutions now being offered for the Chinese problem, and whether they have in them the necessary ingredients to reduce tension and therefore lead us to peace.

A. The talk of a two-China arrangement is perhaps the most persistent and wide-spread. The idea was first officially referred to, I believe, by former President Eisenhower in a press conference on January 19, 1955, when he said that it "was under continuing study." Since then it has been discussed and explored from every possible point of view. Perhaps the most exhaustive treatment of the plan was in the form of an article written by Mr. Chester Bowles, while he was a member of Congress, which appeared in *Foreign Affairs* in its issue of April 1960. In essence the plan calls for the creation of two independent governments, one on mainland China and the other on the Island of Taiwan, to be, as it is today, under the Nationalist Government. Mr. Bowles went to the extent of suggesting that the 12,000,000 overseas Chinese, scattered mainly in southeast Asia, should be persuaded to owe allegiance to the Nationalist Government. The plan is further calculated to solve the problem of Chinese representation in the United Nations where both governments would then have a seat. A modified version of the plan is to create a new Republic of Formosa or Taiwan on the plea that the people on the island are Taiwanese and are therefore entitled to have their own government if they so desire.

After six years of publicity and propaganda in its favor, the plan has not gone very far. Some countries like Great Britain and some members of the Commonwealth, in order to be on the right side with the United States for their own reasons, have expressed their willingness to go along. But the plan lacks the essential elements for success, and the reasons are quite obvious:

1. The plan is vigorously opposed both by Communist China and by Nationalist China, and that should be enough to kill it. There was a time when anything affecting China could be decided upon by London, Paris, Washington, and the other capitals of the

western world. That was in the second half of the 19th century when China was at the mercy of the western powers. But that China is gone—forever. Any policy now having anything to do with China is destined for immediate failure if it is not subscribed to by the Chinese themselves. And no Chinese, of whatever political persuasion, can ever be induced to accept a proposition which destroys the territorial or political unity of China.

2. The idea that the people on the island are Taiwanese or Formosans is a myth from beginning to end. The only pure Taiwanese are perhaps the head-hunters of whom there are still remnants high up on the hills, and even they may be regarded as trespassers. One of China's leading archeologists who now lives in Taiwan has made surveys and excavations on the island, and he is convinced that the artifacts so far discovered by him show that even in prehistoric times the culture on the island belonged to the same pattern as the one on the mainland. In historic times the island came to be occupied by the Chinese as early as the Period of the Three Kingdoms (221–265 A.D.). It was then known as Yi-chou. The first Chinese official to land there was sent by Emperor Yang-ti of the Sui Dynasty (589–618 A.D.), long before there was even any Danish invasion of Britain. For over thirteen hundred years since that time, the Chinese have steadily, though not in large numbers, settled on the island. In 1360 the Yuan Dynasty (1280–1368 A.D.) brought Taiwan and the Pescadores into still closer relationship with mainland China. In the Ming Dynasty, during five years of the reign of Emperor Wan-li (1593–1598 A.D.) the Chinese Government introduced defense measures on the island against the Japanese pirates under Hideyoshi.

The first foreign occupation of Taiwan took place in 1622 when the Dutch held the Pescadores or Penghu Islands and the southern part of Taiwan, though two years later the Pescadores were restored to Chinese rule. Then came the Spaniards to the northern part of Taiwan. But the Dutch defeated them and came into possession of the entire island. This foreign Dutch rule lasted for some 38 years when in 1661 Cheng Cheng-kung (Koxinga), with an army of 125,000 men completely drove away the Dutch and took back the island from them. By 1683 the Manchu Dynasty had become strongly established, and Cheng's grandson surrendered himself to the new rulers in Peking. Chinese administration over the island was thus securely re-established for over 200 years when in 1895, after China was defeated by Japan, it was ceded by the Treaty of Shimonoseki to the then expanding Nipponese empire.

When, in the course of World War II, it was agreed that the island of Taiwan should be returned to China, it was merely an act of restoration to its rightful owner. The Cairo Declaration which contained this stipulation was made public on December 1, 1943, by the President of the United States, the President of China, and the Prime Minister of Great Britain, and it referred to Taiwan as being among the "territories Japan had stolen from China." It said, among other things:

> The Three Great Allies are fighting this war to restrain and punish the aggression of Japan. They want no gain for themselves and have no thought of territorial expansion. It is their purpose that Japan shall be stripped of all the islands in the Pacific which she has seized or occupied since the beginning of the first World War in 1914, and all the territories that Japan has stolen from China, such as Manchuria, Formosa, and the Pescadores, shall be restored to the Republic of China.

Then came the Potsdam Declaration of July 26, 1945, in which Article 8 said:

> The terms of the Cairo Declaration shall be carried out and Japanese sovereignty shall be limited to the islands of Honshu, Hokkaido, Kyushu, Shikoku and such minor islands as we determine.

This stipulation was confirmed by the Instrument of Surrender which was accepted by Japan on September 2, 1945:

> We hereby undertake, for the Emperor, the Japanese Government and their successors, to carry out the provisions of the Potsdam Declaration in good faith.

Over a month later, on October 25, the Chinese Government accepted the surrender of the Japanese Commander of the Tenth Army who was concurrently Governor-General of Taiwan, and the island officially was restored to Chinese rule.

The United States, on its part, made a number of statements and declarations since then which further confirmed the stipulations and commitments mentioned above. The "White Paper" on China of August 1948; the statement issued by the State Department, the so-called Christmas gift to China, which recognized that politically, geographically, and strategically Taiwan now again constituted an integral part of China; the Truman statement of January 5, 1950, recognizing China's right to exercise sovereignty over the island; and finally the admission, in the following month, by the State Department (February 9) before the enquiry of the House Foreign Affairs Committee that the island of Taiwan, since 1945, had become a province of China—all these were re-affirmations of China's sovereignty over Taiwan and the Pescadores.

Mr. Dean Acheson, who was Secretary of State all through this period, further made the American position crystal clear when he explained some of the statements referred to above. On the Potsdam Declaration he said:

> That Declaration at Potsdam was conveyed to the Japanese as one of the terms of their surrender and was accepted by them, and the surrender was made on that basis.
>
> Shortly after that, the Island of Formosa was turned over to the Chinese in accordance with the declarations made and with the conditions of surrender.
>
> The Chinese have administered Formosa for four years. Neither the United States nor any other ally ever questioned that authority and that occupation. When Formosa was made a province of China nobody raised any lawyer's doubts about that. That was regarded as in accordance with the commitments.

On the famous January 5, 1950, statement by President Truman on non-interference in China's civil war (State Department Bulletin XXII, 1950, pp. 79–81) Mr. Acheson also commented:

It is important that our position in regard to China should never be subject to the slightest doubt or the slightest question. Now what has that position been? In the middle of the war, the President of the United States, the Prime Minister of Great Britain, and the President of China agreed at Cairo that among the areas stolen from China was Formosa, and Formosa should go back to China.

Thus the United States stand on Taiwan and the Pescadores, at least till the early days of January 1950 was clear, unequivocal, and precise. To make Taiwan or Formosa anything but an integral part of China now would be a complete repudiation of that position, involving an act of physical amputation which no Chinese would ever accept. How would any Frenchman feel if it is suggested to him that Brittany and Normandy should be made a separate state from France, or that Wales and Scotland be detached from Great Britain, or that Hawaii, Alaska, and even parts of continental United States be made independent of Washington? Such suggestions are simply not made. And yet today responsible people seriously think that Taiwan and the Pescadores can be detached from China!

The Chinese position that the islands are an integral part of their territory is historically, geographically, politically, and administratively undefeatable. It is sheer waste of time and energy trying to argue against that position.

3. To create a new state out of Taiwan, either in the shape of the present Nationalist Government or a new Republic of Taiwan, would naturally appear to the rest of the world as an unwarranted act of interference by the United States in a purely Chinese domestic question. Such a separate state obviously would be sovereign only in name. Its resources are not adequate to make it truly independent. It will have to rely on the United States for economic assistance, and with the anxiety of this country also to keep it within the American "defense perimeter," which is public knowledge, it would have to depend on the United States equally for military assistance. The first act of this new "government" would be signing a mutual defense treaty with the United States whereby

it "grants, and the United States accepts, the right to dispose United States land, air and sea forces in and about" the island. Thus the new "state" would be placed under American control from the beginning for an indefinite period. Neither the Communist world nor even the neutral countries would regard such an arrangement without grave doubt and suspicion. This would also be out of keeping with the spirit as well as with the letter of President Truman's message to Congress on July 19, 1950, when he said:

> In order that there may be no doubt in any quarter about our intentions regarding Formosa, I wish to state that the United States has no territorial ambitions whatever concerning that island, nor do we seek for ourselves any special position or privilege on Formosa.

This was spoken even after the Korean War had broken out.

4. The Nationalist Government on Taiwan cannot subscribe to this plan of detaching the island from the mainland for the simple reason that Taiwan remains in the imagination of all China, so it believes, as the symbol for the reconquest of the mainland. Whether this is realizable is beside the point. The fact is that this hope forms the entire *raison d'être* for its existence. The creation of a separate government completely smothers that hope, however flimsy and insubstantial it may be. To agree to such a proposal would stir up uneasy feelings in its leaders even beyond their graves. For after all these leaders of the Nationalist Government are Chinese, and they cannot be unmindful of what future generations may think of them and of their position in history. As long as they are making their present stand, comic as it may appear, they will be respected and honored in history as being men of conviction or even as patriots. The moment they agree to the formation of a separate government, detached from China, they will be regarded as traitors to their own land, and that would be the most horrible verdict for them to bear. No one in his proper frame of mind could ever entertain such a thought with equanimity. This is one angle of Chinese psychology which it would be wise to consider. Rather than subscribing to such a plan, the leaders in

Taiwan would prefer, the moment they feel that the destruction of China's territorial integrity is becoming unavoidable, to turn over the island to Communist control. They would then at least have the merit of having suffered an honorable defeat and not a dishonorable surrender. I do not have to go into any details on this possibility; the CIA, with its superb organization and unrivaled knowledge, should have information to substantiate it.

In this connection it is pertinent to remind ourselves that in an editorial article of *China Tribune,* a Chinese language Kuomintang daily newspaper in New York, dated March 18, 1961, the writer made the following observation on the two alternatives before the Nationalist Government on Formosa:

> 1. Either mobilize all the forces in Taiwan for an early military reconquest of the mainland. This will be successful because we are confident that wherever our forces land, they will receive support of the local people on the mainland. This step is to be highly recommended. If this is not done, then
>
> 2. It is better to re-open direct negotiations with the Communists instead of allowing the Republic of China to have its demise on Taiwan, or always serving as a "watch-dog" of the Pacific for other countries, or permitting Taiwan to be taken away from China's territorial integrity and unity. This second alternative is of course fraught with danger. But if circumstances force it upon us, we should at least have the courage to resist those who try to dispose of us in any way suited to their convenience. After all it is better that Chinese on both sides, opposed as they are in their views, negotiate and settle the matter among ourselves than that they should serve as puppets in the hands of other countries.

Needless to say, no editorial writer, on so important and so vital an issue, is at liberty to express his own personal views without having cleared them with the proper authorities.

For the above reasons and so long as Chinese acquiescence is essential, the creation of a separate government on Taiwan cannot succeed. If circumstances should compel the existing government on Taiwan actually to surrender itself to the mainland, and this is no mere fantasy, would it not be the greatest fiasco to face the

United States? How would the rest of the world regard this country? What would America do? Outright occupation of Taiwan? That would be even worse, as it would then confirm the worst suspicions of the world.

The creation of two Chinas, in whatever shape or form, will be resisted by all Chinese, just as all the talk about Tibet being not a part of China is being resisted by all Chinese. It is doomed to utter and complete failure. Besides it is fraught with dangers which we should do well to avoid. Would it not thus be better to direct our time and energy to something that is really practicable?

B. The policy of keeping the status quo indefinitely hoping that something beyond our calculation, like the proverbial *deus ex machina,* will neatly solve the problem.

The present situation is the product of the Dulles policy of forging an iron ring round the Communist world. That policy is becoming manifestly unworkable; it has not yielded the results which it anticipated. There is reason to believe that the people in this country are also beginning to realize its inefficacy, and the present administration is likely in time to consider a revision of this policy. To allow it to drift is obviously to have no policy at all. President Kennedy is one who, to quote his own words, "wants to get things done." But action should be preceded by reflection and mature consideration. Is it too much to say that a part of this consideration is to bear in mind the changed military picture between 1953 when Mr. Dulles became Secretary of State and the present time, a period of some eight years?

But to confine ourselves to China. Supposing that in our search for a workable formula, nothing really satisfactory emerges. Are we then to allow the present situation to remain as it is? What will be the consequences of such a step?

The animosity between the United States and Communist China has been intense and will remain intense as long as the United States pursues its present policy. Unless something is done to reduce this tension, the situation can lead to consequences which neither side desires. Already both sides no longer think or act in a completely rational manner. Their responses have become emotional in nature, and that is where the danger lies. Of course it is quite natural for Americans to think that they can do no wrong, and that the fault is all on the Communist Chinese side. But the Communist Chinese feel that they are entirely right in their views. They insist that the question of Taiwan is a purely domestic one and that there should be no external interference of any sort. That, they say, was America's own stand. It was made explicit on numerous occasions before President Truman despatched the Seventh Fleet to the waters surrounding Taiwan on June 27, 1950.

That drastic change of policy is what Communist China cannot tolerate.

If anything, therefore, the present tension is likely to grow more intense until it reaches the point of explosion. That point will be reached when it sees that all hope for a negotiated settlement fails in the actual creation of a separate state in Taiwan under American pressure. It is then that passion will very likely supersede reason. It is at this point that misjudgments and miscalculations will play a decisive role leading to events which sanity and good sense would deprecate. Already Communist China is accusing the United States for having violated in the neighborhood of 160 times the air sovereignty of China. When the situation reaches the point of explosion, another such act of violation may bring irretrievable disaster, just as the assassination at Sarajevo brought on the first World War and the invasion of Poland the second World War. Supposing that a United States plane is shot down by Communist China, the new situation thus created may well go to a point of no return, in which case the two countries can find themselves actually at war with one another, a consummation which neither desires.

If war arises between the United States and Communist China, the consequences will be so frightful as to stagger all imagination. China will be ruined as the United States will not refrain from using atomic power. But neither will the United States be immune from serious injury. China will obviously at once invoke Article I of the Sino-Soviet Treaty of February 14, 1950 and ask Soviet Russia to "immediately render military and other assistance with all the means at its disposal." There is no way in which Soviet Russia can back out on this provision; nor will she want to even if there is a way. She will want to stay out of the conflict, but the temptation to supply the fullest military assistance to her ally will be too strong to resist. For it is clear that at the present stage of world history it is not to Soviet Russia's interest or advantage to see China destroyed by the United States. She would welcome a weaker or more subservient China, but even for that only at the expense of a seriously damaged United States.

A full-scale war between Communist China and the United States, without Soviet Russia's involvement, would bring about results which neither the people in the United States nor the people in China could visualize with any sense of comfort. Who would be the gainer and who the losers? All the "military and other assistance with all the means at its disposal" would include obviously the use of nuclear weapons also.

Further, in the event of such hostilities taking place, the United States is likely to stand quite alone. It will not be as in the case of the Korean War. Neither the United Nations nor the closest allies of the United States will be willing to become involved. Is it then worth the effort for the United States thus to go through this tremendous sacrifice for the sake of a small island almost half way round the world from Washington? I shall plead with the leaders of this country to think more than twice before deciding on so desperate and so profitless a measure.

At this point it is perhaps best to remind ourselves of what President Kennedy said on September 16, 1959:

> We want the question of peace or war for America to be decided by the Congress as the Constitution provided—not by Generalissimo Chiang Kai-shek.

This is a perfectly just and legitimate thought. But to allow the situation to drift, as it does today, would seem to indicate that the United States is allowing events to develop in the direction that President Kennedy and every other American would want to avoid.

As early as ten years ago General Omar Bradley, along with General George C. Marshall, saw the situation very clearly and warned his country of the danger. He was then Chairman of the

Joint Chiefs of Staff. On May 15, 1951, while testifying against the views of General MacArthur, he said that the adoption of these views might well involve the United States in *"the wrong war, at the wrong place, and at the wrong time, and with the wrong enemy* [my italics]. An active involvement in the Far Eastern conflict and the enmeshing of American forces in a major struggle with China would give Marshal Stalin a free hand in Europe." This observation was true then and is even truer today. Can the United States be so unthoughtful as to permit the views of those who want war with China quietly and effectively still to direct and dominate over her policy towards that country?

C. If the analysis of the two widely accepted views vis-à-vis China leads to the conclusion that they are both unworkable, is the situation then quite hopeless? I do not think so. I feel there is a solution. The acceptance of such a solution by the United States would be in her own best interest. And in so far as it helps to reduce the bitter feelings between the United States and China, it will contribute to an easing of the tension all around, and even to the solution of many of the current international questions such as disarmament, southeast Asia, and even Africa and Latin America.

In the article written by Mr. Edgar Snow for *Look* Magazine of January 31, 1961, Premier Chou En-lai was reported to have said the following words:

> It is inconceivable that a peace pact can be concluded without diplomatic relations between China and the United States. It is also inconceivable that there can be diplomatic relations between China and the United States without a settlement of the dispute between the two countries in the Taiwan region.

Chou was not making a demand: he was merely stating a fact as he and his colleagues in the Chinese Communist government see it.

Taiwan and the disposal of the problem of Taiwan in truth constitute the root of all the troubles between the United States and China. As long as that problem is not solved, there is utterly no hope of any improvement in the relationship between the two countries. Conversely, if the two countries can see eye to eye on the question of Taiwan, within twenty-four hours, the atmosphere will have cleared all doubts and suspicions, to so great an extent that we can indeed look forward to a general improvement in all the relations between the two countries. If President Kennedy was provided with the knowledge of that article, which is tantamount to Communist China speaking to the new president, only ten days after he came into the White House, through the medium of Mr. Snow, and if he was disposed to give some thought to it, he could not have suggested, as he did, that as a first step there should be an exchange of correspondents. The Kennedy suggestion was of course not well received, whereupon trouble-makers immediately made capital of the disagreement and said that China had no desire to go along with the new administration. It was an effort on their part as usual to make Communist China carry the burden of the blame. But for Communist China there is no such thing as any first step. The solution of the problem of Taiwan itself *is* the first step, and when that is taken, all the remaining parts of the jig-saw naturally fall into place. If the problem of Taiwan is not solved, then there is no point in doing any other thing at all.

Before offering any solution of the problem of Taiwan, let us use some imagination and try to see the Communist Chinese point of view. I am not saying that we need to accept that point of view. But I think it is always wise to understand or sometimes even to sympathize with the other party's point of view. This is especially true, I dare suggest, with the Chinese, Communist or non-Communist, as their entire culture for thousands of years has been founded on the principle of *li* or of being reasonable and rational.

1. The Chinese Communists, they say, have established themselves on all of China. Their government has achieved order and unity and is carrying out elaborate programs of modernization and industrialization. During the eleven years of its brief history it has done more to consolidate the country than any other government in the memory of living people. Why then, they angrily assert, must the United States try to make mockery of this unity and of these achievements by purposely shielding and supporting a defeated regime on a small island when normally it should have disappeared

long ago? Why must the United States stick a thorn in their side? Is she not deliberately creating trouble for the Chinese Communists? Or is it because a strong and orderly China has really never been to the liking of the United States and the other imperialist powers?

2. Taiwan has always been an integral part of China's territorial sovereignty. Why then must the United States insist on separating it from the mainland? And further, what right has she to incorporate the island into its "defense perimeter" established in front of her very door, but from six to eight thousand miles away from their own coastline? At first the United States used the alibi of the protection of the National Government knowing that that government exists more in fiction than in fact. Now she is trying to play up the role of a separate government on Taiwan while tightening more and more its control over the island. Who can deny that such control is what the United States really is after, and all the rest merely chicanery and persiflage? The fact of the matter is, so the Chinese Communist government argues, that since the despatch of the Seventh Fleet to Taiwan, every action by the United States in that area is calculated to strengthen its hold on the island for its own selfish purposes. The entire world, they believe, is convinced of that.

3. The United States has all along admitted that Taiwan is China's domestic problem. That was made clear and affirmed on numerous occasions, especially by the State Department's White Paper which subsequently was endorsed by President Truman. Why then, the Chinese Communists ask, is a domestic issue thrown into the arena of international politics? The United States has refused consistently to regard it in any other light since mid-June of 1950. Is this not another indication of America's aggressive attitude?

4. And finally, the Chinese Communists argue, nothing that China did and does today is to the liking of the United States and the other imperialist powers. When she held on to her cultural heritage, the Americans said she was too conservative, that her ancient values must be discarded to make room for modernization, and that Christianity must step in to help in the work of a com-

plete overhaul. Now that they are going in for massive industrialization and modernization of her life, the same Americans complain that all the ancient virtues are being torn by the roots and
desiccated. When China turned to the right, America said she
should have turned left. When she turns left, America says she
should turn right. Nothing can please the United States. The only
thing that can please her would seem to be a permanently weak,
helpless and prostrate China so that the Chinese would always be
at her mercy. But that game, the Chinese Communists say, had
been played long enough for more than a century: they are seeing
to it that it is no longer allowed to be played. They have decided to
build a strong China, with a will of her own, commensurate with
the vast contributions she had made to the sum-total of the world's
civilization in the field of the arts, of literature and philosophy, as
in the field of moral science which, in the words of Voltaire, "is
the first of the sciences." And besides, they know, the Chinese
Communists say, that at the present juncture of China's history,
their way of doing things is the only way to establish a well-
organized and incorruptible government and to win national prestige and a respected place in the family of nations. Having accomplished these two primary aims of their revolution, what they will
do in the future will depend upon the circumstances as they develop. Are they so wrong, the Chinese Communists say, in their
present thoughts and deeds?

Whether these arguments of the Chinese Communist government are valid or not we do not for the moment discuss. But certain events have occurred, since the outbreak of the Korean hostilities, which stand out as historical facts, and as such they cannot be
denied. The world knows that there has been a complete change of
United States policy towards Taiwan. Whether the Communist
world had preconceived plans to invade South Korea, which would
perhaps justify such a change, is a matter upon which future historians will have to throw light. But two facts may be interesting.

The one is, as the Council on Foreign Relations says in its annual
publication *United States in World Affairs 1950* that the "absence
of Malik [at the United Nations Security Council on June 25]
strengthened the belief that Premier Kim Il-sung [of North Korea]

ordered invasion on its own responsibility without prior approval from the Kremlin" (p. 218). The other is that only more than one month before the Korean trouble started, Communist China held a conference under the chairmanship of Mao Tse-tung at Peking which planned a complete disbandment of the military forces now that China had become unified under Communist control.

This second fact has not been given sufficient credit. But it is a fact of great importance because it shows that Communist China was far from having any preconceived notion of embroiling itself in the Korean incident, let alone any aggressive designs on Korea, on which later a United Nations resolution was passed. The new government had been barely established. It was only because there was danger to her national security when the United Nations forces under American command threatened to cross the Yalu River that the new government decided to stake everything and plunge into the war. It was not only a momentous decision: it was one of the most difficult and hazardous decisions for any government to make.

Be that as it may, the drastic change of United States policy towards China, immediately upon the outbreak of the Korean War, did give rise to uneasy feelings around the world. The words from the same publication of the Council on Foreign Relations are in this connection pertinent, and I take the liberty of quoting them in full:

> Whether or not the American ground in China was wisely chosen in the first place, it is undeniable that American diplomacy in the second half of 1950 was severely handicapped by the necessity of maintaining it . . . Politically, American intervention [in Formosa] not only raised Chinese communist fury to a new pitch, but was causing widening circles of dissatisfaction and distrust in the free world. Although the President [Truman] has gone out of his way to assure the world that this country had no selfish designs on Formosa, each new American action in reference to that island deepened the feeling that the United States was pursuing aims far removed from those of the United Nations.

Or again:

At noon on June 27, the President announced: "I have ordered United States air and sea forces to give the Korean Government troops cover and support."

It was at this point that the latent divergence between the United States and United Nations attitudes on the Far East first began to reassert itself. In making known the actions taken in Korea in the name of the Security Council resolution of June 25, the President also announced a series of actions which were unrelated to that resolution and, in fact, conflicted with the known views of some governments that had voted for it. "Communism," said the President, "has passed beyond the use of subversion to conquer independent nations and will now use armed invasion and war. It has defied the orders of the Security Council." In these circumstances, he continued, he had been impelled to take certain actions affecting not only Korea but also Formosa, the Philippines, and Indochina. Formosa was, in effect, to be protected from communist attack, American forces in the Philippines were to be strengthened, and military assistance to the Philippine Government accelerated. Military assistance to the forces of France and the Associated States in Indochina would likewise be accelerated, and an American military mission would be dispatched to provide close working relations with them.

Apart from the lack of relevance to the immediate problem before the United Nations, the intensification of the military aid program in southeast Asia was a logical American reaction to the new situation in the Far East. The decisions regarding Formosa, concerning which the United States had thus far maintained a strict "hands-off" policy despite the invasion preparations that were going forward on the Chinese mainland, seemed to require fuller explanation. Under the circumstances now existing, the President asserted, "the occupation of Formosa by Communist forces would be a direct threat to the security of the Pacific area. Accordingly I have ordered the Seventh Fleet to prevent any attack on Formosa. As a corollary of this action I am calling upon the Chinese Government on Formosa to cease all air and sea operations against the mainland. The Seventh Fleet will see that this is done. The determination of the future status of Formosa must await the restoration of security in the Pacific, a peace settlement with Japan, or consideration by the United Nations."

Whatever reasoning underlay this remarkable decision, it was to be a source of inexhaustible complications in the months to come. At one stroke the United States, on grounds of military necessity, had abandoned the policy of non-intervention in China's civil war—authoritatively reaffirmed as recently as January 5 [1950]—and assumed responsibility for forestalling any action in the one theatre of that war where a decisive action remained to be fought.

It was easy to foresee . . . that not many United Nations members would accept the conclusion that action to repel aggression in Korea required action against a supposedly Chinese island a thousand miles away. The Chinese Communists had not attacked Korea; some governments were not even convinced as yet that Mao Tse-tung took his orders from the Kremlin, despite the suspicious uniformity of North Korean, Soviet and Chinese Communist propaganda on all Far Eastern matters . . .

To people whose thoughts habitually ran in an anti-American groove, the American action looked very much like a manifestation of the reckless "imperialism" they had conditioned themselves to expect. The United States, according to this view, was taking advantage of the Korean crisis to lay hands on Formosa for its own purposes. It was noticeable in this connection that the President did not even reaffirm China's right to the possession of Formosa, recognition of which had been the basis of all previous American actions with respect to that island [pp. 207–210].

These words are a strong criticism of the change of United States policy towards China during the last days of June 1950. The Chinese Communists, it is important to recall, did not intervene in the Korean War till November or more than four months later.

National policies are often the products of the circumstances which exist at the time when they are formulated. When circumstances change, it is usually necessary to revise the policies so that they are in keeping with the new spirit. The Dulles policy from which the present stand on Taiwan grew may have good reasons to support it as long as the circumstances responsible for its development remain unchanged. But in this rapidly evolving world they *have* changed, and these changes have been rather startling.

For one thing, the United States is no longer in sole possession of atomic power as she was down to about ten or twelve years ago.

The ICBM development outside of the United States has also drastically changed the situation. The rapid growth of atomic submarines is another disturbing factor, to say nothing of the other advances in technology which have a bearing on military strength. As President Kennedy himself admitted, in his address to the American nation on his return from his recent trip to Europe (*New York Times,* June 7, 1961): "Now we face a new and difficult threat. We no longer have a nuclear monopoly. Their missiles, they believe, will hold off our missiles, and their troops can match our troops should we intervene in these so-called wars of liberation."

Already observers of the international scene now no longer hesitate to say that, while previously the United States can rely exclusively on military power without fear of being challenged and can enforce any policy it desires by virtue of that power, irrespective of what others may feel about it, today the United States must perforce rely on something more subtle, on its powers of persuasion and on its ability to convince others on the strength of its moral rectitude and probity, all of which it possesses and can develop in boundless measure. The time is not too early to make a new appraisal of the existing conditions and to re-define policies more in consonance with these changed conditions. United States policy towards Taiwan since the middle of 1950 has been a departure from its normal traditional course; some may even say that it is an aberration. But in the absence of an absolute military superiority which the United States enjoyed before 1949, the policy needs to be looked into. This is true not only of Taiwan, but of the neighboring areas as well. Laos is in danger of being lost, and so will others be, if we do not re-examine the entire situation. The new developments stretching all the way from South Korea to Turkey are a significant lesson. And further, one other lesson in these areas should be clear to those who have eyes to see, and that is, to seek an understanding with Soviet Russia without prior understanding and agreement from Communist China, does not seem to go very far in the solution of any international problem. Reversing the process will perhaps yield better results.

Let me quote these words, not of a Jeremiah, but of one whose judgment is mature, balanced, and restrained, and who has shown keen powers of observation. Mr. Walter Lippmann, in his article of May 18, 1961, which appeared in the *New York Herald Tribune,* has this to say:

> The revolutions in South Korea and Iran, following the disorders in Laos and South Vietnam, are a warning that in Asia the policy of containment by American satellite states is breaking down. In all four of these countries the governments have been our clients, indeed they have been our creations. All of them are crumbling, and in the last analysis they are all crumbling for the same reason. In relation to the rising popular feeling of independence and the rising popular expectations of material welfare, these American client states are not only corrupt but they are intolerably reactionary. The fact that they are also under the protection of a foreign and non-Asian power is an additional liability.
>
> The Kennedy administration did not form the policy of setting up on the periphery of Asia a semi-circle of American military clients. But it is now confronted with the breakdown of that policy, with the disorders, the dangers, and the pains of having to pick up the pieces. This is an experience which the American people have never had before and it is one for which their leaders have not prepared them. They have not been told by anyone in authority that there has been a radical change in the military situation and what the consequences of that change are. They have not been told that the military situation which existed when John Foster Dulles established this policy no longer exists. They have not been told that he made it work by shaking the bomb at the Communists. That is why so many of them suppose that Mr. Kennedy can make it work with a few Marines and by shaking his fist.
>
> Our moral and intellectual unpreparedness for the reality of things is causing widespread demoralization among us. We must not let ourselves be overcome by it. We can do that best, I think, by recognizing that our present experience on the periphery of Asia is the American equivalent of what the British and the French are experiencing during the liquidation of their colonial empires. For what we are witnessing is the dissolution of the Dulles system of Asian protectorates.

These words are not the words of a scare-monger, but of one who has earned the reputation of being a trained and thoughtful journalist. Mr. Lippmann has the courage to say what he believes to be right. This kind of thinking is beginning to have quite an impact on the minds of other people. Mr. James Reston and the *New York Times* London correspondent, Mr. Drew Middleton, both capable journalists, have started to harp on the same tune. I believe that, as time goes on, more and more people will feel, if they do not already feel, that the Dulles point of view, to say the least, is out of focus with the existing realities, and to continue maintaining it may lead to disaster.

The People's Republic of China is here to stay whether we like it or not. This is a cold, hard fact in our international life. To ignore it is to create an atmosphere of unreality which will do more harm than good.

Today unfortunately in that extensive and populous country there is being fostered a hatred for the United States. That is also a fact. But there is no reason to believe that this is a permanent fixation. We have witnessed a number of emotional somersaults on a national scale within recent years. Friends have become enemies, and enemies friends, and these changes have come about in very short periods of time. Must the 650 million people of China therefore continue to be antagonistic to the United States, especially as we must always bear in mind that in the past they have been on the best of terms? But some beginning has to be made, some gesture given, before there can be any improvement. It is not a sign of weakness, with all the obvious difficulties, to work for some basis where mutual understanding and co-operation are again possible. That is why many people were heartened by what President Kennedy said in his Inaugural Address: "To those nations who would make themselves our adversary, we offer not a pledge but a request: that both sides begin anew the quest for peace."

If that quest for peace is made with earnestness and sincerity, the results may transcend all expectation. Let the United States begin that quest. The United States has always had the initiative to do what potentially is good. She has the strength, the prestige, and the moral power to do so. But I think the first essential factor in that quest is for the United States to retrace its steps back to where they were before the fateful days of June 1950 or indeed to the days when General Marshall was performing his difficult mission in China.

All that is needed is a simple statement by the United States, re-affirming in a few words, that Taiwan is a sovereign part of China, and the results will be electrifying! No practical implementation of that recognition need be made now or even for many years to come. Merely make and accept the principle of China's sovereignty over Taiwan, and within a short time there will be so drastic an easing of the international situation, and the atmosphere will become so clear that many of the so far perplexing problems will open up new vistas of a just and equitable solution.

As to what will be actually done, that is a mere matter of detail. The important thing is to accept and announce the principle of Chinese sovereignty over Taiwan by the United States, and I believe firmly that Communist China will agree to any proposition as to the actual disposition of the island. Neutralization or demilitarization or even a relatively long period of custodianship by the United Nations or any such proposal should be readily accepted by Communist China. If for a specific period of, say, fifteen or twenty years, the United Nations assumes the temporary responsibility of administering the island so that Communist China will agree to making no military or strategic use of it, the time allowed will provide ample opportunity for adjustment of Sino-American relations which will do much to further the cause of world peace. Such proposals, of course, will have to be made, in accordance with prior arrangement, by Communist China after the principle of her sovereignty over Taiwan is generally agreed to and openly announced. She will have to assume the initiative of making these proposals, and, in the case of the United Nations, she will invite that world organization (after she has become a member) to help in the solution of that difficult problem in the interest of world peace. That, for Communist China, would be a concession from her present stand: it would be a compromise which, I think, she will be prepared to accept.

If the island is neutralized or demilitarized, and if the United

Nations is called in to supervise that such neutralization and demilitarization is carried out and then to create a purely civilian administration solely for the welfare of the inhabitants on the island, what need is there for the United States to claim it as a part of its "defense perimeter," especially when the effectiveness of the concept itself behind that perimeter, as Mr. Lippmann reminded us, has virtually disappeared or is now at least being seriously questioned? After all, before 1950, even the Joint Chiefs of Staff, on four successive occasions, as Mr. Dean Acheson testified, made it quite explicit that Taiwan was not essential for American security. If it was not essential then, why should it be essential now? Need it therefore be difficult for the United States to go back to her earlier position?

Under this proposed arrangement of a United Nations custodianship (I purposely avoid the word "trusteeship") the island will grow socially and economically by leaps and bounds. Its people will enjoy a full measure of freedom and liberty which is bound to have incalculable effect on their brethren on the mainland. The present hatred of the 650 million people for the United States will necessarily disappear, for having gained the objective which for years has been drummed into their ears as being unattainable because of American intransigence, the people will then turn to their government for a betterment of their status and living standards, and no power in the government, not even a Communist government, can suppress these popular wishes. If their demands are not met, the government will find itself in trouble precisely as Generalissimo Chiang Kai-shek found himself in deep water soon after the war with Japan was over. As long as the war was being fought, he could exact the people's allegiance. But when it was over, they turned their attention to demanding domestic improvement, and when they found that the government could not satisfy them, their confidence was shaken, and it was not long before that government began to totter to its fall.

There is no reason to doubt why the same trend of development cannot take place in Communist China. Once the principle of Chinese sovereignty over Taiwan is accepted by the United States and the world, no amount of pressure can prevent the people on the mainland from asking what they are entitled to in the way of better living. To exert any such pressure against it would be to look for trouble which no government can overcome.

Under the proposed arrangement the Chinese Communist government could well agree also to having the personnel in the present Taiwan government continue their functions. Taiwan would then, as it rightfully should, become, as Mr. Acheson said, a province of China. Has not Communist China, even as early as a few years back, already offered to appoint Generalissimo Chiang Kai-shek as the governor of the province? Has she not also offered him to become one of the vice-chairmen in the government in Peking? If General Chiang feels that he should enjoy a well-earned retirement after all these years of political and military activity, there is always his native village to retire to, as he had often done previously, or Japan, or the United States, or any other part of the world he may want to choose.

Under the arrangement China and the United States will then be at peace. They may even become friends again, as why should they not when there is such a long record of friendship behind them? But that friendship will be of a different order from what it was before. It will be a friendship founded on absolute equality and mutual respect. And such a friendship at the present juncture of the world's history will be something of priceless value. It will also help to solve the world's racial and color problem which continues to threaten to become the most dangerous of all problems.

Under the arrangement, the United Nations will gain new prestige and stature. It will show to the world what it can accomplish in the way of constructive administration. Further, the people on the island will have a new lease of life, one of freedom and prosperity, and even the present leaders in Taiwan will be provided for. The United States, China, the United Nations, the people in Taiwan—everyone gains and nobody loses. And on the top of all this, the tension in the world is reduced. Frankly, there is no single formula that can do so much in so little time and with so little effort for the world.

The only thing needed is a nod from the United States. Is she prepared to give that nod? I submit it calls for a bold and courageous step after all the propaganda against it during these many years. But I do not doubt that America is equal to the task. The best instincts of American statesmanship will be solidly behind it. For to show courage where courage is needed is in the best traditions of American life, as *Profiles in Courage* has abundantly shown.

To conclude, let me quote from President Kennedy himself, again from the recent address after his return from Europe. After referring to the Communist position in the world, he said:

> But I believe just as strongly that time will prove it wrong, that liberty, independence, and self-determination, not communism, is the future of man and that free men have the will and resources to win the struggle for freedom.

No greater truth has ever been uttered. All men, wherever they are, long to be free and independent. That is part of their heritage as human beings. No one chooses bondage if he can help it. But liberty and freedom must not become the prerogative of a few nations: they must be enjoyed and shared by all. Conditions will have to be created, where they do not exist, to make it possible for freedom to grow. The Chinese people are among the first to desire peace, freedom, and justice. Their culture of such long duration could not have blossomed without them. It is true that during at least the last century they have known neither peace nor freedom nor justice. They have lived under oppression both from within and from without. Between a selfish and grasping bureaucracy and the exploitation of the predatory powers, all they have known are poverty, disease, ignorance, and a despised nationhood. What value can we attach to a very few individuals enjoying their so-called freedom when the vast majority of their compatriots live under such grovelling conditions? These conditions will have to be removed; and in doing this it is necessary to enforce discipline and ask for sacrifice. But these are temporary measures, prologue to the time when "liberty, independence and self-determination" can be enjoyed by everyone in their full measure.

This is the significance of Taiwan in the great drama of development in China. Is America also willing to play a part? Today the island is a fortress, the symbol of a threat and the citadel of war and conflict. It is hidden under a forest of guns. It should not be so. It will have to be transformed into an area of harmony, understanding and mutual accommodation, leading to an eventual unitary administration as an integral part of China. The freedom which the people on the island will begin to enjoy, under this proposed new arrangement, will not be lost to the hundreds of millions on the mainland: its effects on them will be more far-reaching than we think they are possible.

APPENDIX B

THE QUESTION OF RACE AND COLOR:
A Reply to Arnold Toynbee

THERE IS no need to say that racial and color animosity and antagonism have become an increasingly important factor in the relationship among peoples.

The Hindus should perhaps be given the credit for being the first important people to take color (varna) as the basis for social discrimination. It was from this that their famous caste system took its rise. But it was the Europeans and Americans who first exploited the differences of race and color on the international scene. The Americans started with the trade in slaves from Africa, and the problem is still with them. The English exploited them in their colonies. The other Europeans in varying degrees followed the example of the English. And so for over two hundred years the race and color issue has haunted the world. The Caucasian races have derived enormous material advantages from it. For two centuries they have also disregarded the worth and dignity of the human individual of the non-Caucasian world. All this is now rapidly coming to an end, and in this process of change the Caucasian races, owing to their numerical inferiority, have developed a neurosis of fear, fear of reprisal, fear that the non-Caucasian races are uniting to overwhelm them. That explains the uneasiness among the Caucasian peoples. It is for this reason also that they regard the rise of China as a portentous matter. They are apt to see dangers where they do not really exist. In so far as the Chinese are concerned, if I read their history correctly, they are certainly the least racially conscious people on the face of the earth. But even so distinguished a historian as Professor Arnold J. Toynbee seems to have grave doubts about this. For this reason, I find it necessary to write a reply to his article on the subject.

264

PROFESSOR ARNOLD J. TOYNBEE AND "RACE WAR"

PROFESSOR ARNOLD J. TOYNBEE, in his article "Is a 'Race War' Shaping Up?" published in the magazine section of the New York *Times* of September 29, 1963, has raised a number of questions that call for analysis. Though written by an academic historian, it has more than academic interest. It has a direct bearing on the realities of the world situation. It is calculated to influence the thinking of policy-makers in their decisions on new directives. The article has therefore important practical consequences.

My first impression is that many of the statements seem to cancel one another. But the main thesis is clear enough. Fully one-half of the article is devoted to a consideration of China. Mr. Toynbee raised the question, which he said was discussed in Moscow recently, whether the Chinese are "likely to launch a war of revenge against the white race—Russians and Westerners alike." Here he puts the question squarely on racial and color differences. His implications are that such a war is in the making. He urges, therefore, that in order to prevent defeat in such a war, it is necessary that America and Soviet Russia "must act in co-operation with each other, and they must do this quickly." It will only mean "the bankruptcy of American and Russian statesmanship" if they do not succeed in co-operating with each other in the near future" and "put the world in order on their terms"! Mr. Toynbee then concludes by saying; "World order could be imposed tomorrow by the United States and the Soviet Union if they could act together." This is the "double hegemony" that General de Gaulle complained about only the other day. The detente that has now come about through the signing of the nuclear test-ban treaty, in Mr. Toynbee's view, should be followed up at once with other measures of rapprochement in order to prevent China from having a "chance of gaining world domination" which, he thinks, is just around the corner, some thirty or more years from now.

And yet in the final bid for world domination by the Chinese, Mr. Toynbee thinks that it will not be purely a matter of color. "The contest," in his words, "would not be one between the white race and the rest of the world: it would be one between China and the rest of the world; the anti-Chinese coalition would include peoples of all races." Surely the two basic ideas are in conflict. First, the racial war seems to be very much in the making. But Mr. Toynbee evidently does not like to see a war between the white races and the other races. He does not think that the Caucasian races will have the upper hand when they are numerically so inferior. So when the war does come, and since China is the only *bête noire*, it will be the Chinese against the anti-Chinese coalition of all the races of all colors. Mr. Toynbee now feels happier and more relaxed, because "all the races of all colors" who so much hate the Chinese will be thankful to be on the side of the white races in order to put the Chinese in their proper place. There is one exception that Mr. Toynbee allows, and that is Pakistan, which sadly, according to Mr. Toynbee, will be on the side of China because of an identity of interest that has come about only recently as a result of the Chinese-Indian border dispute.

The reasoning here, it seems to me, is unusual. Mr. Toynbee shifts from one concept to another so swiftly that the reader has hardly the time to overcome the confusion created in his mind.

One thing is clear, however. Mr. Toynbee believes, with *his* knowledge and interpretation of history, that the world has been and will be dominated by one section of humanity over the rest. He does not believe in a world of harmony in which there is mutual respect and consideration among all the sections of humanity. The United Nations, in this framework of thinking, would be a superfluous effort.

In this connection it will be interesting to consider the remarks of a distinguished Pakistani made before the Assembly of the United Nations the day after Mr. Toynbee singled his country out as being on the side of the Chinese in this soon-to-be-fought-out war of the races. "The political evolution of the world," said Mr. Zulfikar Ali Bhutto, the Foreign Minister of Pakistan, "is oriented towards an international order based on the consent and co-operation of equal sovereign states." But, he went on to say, there are historians who "look to the imposition of a world order by the unchallengeable power exercised in combination by the two super-states [of the United States and Soviet Russia] as the only alternative for mankind to destruction." Mr. Bhutto then concludes: "Philosophies such as these are a challenge to our faith in the United Nations. The world organization was conceived as an alternative to world hegemony, to the domination of one super-power or more over all the others." His repudiation of Mr. Toynbee's thesis coming so soon in its footsteps seems to be forthright and unequivocal.

My own feeling is that Mr. Toynbee's reading of Chinese history is inadequate. This is not to deny that he remains one of the world's most considerable historians. All I mean to say is that for any one scholar to feel at home and to be able to appreciate the spirit of a variety of civilizations is an impossible task. Mr. Toynbee is a Westerner. He therefore looks at the world with a pair of Western eyes. He cannot help it. When he makes judgments, from his Western vantage point, on civilizations that are dead and gone, no one from the grave will rise to refute him. But he must expect to be contradicted when he speaks about those civilizations that are still very much alive.

I believe there is a rhythm in the history of every major civilization, a sort of *élan vital,* which is the very essence of its being. It is this rhythm that creates a pattern. And it is the pattern that is responsible for what it does and for the way in which it is done. It constitutes the personality of that civilization as there is a personality in a human being. It is therefore not true to say that a nation will react to a set of circumstances in an identical or even a similar way to a nation in another civilization. Chinese painting or art, for instance, is different from Western art. It is guided by its own inner laws. By the same token, Chinese civilization is motivated by a set of dominant ideas and principles that are inherently different from those of Western civilization. The mistake that Mr. Toynbee commits is that he tries to interpret the facts of Chinese history and their meaning from a point of view that is genetically a part of his own being. Neither does this do justice to Chinese history nor can his understanding be accurate.

I cannot go into the many differences that exist between Chinese and European civilizations. This is too tall an order. But there is one difference that has a vital bearing on our discussion, and that is that in Western culture, at least from the Chinese point of view, the element of conflict far outweighs any other element. Conflict as such is not an agent of destruction. The Baconian concept of the conflict between man and nature and the eventual conquest of nature by man for the promotion of human welfare has brought to us, thanks to the Western genius, untold blessings in scientific and technological advance. Likewise the conflict within the human breast, which, according to Hegel, is at the basis of the tragic idea, has produced the wonderful works of Sophocles and Shakespeare.

The concept of conflict, it seems to me, is the recurrent theme in Western culture in the more than two thousand years of its history. It is predominant in Homer in the destruction of the Trojans by the Greeks. It is predominant in Roman history. Virgil could have very well made his hero Aeneas settle down on Carthaginian soil and together with Dido, firmly bound as they were by love, he could have created a new empire embracing both the northern and southern shores of the Mediterranean. But, no, in the interest of racial purity—for Dido was of Phoenician origin—he must establish a separate realm and launch a vigorous campaign against Carthage, *Delenda est Carthago!* Here is as good an example as any of coexistence offered to Aeneas by Dido on a silver platter, and he kicked it in her face.

I can go on to show example after example in Western civilization where the idea of conflict plays a major role in its development. The idea in fact is quite common to all civilizations that have created epic poetry. The Aryans, to whom we owe the *Mahabharata* and the *Ramayana,* came into India, as Mr. Toynbee pointed out, toward the end of the second millennium B.C., met the inhabitants of the Indus Valley who were culturally on a higher level, and without hesitation put them to the sword and made an end to what we now call the Mohenjo-Daro civilization. The ancient Iranians, another branch of the Aryans, conceived in their *Zend Avesta* the idea of Ahura Mazda and Ahriman, the forces of good and evil, which were in eternal conflict with each other. The Greeks further developed the idea of dichotomy of the intellect and the senses, which seems to have split wide the Western personality for so long that only recently existentialists and Zen Buddhists have been called in to repair the damage and restore the sense of unity.

I am not trying to attach any value judgment to this concept of conflict. I am merely stating what I believe to be a fact, a very important fact, in the constitution of Western culture. Unless there is an awareness, among the Western peoples, that this concept is incompatible with the new world order that we are all trying to create, one in which there must be developed a spirit of conciliation and of mutual respect and accommodation, this concept will continue to be a disturbing factor in international affairs. The world will continue to witness marvelous accomplishments in technology, in going eventually to the moon or to the distant stars, but this little spot known as the earth will continue to flutter in a state of uncertainty and insecurity.

What then is the pattern in Chinese history? Instead of conflict and the principle of progressive advancement through conquest, which itself is based on the idea of opposition, we have at work the principle of adaptation, of appropriation, of the manifold elements of nature and the universe as being complementary to one another. In all of China's leading thinkers this concept was expressed in a variety of ways. By the time we come to Confucius and Lao-tze, the idea was no longer a matter of discussion: it had become deeply ingrained in the very tissue of Chinese thinking. Hot and cold, moist and dry, high and low, black and white, emptiness and fullness, light and darkness—these do not stand opposed to one another any more than the male is opposed to the female or the negative to the positive. Each is indispensable to the other for the fulfillment of its being. Without what is normally considered the opposite there can be no concept of completeness. This basic thought must have developed in the formative period of Chinese history, out of a peculiar set of circumstances that made the life of the early farmer, then as it still does now, difficult and precarious. Sustained and continual supplication of the divine forces was an essential condition to prolong life and to confer blessings on it, and out of it all was developed a religion or philosophy of harmony, harmony between man and man, harmony between man and nature, which has given a peculiar stamp to Chinese civilization. It was embodied in the *Book of Change,* where the unceasing process of mutual adaptation and reconciliation became the source and fountain of the creativity of the universe. It found expression in the concept of the yin and yang, whose infinite mobility and interaction provide us with the manifoldness of life. And in popular mythology it takes the form of the dragon.

Yes, the dragon, which is as definitive and as final a dividing line between the Western and the Chinese worlds as one can imagine. The dragon in Western civilization, from the early days of the Greeks, was a symbol of evil to be overcome, conquered, and then slaughtered. It was a monster to be eliminated as an obstacle in the realization of man's wishes and ambitions. It was in the way of the argonauts when they were in quest of the Golden Fleece. It was known as Python, which haunted the caves of Parnassus and was killed by Apollo. It took the form of the nine-headed Hydra of Lerna, to be slain by Heracles. Medusa, one of three Gorgons, was likewise in the shape of a sea serpent or dragon, with golden wings, brazen claws and enormous teeth, whose head was cut off by Perseus and presented to Athene to be set in her shield. And then the fire-breathing dragon of the early Saxons in Beowulf and the familiar paintings of St. George thrusting his spear into the belly of the dragon. Everywhere the dragon in Western art and thought symbolizes the principle of evil to be conquered and annihilated by man.

But the dragon in east Asia, in China and Japan, is not the grim and ugly monster of the West. It is a projection of man himself when he has reached his ultimate, of his strength and goodness when the cosmos within him has arrived at a state of orderly progression. It is the spirit of change, of life's creative force, and therefore of life itself. It is life's fulfillment, and so it can assume an infinite variety of shapes and forms. Mr. Okakura has done better than anyone I know in giving us a poetic description of the dragon. "Hidden in caves in the highest mountains or coiled up in the measureless depths of the ocean, he bides his time until he returns to work. He ascends in the storm clouds, he washes his mane in the darkness of the seething whirlwind. He plunges his claws into the lightning, his skin gleams like the bark of the pine trees when the rain runs down the trunks. The tornado is his voice which, resounding through the moldering leaves of the forests, heralds the new spring." The dragon is the symbol of renewed life, of eternal spring. He does unceasing work for the benefit of man. He is nature brought into consonance with the spirit of man.

This poor dragon needs some explanation because he is so sadly misunderstood in the West. Along with the concept of yin and yang and the *Book of Change,* the dragon concept is one of creativity through absorption, reconciliation, and harmony. That was why Confucius compared Lao-tze to the dragon when they met. In the realm of humanistic values, of man's relationship with other men in the Confucian view of life, in the realm of cosmic values, of man's relationship to nature in the Lao-tze view of the universe, the idea of harmony and of a higher unity is, I think, fundamental. That has had far-reaching consequences in the shaping and molding of Chinese history. It is for this reason that Mr. Charles P. Fitzgerald made the perceptive remark that "the history of China is a record of an expanding culture, not that of a conquering empire."

I hope that this background information of Chinese history throws out of focus Mr. Toynbee's assertion that China today is openly "making a bid for world domination." There has not been any such thing as conscious domination of other peoples in Chinese history, and by its very nature and the inner law of its being, which no one can renounce, not even Marxism-Leninism, I do not believe that such domination can arise. Mr. Toynbee further says, "Of all human communities anywhere in the world, China has, in fact, been by far the most successful, so far, in uniting a large part of the human race over a long period of time." If this is true, and I think it is, it has not been through military force but through moral persuasion. As long as twenty-five centuries ago, Mencius

was making the distinction between subjugation by force and subjugation through virtue, and he was convinced that the latter was
much the more effective of the two. But it is the prevailing view
that China is bent on aggression and expansion through military
means. That, I think, is mistaken and should be corrected.

First the Huns, the same Huns who ultimately brought the
downfall of the Roman Empire, then the To-pa Tartars of the fifth
century, then the Khitans and Jurchens of the Sung Dynasty, then
the Mongols, then the Manchus, and finally the Western world—
all these came marching into China and tried to subdue and conquer her. Surely no country has been more sinned against than sin-
ning. And yet, irony of ironies, this country, which, through the
centuries and its long history, has been a victim of aggression, is
today branded as the most aggressive country in the world! Are we
to believe this? With what can it carry out its policy of aggression?
With an industry that, according to the opinion of a recent Belgian
parliamentarian, will take at least some eighty years to be on its
feet, or, as the Communists themselves admit, a minimum of half a
century?

China does not feel that she has the "birthright" or the "mandate" to rule the world. This is a false view of the Chinese people.
All they feel is that every nation and every people should come together and be of mutual help to each other, even to the extent of
assisting those who have fallen or perished. *Hsin mi kuo, chi chüeh
ssu.* These six characters have been the cornerstone of Chinese political thought from time immemorial as have been four other
characters *yu chiao wu lai.* What makes Confucius' teaching so
vital and so pertinent today is the thought that between all human
beings there should be no distinction of class, race, or color: the
only distinction is the degree of one's education and cultural at-
tainments. This is the cohesive power, the unifying element which
through the centuries has brought China from her modest beginnings in a small area of the Yellow River valley to what she is
today.

With due apologies to Mr. Toynbee, the idea of a hegemony of
any one state over the rest of the world or of a "double hegemony," in any shape or form, does not exist in the mind of the

Chinese. The spirit of China's ancient tradition will continue to assert itself for a world of order and harmony in which each nation or race has the full opportunity to contribute its maximum good for the fulfillment of all mankind. The world will then attain what Confucius calls *Ta Tung*, the Great Commonwealth. That spirit is the very spirit of the United Nations.

APPENDIX C

TWO LETTERS ON THE SINO–INDIAN BORDER DISPUTE

STATUS OF McMAHON LINE

INDIAN POSITION IN BORDER DISPUTE WITH CHINA QUESTIONED

The writer of the following letter has held posts in Nationalist China's diplomatic service. He is the author of "Within the Four Seas," a study of world peace, and is on the faculty of the Fairleigh Dickinson University.

TO THE EDITOR OF THE NEW YORK TIMES:

What, according to the record, is the McMahon Line, which India insists is the boundary between China and India and which Communist China considers to have no legal basis?

The line forms part of the Simla Convention of 1914 on which Great Britain, acting on behalf of the then British India, China and Tibet were represented. It is 850 miles long and was "desired" by the British delegate Sir Arthur Henry McMahon as the boundary between Tibet and northeast India. Neither its latitude nor its longitude was mentioned. It was to extend roughly 100 miles north from the plains of India.

The draft of the Simla Convention was initialed by the three representatives on April 27, 1914. Two days later the Chinese representative was disavowed and withdrawn by the Chinese Government owing to opposition from many parts of the country. The British Minister at Peking then warned the Chinese Government on June 6 that, regardless of Chinese wishes, the final convention was going to be signed by the British and Tibetan authorities. This was

274

done on July 3. The first World War broke out a month later and the whole matter entered the stage of suspended animation.

The convention and exchanges of notes signed by the British Tibetan representatives have not been made public until now and probably never will, not having reached the status of legal documents. They fell short of the essential requirements to make a treaty or convention valid and have therefore no standing in international law. That seems to have been the clear understanding even of Sir Charles Bell, who, as a British official, took part in the Simla Conference as a member of the Tibetan delegation! The Dalai Lama himself did not ratify the convention. China did not even sign the convention, let alone ratify it.

That the Simla Convention has no legal value seems to be further borne out by the fact that it is not even included in the comprehensive "Treaties, Engagements and Sanads Relating to India and Neighboring Countries" compiled by C. U. Aitchison under the authority of the Foreign and Political Department of the Indian Government. Aitchison was then Under Secretary of the Foreign Department and the compilation was in the nature of an official publication.

The interesting question to ask is whether the Indian Government, in claiming the McMahon Line as the boundary, has made a thorough and careful study of its legal position. From "an objective reading," as Secretary Herter has said, "we have no basis to go on." What basis then has the Government of India to go on? I think the world is entitled to know if India desires its sympathy and support.

The Indian note of November 8 deprecates "the activities of the old imperialist powers" against whom both India and China struggled in the past. That is quite correct. But would India allow herself to take advantage of the fruits of these same imperialist activities directed against China when it is now to her interest to do so?

It is important to let my Indian friends know that the views I have expressed are the views of all Chinese, wherever they are, and irrespective of their political beliefs and affiliations. Clearly the Indian people are being put to a severe moral test. We shall all feel happier if some Indian scholar states the Indian point of view. All we wish is a clear and impartial presentation of the historical facts. There should be no difficulty in solving the unfortunate boundary issue when these facts are established.

Chang Hsin-hai.

Teaneck, N.J., Nov. 29, 1959.

THE SINO-INDIAN BORDER

NEHRU'S VIEW REGARDING SETTLEMENT OF PROBLEM DISCUSSED

The writer of the following is Professor of History and Government, University of Hartford, and author of books on Tibet.

TO THE EDITOR OF THE NEW YORK TIMES

Your editorial of Jan. 2 criticized Mr. Nehru in the following words: "By the standards India has now set Communist China is not an aggressor on India's Himalayan frontier but simply a rectifier of borders outlined under colonial rule."

I wonder by what standard Communist China can be called an aggressor so far as the Sino-Indian border dispute is concerned. Regarding the western sector of the disputed border, Mr. Nehru himself admitted in 1959 that "this was the boundary of the old Kashmir state with Tibet and Chinese Turkestan. Nobody had marked it." Chinese troops, whether Nationalist (until 1949) or Communist (thereafter), have only guarded a traditional, customary line there and have never encroached upon Indian territory. While Pakistan has never raised any objection to the Chinese position, Mr. Nehru now claims as Indian territory an area of 38,000 square kilometers, to which neither British nor Indian jurisdiction has ever extended and within which the Chinese Communists from March, 1956, to October, 1957, built a motor road from Yehcheng in Chinese Turkestan to Gortok in Tibet without even being detected by the Indian Government.

As to the eastern sector, the so-called McMahon Line was imposed on the Tibetan representative on March 24, 1914, at Delhi by Sir Henry McMahon behind the back of the Chinese delegate. It was never discussed at the subsequent Simla Conference. Nor was it ever recognized by any Chinese Government—Imperial, Nationalist, or Communist. It aroused the displeasure of the thirteenth Dalai Lama (Sir Charles Bell's account) and the Lhasa Government also expressed strong dissatisfaction with it.

Chou En-lai in his note to Nehru of Sept. 8, 1959, declared that "the Chinese Government absolutely does not recognize the so-called McMahon Line, but Chinese troops have never crossed that line." On the other hand, Chou charged in the same note that since the outbreak of the rebellion in Tibet Indian troops not only overstepped the line, but also exceeded the boundary drawn on current Indian maps, which in many places cuts even deeper into Chinese territory than the McMahon Line.

It is more fair to say that by the standards India has now set Communist China is doing what Mr. Nehru thinks fit and proper, i.e., liquidating anachronistic colonialism—with the only difference that Portugal actually ruled Goa for more than four centuries, while the British colonial power in India only outlined the border now claimed by Mr. Nehru, but did not establish it legally for a single day.

In your editorial of Jan. 4 you commented further that "India was, of course, the first to set an example in the application of the 'double standard' through its invasion of Goa."

I do not think that one should blame India too much for having used force to liberate a part of her own territory from colonial rule. It was against colonial rule that this country began its independent career. But what has perplexed the world is rather Mr. Nehru's liquidation of French and Portuguese colonial rule in India while inheriting the benefits of British rule there. A study of his policy toward Bhutan, Sikkim and Nepal, his suppression of the natives in Assam and his strong-arm action in Hyderabad and Kashmir would reveal the meagerness of his departure from British colonial precedent.

Communist China has settled her border issues with Burma and Nepal amicably. There is no reason why the Sino-Indian frontier question cannot be similarly settled, if only one standard is applied by the Indian leader.

Tieh-Tseng Li.

West Hartford, Conn., Jan. 7, 1962.

INDEX